INNOVATIONS IN M.. .C. .__ .. PUBLISHING

This book examines the key developments in the UK magazine industry since 2014 and explains in detail how the business has innovated to survive.

Innovations in Magazine Publishing explores the key issues that publishers and editors have had to grapple with in recent years and demonstrates how they have changed their business models and encouraged innovation and creativity. Written in an engaging and accessible style, the authors and contributors have drawn on years of industry expertise and contacts to examine the massive changes that have taken place in the areas of content creation and advertising in the last decade. Beginning with a highly useful summary of UK magazine publishing history, the book then provides a detailed focus on how magazines have had to adapt to a declining revenue picture in both copy and advertisement sales. This discussion considers changes in ownership and the supply chain, mutual dependency on social media, the rapid growth of the independent sector, investing in brand and product extensions, and how media companies themselves have changed to meet the demands of the new era. The important issue of ethnic diversity within the UK publishing industry is addressed and the introduction also includes a discussion of the effects of the Covid-19 pandemic on the industry, and how the magazine business will need to respond to whatever the future may bring.

This comprehensive overview of the current state of the industry is a vital resource for students, researchers and professionals in magazine journalism, as well as for those studying media and journalism studies more generally.

Simon Das is Senior Lecturer in Magazine Publishing at the University for the Creative Arts (UCA). He was previously managing editor of UK black music monthly *Touch* magazine, a supplement project editor for *Time Out* and a freelance journalist for *Arena* and *i-D* in London, *el País* newspaper in Madrid and *The Fader* in New York.

David Stam is Associate Lecturer in Magazine Publishing at the University of the Arts London. He has been Managing Director within Reed Business Information and a Board Director of IPC Media. He has worked as a consultant for TSL Education, *The Economist* and *The Spectator*. In 2014, he co-edited *Inside Magazine Publishing* with Andrew Scott.

Andrew Blake is Associate Lecturer in Magazine Publishing at the University of the Arts London, having taught at the Universities of East London, Winchester and Southampton. He has written about many aspects of contemporary culture.

INNOVATIONS IN MAGAZINE PUBLISHING

Edited by Simon Das, David Stam and Andrew Blake

Routledge
Taylor & Francis Group

LONDON AND NEW YORK

First published 2021
by Routledge
2 Park Square, Milton Park, Abingdon, Oxon OX14 4RN

and by Routledge
52 Vanderbilt Avenue, New York, NY 10017

Routledge is an imprint of the Taylor & Francis Group, an informa business

British Library Cataloguing-in-Publication Data
A catalogue record for this book is available from the British Library

Library of Congress Cataloging-in-Publication Data
Names: Das, Simon, editor. | Stam, David, 1953– editor. |
Blake, Andrew, 1955– editor.
Title: Innovations in magazine publishing / edited by
Simon Das, David Stam, and Andrew Blake.
Description: London; New York: Routledge, 2021. |
Includes bibliographical references and index. |
Identifiers: LCCN 2020046052 | ISBN 9780367337001 (hardback) |
ISBN 9780367337018 (paperback) | ISBN 9780429321368 (ebook)
Subjects: LCSH: Periodicals–Publishing–Great Britain–History–21st century. |
Periodicals–Publishing–Great Britain–Management. |
Periodicals–Publishing–Economic aspects.
Classification: LCC PN5124.P4 I55 2021 | DDC 052/.0941–dc23
LC record available at https://lccn.loc.gov/2020046052

ISBN: 9780367337001 (hbk)
ISBN: 9780367337018 (pbk)
ISBN: 9780429321368 (ebk)

Typeset in Bembo
by Newgen Publishing UK

CONTENTS

EDITORS AND CONTRIBUTORS

Andrew Blake is an associate lecturer at the University of the Arts London, having taught Cultural Studies and/or Music at the Universities of East London, Winchester and Southampton. He was joint editor of *Buy This Book: Studies in Advertising and Consumption* (1997) and contributed to the third edition of *The Advertising Handbook* (2009). Writing on other cultural matters includes contributions to *The Cambridge History of 20th Century Music* (2004) and *The Bloomsbury Companion to Rock Music Research* (2020). His book *The Irresistible Rise of Harry Potter* (2002) has been translated five times.

Simon Das is Senior Lecturer in Magazine Publishing at the University for the Creative Arts (UCA). Having developed and taught on media and magazine publishing courses in UK higher and further education for the last 13 years, he was previously managing editor of UK black music monthly *Touch* magazine, a supplement project editor for *TimeOut* and freelanced as a journalist for a number of magazines including *Arena* and *i-D* in London, *el País* newspaper in Madrid and *The Fader* in New York. Simon holds a first degree in Business Studies, a Master's in Higher and Professional Education and a PhD in media management and cultural theory from the University of Westminster, where he researched managing creativity in magazines. Simon is a member of the Chartered Institute of Marketing and was the co-founder of the Creative Industries Management Research Hub (CIMRH) at the University of the Arts London (UAL).

Helen Powell is Associate Professor in Creative Advertising at London South Bank University, where she leads the BA (Hons) Creative Advertising with Marketing degree. Her research sits at the intersection of promotional culture and consumer behaviour and in the field of temporality and digital culture. Helen is co-editor of *The Advertising Handbook*, now in its fourth edition, and *Promotional Culture and Convergence*, both published by Routledge.

Christine Stam graduated from the University of Bath in 1976 and spent the first years of her working life as a pharmacist, before the marketing bug took hold. After more than 20 years working in the pharmaceutical Industry and as a consultant, she took to academia and studied for an MA in Intercultural Communication with International Business at the University of Surrey. A PhD in English Literature followed closely behind in 2009. She has been married to David since 1978 and they have two children and three grandchildren.

David Stam joined Thomson Magazines in 1976 after graduating from the University of Bath. Moving through a succession of roles in advertising, publishing and circulation, he was appointed as Managing Director within Reed Business Information in 1993 and of the market leading distributor Marketforce (UK) in 1995. In this role, he also served as a Board Director of IPC Media. In 2006, David developed an active consultancy career working for blue chip magazine publishers including TSL Education, *The Economist*, DC Thomson and *The Spectator*. He has served as an ABC Council Member and has advised PPA. In 2014, he co-edited *Inside Magazine Publishing* with Andrew Scott. David is an Associate Lecturer at the London College of Communication, part of the University of the Arts London (UAL).

PREFACE

The editors of *Innovations in Magazine Publishing* share a passion for jazz and it was at a gig – in pre-COVID days – at the Royal Albert Hall for the amazing fusion band Snarky Puppy that the idea for this textbook took hold. What was our thinking? Simon had just been awarded his PhD in the field of magazine innovation, management and creativity and wanted to find a wider audience for his work, especially amongst media undergraduates. David felt there was a need to refresh the successful 2014 book *Inside Magazine Publishing* for the new decade with the emphasis on innovation, and Andrew wanted to commit to print some of his research-based lectures at the University of the Arts London (UAL) in the area of international publishing and diversity. Routledge as ever were positive and supportive for a new text on the popular subject of magazines.

When the concept for the book was put out for peer review, it was suggested that Christine Stam's chapter on the history of magazine publishing was updated and reprinted from the 2014 edition, as it has proved very popular with students and staff alike looking for a concise history of the medium. We were also delighted to be joined by Helen Powell who has contributed a chapter on how magazine advertising has changed over the years and will continue to do so. Our team was complete.

Research and early drafts were undertaken in the winter and early spring of 2020 and then – at 8.30 pm on Monday, 23 March 2020 – the lives of everyone in the UK changed. Lockdown.

The three editors have all seen severe recessions in the media business before but never anything potentially as damaging as a prolonged lockdown of commerce. Once we had mastered the intricacies of Zoom and Teams and could visually communicate once more, we decided that we had to carry on and fulfil our Routledge schedule. There would have to be some minor changes to the original synopsis as, for the best of reasons, not all of our original contributors could write for us. Coping with childcare and eldercare, home schooling and contributing to an academic work 'from home' was far from easy. Physical library access was not possible, so all research and fact finding now had to be done online. But as our long 'thank you' list shows, many key industry players did contribute and helped us bring *Innovations in Magazine Publishing* to you – on time.

We wish to pay sincere thanks to the following people and organisations who have helped in various ways in the book's production. Firstly, our thanks to Anne Coddington, Frania Hall, Keith Martin and other colleagues and students at UAL. Teaching on the BA degree in Magazine Journalism and Publishing and the MA in Publishing has allowed us to present some of our research in the classroom, and many of the students on those degrees (too many to name) have provided useful responses which have tempered and refined our ideas.

Many thanks to Christopher Phinn, Sharan Dhaliwal and Mark Hooper for the extended drop-in pieces in chapters 3, 7 and 8, respectively. To Ian Cleverly, Simon Collis, Dan Flower, Robin MacMillan, Joe Pidgeon and Marcus Rich for assisting Simon with interviews. To Adrian Hughes of Marketforce and Tim Weller for providing background for Chapter 3, and the team behind the new look *Goodwood Magazine* featured in Chapter 3. To Jeremy Leslie of magCulture and Steve Watson of Stack for advice on independent magazines, and Ranj Begley for providing data on Readly.

Magazine media is a business which changes fast in terms of its portfolio profiles, its 'dramatis personae' and of course the data and numbers which surround it. Thanks to Jim Bilton of Wessenden Marketing; what would the industry do without his detailed and insightful monthly newsletter? Also to Zenith, Dentsu Aegis, Enders Analysis, Plum Consulting and Magnetic for allowing us to extract reports.

A word of explanation to avoid possible confusion. In 2001, the US publisher Time Inc purchased IPC Media formerly known as IPC Magazines. The business was in turn rebranded TI Media and was sold to a finance house in 2017. In 2020, the company was purchased by Future plc. Readers please note that certain titles will have been referred to in these different ownership contexts.

The magazine publishing industry has experienced many challenges, opportunities and threats since the millennium. These have been as varied as the onset of new digital media and decline in advertising revenue, competition for consumers' time, a general financial crisis around 2008 and now changes to work and leisure driven by COVID-19. The latter may well be the hardest nut to crack. Maybe the size and shape of companies portrayed in this textbook will change between our copy deadline data and publication. But Virus, do not underestimate us: magazine publishers are innovative, creative, hardworking and occasionally a little crazy. These attributes continue to serve the industry well and we trust that *Innovations in Magazine Publishing* will both inform and inspire publishers and editors – of both large and small enterprises – to turn challenges into opportunities, and for students to increase their understanding. We wish you well in uncertain times and we trust that you value and enjoy this book.

Simon Das
David Stam
Andrew Blake
September 2020
London and Norfolk, UK

ACKNOWLEDGEMENTS

The editors and publisher would like to thank the following companies and individuals for permission to reproduce photographs and illustrations:

Phil Roeder for the cover photograph

The Spectator, *The Face* and *Decanter* (Future plc) for the cover images in Chapter 1

Future plc for images of *The Field*, *Country Life*, *Woman*, *Woman's Own*, *Woman's Weekly* and *Marie Claire* in Chapter 2

Hearst Magazines UK for *Cosmopolitan* in Chapter 2

University of Reading, Special Collections for the photograph of Blackpool Station bookstall in Chapter 2

TCO London for illustrations in Chapters 3 and 8

magCulture and Readly for photographs in Chapter 3

Cycling Weekly, *Rouleur* and *Hole & Corner* for cover images in Chapter 4

Magnetic and DStudio for the image in Chapter 5

How to Spend It (*Financial Times*), *Burnt Roti*, *New Internationalist* and *Monocle* for the cover images in Chapter 6

Trevor Nelson for the image in Chapter 7

Private Eye magazine (www.private-eye.co.uk) and Athenaeum Nieuwscentrum for the photographs in Chapter 8

Dentsu Aegis, Plum Consulting and Zenith for allowing the reproduction of the tables in Chapter 5

Photographers Simon Turtle and Ken Moreton for kindly allowing the reproduction of the photographs in Chapters 1 and 4, respectively. Please note that the photograph of *Stylist* in Chapter 4 was taken before the 2020 pandemic.

INTRODUCTION

Simon Das, David Stam and Andrew Blake

Innovations in Magazine Publishing follows a number of significant academic publications which demonstrate the health of the subject matter as a field of enquiry. Since the appearance of *Inside Magazine Publishing* co-edited by David Stam (Stam and Scott 2014), a number of key texts have been published, including Cox and Mowatt's very comprehensive industrial history *Revolutions from Grub Street: a History of Magazine Publishing in Britain* (2014), and the fourth edition of Jenny Mackay's stalwart introduction *The Magazines Handbook* (2018). Beyond these (very useful) texts, we should mention two compendia of scholarly work on magazines. The first of these, *The Routledge Handbook of Magazine Research: The Future of the Magazine Form* (Abrahamson and Prior-Miller 2018), is a book useful for students and scholars alike. Its individual chapters cover a very wide range of topics directly related to magazine research. Each of these essays summarises the current state of knowledge, and identifies possibilities for further research, and each has very useful footnotes and bibliographies. Though the coverage can seem over-focused on the USA (and it has disappointingly little to say about its subtitle, the future of the magazine form), its scope is broad enough for us to say that no student of magazines, their histories and potential futures should be without this book. We would hope that it is kept up to date.

The second book, a more recent compendium, is *The Handbook of Magazine Studies* (Sternadori and Holmes, 2020). This is similarly epic in size, but less focused in approach than the *Routledge Handbook*, and as a result, the contents are more variable in format and tone. There are useful discussions of research methods; some straightforward explorations of genre; and some historical overviews – all of which can act as companions to the entries in the *Routledge Handbook*. Reflecting interests current at the time of the book's compilation (the height of the #metoo movement), there are some interesting essays on sex, gender and power in magazine publishing, alongside more general reflections on magazines, politics and identity.

From this book's point of view, Tim Holmes's discussion of *Porter* magazine as a new 'hybrid' form of infomercial publishing is the star of the show. Although *Porter*, launched in 2014 as the print 'face' of an online retail company, is now itself online-only and may already be a fading experiment, in relation to innovation it's certainly a creative response to changing conditions, and therefore a model we need to note and learn from (Holmes, 2020).

Innovations in magazine publishing – a book about 'dichotomies'

Since the famous twentieth-century economist Joseph Schumpeter proffered his 'endogenous' theory of economic growth, showing technology as both a destructive and a creative economic force, 'creative destruction' has become part of what we understand about innovation. In the last 20 years, this force, for good or bad, in the form of digital and internet-based technology has come to radically change not just products and services of all kinds, but entire industries and arguably even the fabric of society itself. With sight of the coming age of ubiquitous media (everybody as a publisher), free content and 24/7 global internet connectivity, magazine publishing has faced at least a decade of pathological predictions of disruption of what was an innovation of the eighteenth and nineteenth centuries. The late Felix Dennis, one of the great magazine publishers of the twentieth century, predicted 15 years ago that by now, print magazines would struggle to survive (Dennis, 2004). In one way, he was right, however in many other ways, he was wrong.

Innovations in Magazine Publishing is about this very dichotomy – the story of *destruction* (magazines in the digital era largely replaced as a weekly or monthly communicative vehicle of media, media sales, and the world of fashion and consumerist promotion) and the story of *creativity* – the fact that publishers have done much more than just 'clinging on' to existing forms of publishing and distribution. As Simon Das explains in the opening chapter, the last decade has seen a structural split neatly reflecting this disruptive/creative force of innovation. Similarly David Stam's overview of the contemporary magazine publishing industry (Chapter 3) outlines, on the one hand, legacy magazine businesses that have consolidated into larger companies in the last decade, tapping into global investment capital; while at the other end of the spectrum, publishing has fragmented into smaller organisations of networked creatives. All are facets of an industry reinventing a magazine 'metaphor' for the digital twenty-first century for readers who, as Andrew Blake explains in Chapter 6, often hold new forms of identity in a globalising world. The specific question of whether such networked creativity can be harnessed in magazine workers across this spectrum is an area of investigation for which the case studies in Chapter 4 add unique insights from the intersecting field of media management. With most media studies focused on end products or marketing, a 'missing middle' has been exposed, neglecting the examination of innovation as related to the creative process itself.

The more explicitly 'creative' end of this magazine publishing spectrum is undoubtedly that of 'independent magazines'. In Chapter 8 (by David Stam), printed magazines are discussed as a valued counterpoint to the often ephemeral nature of digital media. From scarce and niche (such as *Hole & Corner* and *Burnt Roti*) to abundant and 'free' products (such as *Stylist*), publishers of magazines somewhere in-between have pioneered being digitally mediated services for specialist audiences. In an interview in Chapter 1, the managing director of *Decanter*, Robin McMillan, points to a new confidence from mainstream 'legacy' publishers, those who have defied the unfavourable digital environment of the last decade.

Environment and context is often said to be everything when examining any field, phenomena or industrial system, and any study of the media cannot ignore the special, totemic nature of magazine publishing as a cultural media industry. Aside from its new and current affairs origins, Christine Stam's history of magazines (Chapter 2) shows that magazine publishing was, as an industry, inextricably linked to the most well-known brands of the last 100 years, becoming innovators of a paid-for media vehicle for the promotion of consumerism itself. Andrew Blake's chapter on international magazines (Chapter 6), meanwhile, points to the constant innovations in product over the last 40 years, through which both publishers and advertisers address new global readerships, including the very wealthy and the aspirant well-paid.

The largest golden goose of the magazine industry's past can therefore be seen as display advertising sales for segmented audiences. As the book acknowledges, this is also perhaps the most changed aspect of the publishers' world since the Millennium, and no examination of the magazine media business would be complete without a considered look at the economics of advertising. In Chapter 5, Helen Powell's examination of the role of advertising shows in granular detail what the shift to digital or programmatic advertising means to the magazine business today – and importantly what it might mean in the future.

Magazine futures: dark clouds and silver linings

Sometimes the future itself, however, arrives more rapidly, and more destructively, than anyone can expect. At the time of writing, nothing could be more pertinent to examining the external environmental 'shock' of the COVID-19 pandemic. Although its impact is not the focus of Chapter 1 (where the last two decades of neoliberal economics are assessed), the global pandemic will undoubtedly accentuate some of the negative effects of the business environment – but, in the spirit of the Schumpeterian message within, there may lie a silver lining to the dark clouds above.

In March 2020. the UK, along with most world economies, went into lockdown to staunch the spread of COVID-19. What happened and how did this affect the publishing industry? Your editors are not futurologists, and this wicked virus continues to challenge predictions – but as a generalisation, a number of the behavioural changes driven by coronavirus have speeded up trends which were already present in the marketplace – and they are not all bad.

For a period of at least six weeks, all but essential shops closed. The UK's largest newsagent, WH Smith, kept certain High Street stores open for reduced hours but its important Travel stores division was severely hit as office workers turned to working from home and international air travel was only for essential purposes. The summer of 2020 saw the resumption of full-time trading on the High Street, but with shoppers wearing masks – a practice not exactly conducive to shelf browsing for books and magazines. Because of the depth of its range and the supportive policy to stock the specialist press, many titles lost significant sales in this period, but hobbyists and followers of niche sports are nothing but enthusiasts and publishers saw an uptake in postal subscription sales to help offset falling retail sales.

Supermarkets, convenience stores and independent newsagents remained open throughout the worst weeks of the pandemic. Publishers reported higher sales in these outlets, particularly for mass selling titles such as TV listings and celebrity weeklies. However, distributors often found it hard to send extra copies into this market channel as retail staff were under great work pressure and, unsurprisingly, prioritised food sales. Again, subscription sales prospered, but as we write, retail customers are slowly returning.

The pandemic accelerated the existing trend from retail into subscriptions, and it also aided the move to digital. The experience of a digital magazine is not the same as for the print version and some undoubtedly find it less satisfying, but the download is instantaneous (which means no queuing two metres apart outside your supermarket) and is often more cost effective than the normal cover price. As David Stam describes in Chapter 3, you can also take an 'all-you-can-read' approach by subscribing to services such as Readly and Cafeyn at a highly attractive price. Certain membership titles also took the opportunity to go digital; one of these, *The Goodwood Magazine*, is examined in Chapter 3.

In Chapter 5, Helen Powell traces the decline in traditional paid-for magazine advertising space, pointing out that even the largest publishers find it tough to compete with the social media and search engine giants of the internet age. Coronavirus will undoubtedly have hastened this sad trend; but as the world emerges from lockdown and seeks to discover a 'new normal', marketers of consumer goods and services are looking to build rapport with their markets. At a time when everyone is concerned about rising levels of unemployment, redundancy and health issues – both physical and mental – brands want to be seen as compassionate, caring, inclusive and sympathetic. Your editors argue that there is no better way to portray these noble attributes than through the pages of trusted magazines in the form of content marketing.

As Simon Das and Christine Stam describe in Chapters 1 and 2, respectively, magazines have been storytelling in words and pictures for centuries. Their practitioners are experts at it and their readers – as the excellent research by Guy Consterdine (2005) shows – trust what they say and value the relationship with their chosen titles. There is no doubt that the traditional advertising revenue stream for titles is running dry, but there are opportunities to be grasped by publishers in the growing area of branded content, both in print and digital. Chapter 8 describes the endeavours of a new type of media business that is well placed to take advantage of such opportunities, TCO London. Businesses will have to learn to adapt – in particular editorial colleagues will have to lessen the grip on so-called 'Church versus State' but the unique relationships that magazines have with their readers can come to the fore to help deliver the new found objectives of client companies.

Trust is a key word here, and there is little surprise in the unfolding success of the UK news weeklies sector. Titles such as *The Economist*, *The Spectator* and *The New Statesman* invest and deliver high quality writing, carefully subedited and fact checked to cement reader loyalty trust. In a world of fast, sometimes fake, news this is a cornerstone of their business model and the genre has seen significant subscription success during and post lockdown. These magazines are amongst the longest serving of the UK market and undoubtedly have a healthy future in an uncertain world.

One story that knocked coronavirus off the front pages in the summer of 2020 was Black Lives Matter (BLM). Whether in metropolitan America or in the UK's West Country, people of every colour and creed came out to register protest and to say – BLM, of course they matter: in education, health and equal opportunities people of colour must have the same expectation of opportunity and success as their white countrymen and women. Sports players took the knee behind closed doors at cricket and soccer games, and a statue of a historical slave trader was toppled into the Bristol docks.

Your editors had planned a chapter on diversity in the magazine world long before BLM hit the headlines; but the movement has given this important issue focus and impetus. In fairness, the industry has long been a good example of gender diversity, but as Andrew Blake and Simon Das explain in Chapter 7, much less so in terms of ethnicity. While the 'ethnic media' (including influential UK publications such as *gal-dem* and *Burnt Roti*) have made significant provision for the diverse readerships who now inhabit urban areas in the UK (as they do in the rest of Europe and North America), too often mainstream magazines promote positive representations of that population, while their employment structures are much more conservative. Again, we hope that the dramatic events of 2020 will produce a beneficial change to the industry. Here is one area where the 'new normal' needs to be genuinely new, and not a cut-price version of the old. Without innovation in employment structures and practices that at least matches the technological and business innovations described in this book, magazine publishing is in danger of becoming a cultural anachronism in a changing world.

A roadmap for the future of magazines

In the last ten years, the publishing industry worldwide has reeled from the structural shock of digital media and the cyclical revenue downturn of the post-2008 financial crisis. There have been title closures and some of them significant, such as the cessation of the *Marie Claire* print edition in 2019. But the business has also shown resilience with editors and publishers, of both large and small players, creating new ways of mediating content with resulting revenue streams. This new title, *Innovations in Magazine Publishing,* is a roadmap for the future – a future only navigable by rising to the challenges of ever more digital technological change, new advertising and business models and the management of a creative and diverse media workforce. We trust that this book will be helpful to students and practitioners alike, when considering these complex issues.

References

Abrahamson, David, and Marcia R. Prior-Miller (2018), *The Routledge Handbook of Magazine Research: The Future of the Magazine Form,* 2nd edition, New York: Routledge

Consterdine, Guy (2005), *How Magazine Advertising Works*, 5th edition, Periodical Publishers' Association

Cox, Howard, and Simon Mowatt (2014), *Revolutions from Grub Street: A History of Magazine Publishing in Britain*, Oxford: Oxford University Press.

Dennis, Felix (2004), 'The four horsemen', *British Journalism Review*, vol. 15 no. 3, pp. 45–50

Holmes, Tim (2020), 'Case study: *Porter* magazine: a case study in hybridity', in Miglena Sternadori and Tim Holmes, eds., *The Handbook of Magazine Studies*, Hoboken, NJ: John Wiley, pp. 154–162

McKay, Jenny (2018), *The Magazines Handbook*, 4th edition, London: Routledge

Stam, David, and Andrew Scott (2014), *Inside Magazine Publishing*, Oxford: Routledge

Sternadori, Miglena, and Tim Holmes, eds. (2020), *The Handbook of Magazine Studies*, Hoboken, NJ: John Wiley

1

MAGAZINE PUBLISHING INNOVATION

The 'drivers' and implications of technology

Simon Das

This opening chapter examines the underlying factors behind what is discussed as the magazine industry's battle for relevance in the twenty-first century. While the examination of the magazine business today and its history (discussed in Chapters 2 and 3) provides examples of publishing innovation, the aim of this chapter is to reveal the external 'drivers' behind innovation in the digital era at an industry level and the business and strategic implications for dealing with them.

In an attempt at explaining the way publishers have, and need to further, innovate, the focus on digital 'disruption' is analysed by discussing innovation theory, the magazine business over the eras and its recent socioeconomic and technological context. Estimating the drivers of innovation in the digital era, a detailed PEST analysis (an analysis of the political, economic, sociological and technological environment) is provided for the magazine industry, before examining a current innovation publishing case study in TI Media's *Decanter* magazine.

As the industry-wide discussion and case study shows, publishers adopting both 'sustaining' and 'disruptive' innovations provide ways forward in the context of where media and 'tech' are inseparable, but legacy business remains crucial and relevant. Innovation in areas such as online platforms, business-to-business services and premium subscriptions are therefore proffered as strategic implications for a 'mixed mode' future for a media business in the twenty-first century.

Innovation theory

Innovation is not just about improving turnover or profit in a company. Although the economic imperative of aiding a company's fortune's is undoubtedly part of the picture, innovation is also about a growth in knowledge; an improvement in human experience, improvements in efficiency and quality and creativity of what companies do and how they do it. According to innovation management theorists such as David O'Sullivan, innovation is the "process of making changes to something established by introducing something new" (O'Sullivan & Dooley, 2009a, p. 3). As we shall discuss, these changes in the magazine world can be to the products a publisher provides (print products, digital content), the processes they employ (such as how magazines reach audiences or how they are edited) and in the services delivered (such as business-to-customer events or business-to-business advertisers and branded content clients).

Why innovate? The drivers of innovation

External factors are said to drive innovation. Nothing can remain static in the dynamic climate and markets that any company operates in. It is therefore untrue that innovation is created in a vacuum and produced for its own sake, despite the often quoted intrinsic need to be 'an innovator' or to be 'disruptive' – there are always extrinsic factors driving this. Changes in the market and the wider technological environment often dictate the need for innovation. According to O'Sullivan & Dooley (2009a, p. 12), the drivers of innovation are specifically: emerging technologies, competition, new ideas from customers and partners and changes in the external environment. Such external factors are sometimes called 'socioeconomic factors' and in many business studies analyses since Aguilar's *Scanning the Business Environment* (Aguilar, 1967) are often assessed by a form of PEST analysis: one specifically examining, *political, economic, sociological* and *technological* factors driving change.

Disruptive innovation theory

Product innovations can be incremental, slow or more radical and even 'game-changing' in nature. Many digital innovations of the last decade are said to be in this radical bracket, so much so that they are often called 'disruptive innovations'. In the business lexicon of the present era, this term is often synonymous with the word 'tech', disruption is seen perhaps increasingly as a form of pure tech innovation. In the digital era, 'disruption', has become more than just a widely cited objective, it has become something of a business mantra. Part of a David and Goliath narrative, it inspires pitches in boardrooms, VC (venture capital) offices and press releases, where start-up companies espouse being disruptors in the vein of Apple's Steve Jobs, Facebook's Mark Zuckerberg or Amazon's Jeff Bezos. According to the most widely cited originator of disruptive innovation theory, Clayton Christensen, the term 'disruptive', however, is perhaps too loosely applied to "any situation in which an industry is shaken up and successful incumbents stumble" (Christensen et al., 2015, p. 45). Being disruptive is seen as a tech business imperative – a way to be technologically smart in a period where innovations have arrived in established marketplaces, eliminating established industries at an unforeseen rate.

Long before the rise of the tech giants, disruptive innovation theory was developed as a strategic warning tool for established businesses to avoid what was empirically shown by Clayton Christensen as a form of pathology in business success. Asking why innovators are often displaced by entirely inexperienced companies, disruptive innovation was framed by Christensen as a type of 'innovator's dilemma' – the name used to entitle his following book (Christensen, 1997). A warning of 'sticking to what you know at your peril', DI theory shows us a recurring pattern of industrial decline caused by new entrants in markets offering very different, often unknown and 'low-end' products in established markets. By gaining small traction at lower ends of markets, unknown innovators improve what Christensen terms product 'performance', and end up accessing more lucrative and higher end markets. Left unchecked, predicts the theory, new entrants' performance can escalate, before disrupting existing companies, markets and even entire industries: a pattern seen by a number of different business scholars across sectors, industries and markets.

The explanation of why disruptive innovation happens in this way might be summed up by a customer view: 'you didn't know you even wanted a specific innovation, until you realised you couldn't live without it'. It was, according to Allworth (2011), the guiding business philosophy of Apple's founder and former CEO Steve Jobs – defining a 20-year period where each new class of electronic product launched entered fields that Apple had no business competency in when launching. An exemplar of Christensen's disruptors' model, Apple launched the iPod into the portable hi-fi market when Sony and others had 30 years of market leadership; they launched iPhone into mobile telephony when a duopoly of Nokia and Ericsson dominated smartphones globally; and even took on the entire music retail and streaming industry when they were known only for home computing and creative desktop publishing (iTunes and Apple Music).

Although some extremely successful tech innovations in the last decade, for example Uber, are said by Christensen to *not* be disruptive innovation (Uber has not changed the field of taxis to an alternative type of transport), disruption has changed our landscape. Some clear examples that do fit Christensen's model are the social media 'aggregation' platforms of Facebook, Twitter and Instagram disrupting newspaper and magazine publishing. In media, Netflix has been seen as the end to a 30-year-strong global video rental business and in leisure, Airbnb today threatens an entire strata of the hotel industry, with its endless supply of user generated low-cost rentals. In rapidly changing times, the big innovations of the last decade all started as low end or marginal concepts (Airbnb was originally a student 'sofa sharing' service), but all employed digital technology to radically reinvent the established order of things and thus provide a level of Christensen's product (or service) 'performance' that customers could not have imagined before they existed. They often did this by offering something initially free, low cost and often less high-end than established rivals.

A century of magazine innovation: scale to specialisation

Adaption and adoption since the last century

Forms of disruptive technology have always guided the hand of business innovation in magazine publishing. New and innovative products, ways of reaching audiences and new business models is not something new to magazine publishing – it is part of a story in publishing revealing them as adaptors and disruptors in the twentieth century, and even before – in the early nineteenth century, magazines themselves were disruptive to the traditional press, newspapers and even book publishers (see Chapter 2). An examination of this industrial history of "adoption and adaptation" of technology by magazine publishers (in Das, 2016, Cox & Mowatt, 2014 and Stam & Scott 2014) shows us that magazines have seldom sat still as a media 'product'. The varying of form, features, distribution, advertising and content is testament to so many magazine titles being the most enduring and long-running media brands today. As discussed in Chapter 2, titles or brands such as *The Lady, Tatler* and *Vanity Fair* all date back to the mid-nineteenth century – and *The Spectator* even further, being in continuous business since 1828.

Over this period of time, publishers have therefore had to change what they do, how they do it and who they do it for, driven fundamentally by technological change, cultural shifts (in work, leisure and domestic roles) and the growth of literacy and consumerism as part of it. Magazine publishing, like other industries after the Industrial Revolution, was underpinned by the technological affordances of the era: technology and socioeconomics going hand-in-hand. As far back as the

PHOTO 1.1 Three hundred years of *The Spectator* magazine. Richard Steele and Joseph Addison's original version of 1711 and a recent cover from the modern publication (2011).

beginning of the last century, the technologies of moveable fixed type printing, colour reprographics of photography, gravure and offset lithographic printing – all afforded the production of colour printed periodicals for the masses. Such changes defined the industrial structure of magazine publishing but did not emerge in isolation. These technologies merely served the growing demand for news and specialist media, one fuelled by Britain's industrial expansion of rail infrastructure, and a growing middle-class of readers with new pastimes. In terms of industrial structure, publishing magazines meant bigger and bigger magazine companies: and the later nineteenth century becoming a time of amalgamation, investment and vertical integration of presses, and the swallowing-up of smaller publishers and newspaper publishers into ever larger entities.

Early twentieth century: new magazines for new tastes

Referring to this era, magazine-industry historians Cox and Mowatt describe how Amalgamated Press, Newnes and Odhams were all acquired by Daily Mirror Newspapers, creating a "virtual monopoly of Britain's consumer magazines" (Cox & Mowatt, 2014, p. 13) in the formation of the International Publishing Company (or IPC). Fuelled by post-war lifestyle changes and birth of mainstream consumerism, without competition from the geographically distant US corporations or European publishers (who did not enter the UK market until the 1980s), IPC is referred to by Cox & Mowatt as being Britain's mid-century 'Ministry of Magazines' (Cox & Mowatt, 2014, p. 91) – an organisation that by 1960 was bigger than the BBC.

Throughout the mid-twentieth century, this picture of industrial growth continued, but began to look different and more fragmented as broadcast media became the disruptive technology of the time, in the form of radio and then television. This was a time for more new ideas in magazines, from publishers that faced new competition from more media channels, and larger state-owned mass media broadcasters (such as the BBC). With the drivers of innovation identified from a growing Post-War boom in consumerism, news and current affairs, leisure pursuits and hobbies became the magazine industry's focus as they mined diverse, and even esoteric tastes from more varied audiences. Innovation through the process of 'segmentation' (the search for more subgenres in specialist audiences) also capitalised on specialist advertising revenues, allowing magazines a different way to compete with the mass media 'reach' of radio and television.

The 1980s and 1990s: segmentation and new audiences

By the 1980s, the new drivers of innovation furthered this process of discovering new and specialist readerships. Eased by liberalised labour markets (the major theme of the Thatcher-Reagan era), the *laissez faire* economic ideology of the period broke the traditional newspaper unionised print and typesetting strangleholds. The resultant growing Anglo-American magazine sector (by publishers such as Hearst, Condé Nast and the National Magazine Company), however all neglected a new social change – and with it an opportunity to connect with a demographic of working women. The new lower socioeconomic taste for 'chatty' women's journalism emerged, and with it the arrival of European publishers such as Germany's Gruner & Jahr and Bauer Media, who sent shockwaves across the publishing sector with the launch of the so called 'throwaway' titles such as *Prima* in 1987, before other European entrants arrived. In the wake of yet more consumer demand for women's celebrity fare, the high society voyeurism in *Hello!* (published by Spain's Sancho Junquez family) saw later and greater French incursions into the UK market with their Gallic counterpoint to the 'feminism' of Anglo-American women's staple *Cosmopolitan*, in the form of *Marie Claire* – a title that was a market leader until the 2010s.

Magazines in the new millennium: towards new niches

Heading towards the digital era, the 1990s to 2000s saw ever more specialist magazines emerge, and the innovative ability to address many 'niche interest' areas, especially for younger audiences never previously catered for. Launches in lifestyle, music magazines and men's fashion – niches previously thought impossible to mine – were innovative areas for new, smaller publishers with creative ideas and more flexibility than major publishers. The drivers of democratised tastes, the rise of an information society and a dissemination of computing into homes, were bolstered by a labour market of freelance creatives and the advent of digital desktop publishing technologies. One company that emerged as a future specialist innovator in this era was the small Peterborough based EMAP – which became the home to pop music magazine *Smash Hits*, before it helped editor Nick Logan launch a slew of 'stylepress' titles such as *The Face* and *Arena* (through his own company called Wagadon), alongside a number of number of home computing and computer games magazines. Alongside newcomers Dennis Publishing (owned by Felix Dennis, famed for 1960s counterculture magazine editor *Oz*) and Future Publishing – these publishers capitalised on the hugely growing consumerism around home entertainment, home computing and high street fashion. Creating a combined computer gaming, gadget, fashion and lifestyle sector that, at its height, these combined areas grew to around 25 per cent of all magazine sales by the turn of the millennium (Key Note, 2004). Innovation driven by the inexhaustible taste for information technology, popular music and fashion culture and the second wave of the post-war youth culture and consumerism explosion in the late twentieth century.

The digital drivers of the digital era: PEST analysis

T for technology: magazines in the digital era

During the last decade, the industry has faced immense challenge – one that's even been called an existential threat to the magazine itself – from a variety of digital

PHOTO 1.2 Montage of covers from legendary 1990s style guide *The Face*.

platforms and the way they reinvent what has become known as media 'content'. The ability for consumers, through a variety of increasingly mobile devices, to instantly receive and share multimedia content, from digital-only magazines through to HD television and radio, is now the norm through everyone's mobile phone. Contrastingly, this democratising of words, content and publishing has not led to unmonetised sharing. The new economic reality of media has become one reliant on living with technology giants of Facebook, Google, YouTube and Amazon – monolithic giants who dominate the competitive media landscape. Magazines as media products (and advertiser services within them) today operate in a complex user 'media mix', alongside their readers' ever-present mobile phone connectivity, with its social media feeds, news services and the linked on-demand digital services of mainstream television broadcasters and tech giant backed content creators such as Apple, Amazon and Netflix.

Although digital technology started to have an effect on the industry in the 1980s, with a wave of youth culture launches by independent magazines aided by the advent of desktop publishing software such as Quark's page layout software coupled to network-friendly personal computers (namely Steve Job's Apple computers, and his MacOS operating system), the last decade has been the era of the end of this beginning. Before the maturation of internet technologies, publishing was some-thing that required specialist skills, equipment, software, distribution channels and considerable outlay. In recent decades, 'to publish' has come to include even the meaning of pressing a button marked 'publish' on a web-based back-end of a blog or a social media story on Facebook or Instagram. Everyone, by this definition, is now a publisher – but only a few publishers own a platform that everyone uses. Looked at from a functionality point of view, why go to an individual publisher's platform when you can go to a 'node' where thousands of publishers' content can be found? According to Lucy Küng, the majority of legacy publisher's digital traffic (including magazine publishers) is on one of the monolithic 'tech' companies' platforms: Google, Facebook (including Instagram), Amazon or Apple. 70 per cent of this is accessed via a mobile (Küng, 2018).

Theorists therefore point out that the last decade cannot be one defined, as in previous decades, by industrial development of 'high tech' or even 'new' technology. It is more revolutionary than that. There is no such thing as new 'technology' when changes in technology and media usage are so rapid, fundamental and widely spread. The evidence in language is that we have a new all-encompassing term for anything innovative at all in the present era – it's simply called 'tech'. Akin to nearly all other industries (e.g. in the automotive industry Tesla cars might be described as 'tech on wheels'), in the media industry, according to Lucy Küng: "Technology has become media itself now, absolutely intrinsic to the creation of content, to the distribution of that content, to the quality of that content, to building a relationship with audiences, and to scale and therefore competitive sustainability" (Küng, 2018, p. 1). If everyone is a publisher, it is because technology that everyone has access to (for free) is no longer a portal or 'conduit' for content delivery – the tech *is* the content itself.

S for sociological: society and technology in the digital era

Given this view of technology, it might seem confusing to consider that it is per-haps not technology per se that is the external driver for innovation, but society itself. According to a more sociological view, technology and society cannot be prized apart. While it is true that technology has been rapidly evolving – it has done so, both for and because of, technology. Explained by famed digital sociolo-gist, Manuel Castells: "We know that technology does not determine society: it *is* society. Society shapes technology according to the needs, values, and interests of people who use the technology" (Castells, 2005, p. 3).

What might be termed 'digital philosophy' or anthropology since Manuel Castells, many have referred to the last two decades of 'the information age' as being explained not just by information technology, but by its novel connectivity as a 'network society' (Castells, 2000). In the last decade, his social theory has explained an interconnectivity and power that traditionally 'loose' systems such as networks can have through digital technology. In the past, a network was a structure suit-able only for informal organisations (e.g. friendship networks) – they could never act in the way vertical organisations ran companies, armies, even nations. The new connectivity of work, industries and even social grouping in the last decade, has the power to transcend corporate, national and even continental boundaries by the affordance of internet-based technology. In the view of sociologists optimistic about such networked power, such as David Gauntlett (2011), this network society affords the ordinary person on the street a 'making' culture, free to do things in way that breaks down the gatekeeping of consumerism, thus liberating human creativity and the bonds between producers and consumers.

Others point out the potential dangers of such dramatic social change facilitated for 'free' by the large tech giants, having monopolised data on our on-demand 24/7 world. If there is a 'downside' to this new sociology, it is perhaps that digital technologies have also turbo charged the growth of a group outside of this rather utopian 'creative class' of thought leaders. Those economically precarious as part of the 'gig economy' (freelancing for example, so much a part of the creative indus-tries and many others), perhaps have not had as much to rejoice in the digital economy. In the last five years, we have seen a related darker side of digital tech-nology, especially with regards to social media– and the associated rise of what Andrew Keen once hailed as a modern 'cult of the amateur' (Keen, 2007). In such a world, where once marginal views and political populism have been on the increase as the internet 'disintermediates' trusted and professional publishing voices, placing experts and the mainstream media channels on an equal footing with the blogger, the social 'influencer' and anyone with a viewpoint.

Regardless of importance and validity of such concerns about the digital society, a macropicture of the UK, after decades of internationalisation and cultural diver-sity through generations of immigration, reveals a digital 'turbo charging' in the last decade of what was nascent in the 1990s: changing social attitudes, consumption habits, working patterns and leisure pursuits. Many former cultural norms from a generation ago are today unrecognisable. Those optimistic about such a shift will consider a more digitally connected society as one richer in social capital, more invested in one another and see it to have improved education and understanding. We might consider evidence of this by recalling the social stigma of only two decades ago about things such as gay marriage in middle-class England; the racial prejudice in sport or the subtle exclusion in the workplace of people on the basis of disability or even gender. Although these remain, of course, present-day issues, there is no doubt that society has evolved enormously in such areas, especially amongst the culture of the 'Millennials'. These are said to be a generation born as 'digital natives' (and therefore not 'digital migrants' who entered the internet era as adults), a generation at ease with the speed and pace of adoption of new social norms – and a group that is said to transcend class, region or border boundaries.

Despite such huge and progressive drivers of societal change in the UK as elsewhere, this does not signify a youthfulness of society *per se*. Demographers will be quick to point out that the last decade was a time where an ageing population came to dominate the demographic make-up of British society. Never in history has there been such an intergenerational schism between the younger 'digitally native' drivers of technology and the older economic beneficiaries of capital and land. This is perhaps justified as only sustainable in the societal trade-off espoused by Gauntlett (2011), as when it comes to Millennials – this is a demographic said to be less materialistic. Several generations after the post-War 'Baby boomers', Millennials consume less, make choices based on more ethical and sustainable basis, and co-produce 'value-added' economic outputs in more socially constructed and participant ways: perhaps in the creativity of social media, up-cycling products or in the remixing of art and music. In fact, they are, according Richard Florida, an entirely new 'creative class' of people – ones geographically free of nations, tied instead to any global place where the three 'Ts' of tolerance, talent and technology coincide (Florida, 2004).

The magazine mass-media model of sales volumes in specific nations and regions at a low prices is, therefore, one increasingly out of kilter with such social changes, especially those of a new 'creative class' sensibility. Although, in an ageing population, where printed titles in certain genres remain very strong (e.g. in TV listings magazines), we can see that the specific driver of change is that society sees media, overall, as a less 'valued' source of both information, entertainment (and more perniciously trust in news) and its dissemination of taste and shared experiences. These areas for magazines have become the spaces and new battlegrounds for publisher 'verticals', or 'communities' that the industry aims to keep, consolidate and reinvent for a new generation: one more as 'participants', over the former assumption of people as 'readers', 'browsers' or 'audiences'.

P for political: the rules of no regulation

The political environment for publishers is often thought of as one that seldom changes. However, some regulatory frameworks – or the lack of them – have become powerful drivers for change in media described above – one that has shaken the magazine industry to its core. Although publishers in the past have dealt with (and even lobbied against) regulation on a number of areas from freedom of speech, libel law through to pornography (e.g. the 1990s near censorship of men's consumer lifestyle 'lads mags' in the UK), all of these pale into insignificance compared with the recent impact of a decade of what might be called 'silence' from government on market regulation and competition in media and telecommunications.

The largest political driver to innovate is therefore not the politics, but the lack of governmental rule in the controlling of media markets, or more precisely, the regulatory freedom afforded by liberalised markets and the absence of international protectionism in markets such as the UK's. Considering the scale of the recent rise of the tech giants such as Facebook (excluding the equally powerful entities of Google and Amazon), can be seen as dominant in all nearly all aspects of content and news dissemination – not just in the sharing of publishers' and users' content through both Facebook and Instagram social media and stories, but also as being the world's largest messaging, telephony and videoconferencing telecommunications company in the world with WhatsApp.

This astronomic rise in what might be called the economic 'gatekeeping' ability in recent years has aggrieved some of the highest spokespeople in magazine publishing. According to James Hewes, CEO of FIPP (the International Federation of the Periodical Press), the emergence of the technological giants of Google and Facebook ten years ago was not seen as a threat to magazines, but an opportunity. It is now, however, perceived in a very different way: "The direction of travel is very much towards regulation. Market pressure or regulation will eventually break them up" (Hewes, 2020). According to Hewes, the big mistake that the magazine industry made was to treat tech giants as 'public utilities'. In a recent interview, he explains that these companies "have no obligation to treat us fairly, unless the government legislates. I think we forget that. I think we always thought it would be in Facebook's interest to keep us happy. It wasn't" (Hewes, 2020).

E for economic: the new business of being 'free'

The last decade's economic environment in the wake of the 2008 financial crisis and the following generation of austerity measures (including public sector pay freezes and cuts in public spending) lead to stagnant economic growth in mature Western economies such as the UK's. This climate has unsurprisingly coincided with the growth of many free at source digital services – when money is tight, why pay for something that you get on the internet for free? Popularly theorised by the likes of *Wired* magazine's editor, Chris Anderson (Anderson, 2006, 2009), from the beginning of the last decade, the digital era offered a 'radical' zero price to consumers for many services and media products. For the media industry, the resultant untested business model of giving content away for free in the internet age led to a paradigm shift by publishers, especially newspapers and content aggregators, desperate to tap into gaining huge digital audiences. By 2010, the new 'added

value' of media economics became, not lifetime value, unit sales or even revenue, but the new digital 'metrics' of hits, page impressions, unique users, social
media 'shares' and 'likes'. When news, entertainment, encyclopaedias and direc-
tories, maps, reviews, advice and social groupings increasingly became part of the
user-generated internet world hailed by the digital media evangelists as part of
new sharing economy of 'making and connecting' (Gauntlett, 2011), magazine
publishers faced the prospect of not being able to sell their products to audiences
in the near future.

Those who hailed the 'death of print' soon after the Millennium dot-com boom,
for example Dennis Publishing's former owner Felix Dennis in his famous 'Four
Horsemen' paper (Dennis, 2004), were both quick to see the future decline in print
magazine circulations and the need for digital content (and in the potential for
digital advertising), but at the same time wrong in suggesting the scale and speed of
impact on the industry. In an overview, the picture of the last decade is one of relief,
yet also woe. On the one hand, magazine circulations have not declined evenly, or
plummeted across the board to an insignificant level in the way predicted: a positive
for the legacy industry and their brands. On the other hand, there is no doubting
that headline total magazine circulations have massively dropped (according to
Mintel, 2019 in the five years between the years 2014 and 2019 alone by 26 per
cent) and exploiting digital magazine sales and a transfer of advertising revenues
from print to online has not compensated for this decline: a huge challenge for the
industry.

While declines in circulations were more obvious to predict, what blindsided
the magazine publishing industry was the changing economics around their main
source of income – advertising. The economics – not of paid-for content but that of
selling display pages – in the end, presented the real existential threat to magazines.
Magazine publishers were the historic masters of advertising, and increasingly relied
on it for 'subsidising' their cover prices by the 2000s (Sumner, 2001): magazines
sold because they were inexpensive to the readers, being effectively 'paid-for' by
advertisers.

During the Noughties, when the social media tech giants grew to a global size,
they initially had no such experience in advertising sales – and little interest in it.
According to FIPP CEO James Hewes: "Facebook have gone from zero to being
basically the second biggest player in the digital advertising market. The problem is
they keep all the revenue" (Hewes, 2020). This left magazine publishers between a
rock and a hard place by 2010, faced with one of two options: They could either
provide their content via social platforms for free – and get no reward; or they
could engage online communities through search engine optimisation (SEO) and
push audiences to their own magazine platforms. Although this seemed like a good
strategy, the 'new' economics of digital advertising showed that sales revenues in this
space were tiny, based on programmatic tariffs for online magazine metrics nowhere
near the astronomic, targeted 'reach' of Google, Facebook, Instagram and YouTube.
Anderson's new world of near 'free' economics, it seemed, applied nearly as well to
the lucrative business-to-business sphere of media advertising sales, as it did to how

PHOTO 1.3 The late Felix Dennis who gave the landmark Four Horsemen speech in 2004. Photo Simon Turtle.

people received their news, pastime pleasure reading or trivia about people with extraordinary pet cats.

A case study in 'mixed mode' innovation: *Decanter*

Established magazines facing the dilemma of whether to do something 'disruptive' or fail, often end up opting for what might be called a 'mixed mode' of innovation: mixed in the attempt to find new customers and advertisers through untraditional and disruptive means, while also serving an established audience, upholding market position and brand equity in legacy. This pragmatic approach to dealing with the PEST 'drivers' discussed, has the benefit of firstly building what Christensen calls 'sustaining' innovation into a market (getting better at what you do), while also learning about new markets and testing the water for newer 'disruptive' concepts. While publishers might be well aware of drivers for innovation

PHOTO 1.4 Two 2020 covers from *Decanter* – the magazine for wine connoisseurs.

predicting disruption on a wider level, managing decline can be both simple and lucrative – especially if the decline is a slow disruption. As the international trade body for magazines, FIPP proffers:

> Weekly lifestyles, TV magazines, and gossips were once the most profitable magazines, yet are the most affected in the last ten years. All of that content is largely going to go to digital platforms. That market is eventually going to disappear. I wouldn't say ten years, but eventually they [the readers] are going to die, and the market with it.
>
> *Hewes, 2020*

In the case of *Decanter*, surviving and thriving in the digital era is concerned with working both sides of this innovation street; acknowledging their legacy as one of the best-known specialist wine magazines on the newsstands and super-market shelves, but also their future as a 'premium' digital content provider, a database for shoppers of wine, and an important social media and public relations-driven event organiser. In a recent conversation with Marcus Rich, former CEO of TI Media (now Future plc) (Rich, 2020), of all the 40 magazine brands they publish, he cited wine magazine *Decanter* as one of the most 'innovative' during the digital shift.

Decanter magazine sees the print product only at the symbolic centre of their business: the sales of the magazine are not the central to their business strategy. As such, this is a magazine that despite its legacy (launching in 1975), does not even seek a circulation certificate (print and digital) from the Audit Bureau of Circulations (ABC). Instead, *Decanter* is concerned with connecting as many different readers in as many ways as possible. *Decanter* maintains these contact points digitally, socially, through premium 'paywalled' digital content and interestingly, being a brand that convenes events – and influential ones at that. In doing this, *Decanter* has a large following – it has amassed both a consumer audience (who want to read about wine) and importantly a new business-to-business (b2b) customer in the form of paid-for 'advertisers'. This b2b aspect comes mainly from the winemakers and distributors who want to be represented at international events, and who covet the awards and prizes given by the magazine. This is a magazine, therefore, as an 'expert', as an authentic voice and gatekeeper of knowledge about a specialist consumer area. *Decanter* digitally connects people 'at a distance' through new media channels (both free and premium), but is also 'close enough' to see their faces (and their ticket receipts) at a number of events; most importantly, a yearly prestigious *Decanter* Awards ceremony.

MANAGING INNOVATION FOCUS: A LOOK INSIDE *DECANTER* MAGAZINE

An interview with Robin McMillan, Managing Director of *Decanter*, Future plc (previously TI Media)

Tell us a little about yourself. Have you been MD at *Decanter* for long?

I joined two years ago. I have never been a magazine publisher or even an editor. I don't have a media background. I came from retail, I was at The Wine Society and Berry Bros, before that. *Decanter* felt similar though, in that it is a quintessentially English brand, but also very global.

When did *Decanter* first publish its magazine?

We've been going since 1975! That's a good history for a consumer magazine. But in the wine business, that's of course not that old: The Wine Society goes back to the 1870s

Magazines don't traditionally have MDs. Who does what at *Decanter*?

I'm acting as editor in chief – though that job title is one we've been looking to fill for quite a while. The skills and backgrounds have changed in publishing. We have really good editorial people. We have great print experienced people, great digital people and also someone specialist running the premium digital side (paywall). However, everyone now works under a single content hub. The process starts with 'what's the content?', and then we decide where it's going – so it's 'platform agnostic'.

Given this brand history, are there a lot of competitors?

In the UK, from a purely magazine perspective, there's not actually a great deal of competition – the whole field has narrowed down. But, then we're increasingly thinking globally and internationally. Nearly a third of our readers are from the US and around 16 per cent in Europe. Competition in those territories is much stronger: *Wine Spectator*, in the US, for example.

You're best known for your events. Are magazine sales less important now?

I really try to avoid the 'this is more important than that debate'. The commercial numbers may make that true, but everyone's point of reference to *Decanter* the brand *is* the magazine. Before I joined a couple of years ago, my assumption was that print was on the way out. Actually I think it's the opposite.

That may come to surprise people who point to declining print circulations…

Well, print just has to adapt its content and positioning to the 'new order' of tech out there. There are now a lot of 'touchpoints', but the one constant element is print. They understand what that is. They are familiar with the magazine. I say: 'What a fantastic vehicle to show what this new world might look like.' It's a really important part of the mix.

And what about the other, digital, elements in the 'mix'

Our differentiated offer is the best example of this mix. So, some people might go to our events, some might be aware of the awards, but not necessarily both, others may subscribe to our digital premium content on the app, but not be magazine subscribers, others may simply occasionally look at our content on the dotcom site. I don't think there are models out there for this new 'digital' world! The journey from print to… 'whatever' is a question mark. It's a case of trying a lot of things and seeing what 'sticks'! The challenge for me is to keep the consumer looking-in and seeing *Decanter* as a cohesive brand.

What's the most 'innovative' thing you've done in the last couple of years?

Decanter Premium, without a doubt. We're in a 'test and learn' environment with the premium content in digital. It's going well, with around 7000 subscribers in two years. The magazine gives the content people are used to: profiles, reviews, columnists and so on. Premium is designed to give that too as well as extra breadth and depth and immediacy of content. If we had a selection of 'Top 500 wines' on the premium app, perhaps only 50 of those would be on the main website. There's also exclusive access to events. We did a trial where Premium users had an exclusive first hour of an event. That went down really well. The wine producers loved it too, as they knew this was a group who paid extra and are extra interested in wine.

Do people who buy a subscription to the magazine get Premium?

No. What we call the 'bundling' side of things is something we are looking at. Under the banner of innovation, we're almost creating faster than we can bundle. We've got the magazine, Premium content, and the Premium app. Systems wise – that's a challenge. It's also something we're learning about. One recent reader feedback read, "I've been a subscriber for 15 years, why should I pay for all this separate new premium content?" It's a fair point. Where we want to get to, is to buy into *Decanter* at any level you want: we stand for discovery, enjoyment, pleasure. As we bring the brand together, the idea is to bring a single offer together, giving you access to the whole *Decanter* universe.

Given your awards and events, are you a partly B2B magazine business?

I believe we're consumer led – that's our legacy, and the trade tend to follow as the content appeals to them too – and the wine trade is very important to us. Our wine awards are the largest in the world. That means the producers, the trade, distributors etc get that level of recognition, to help get into new markets, to meet new consumers. That's all trade. So our experience is, if we make magazine or premium content that appeals to the consumer, then it tends to appeal to the trade as well.

What about advertising and marketing? Is this a big part of the team?

Yes, we've got a large sales team, as there are four sides to the business: print, digital, Premium and events. Out of a team of around 35, 8 are editorial.

Our commercial team are not just selling display advertisements, they are visiting wine producers across the world, asking about ads; helping to create advertorials; asking about entering our awards or perhaps taking them to a tasting event in London, Shanghai or New York. They get to know who does what in the industry, and they even arrange bespoke promotional deals, like the *Decanter* awards stickers you might see on wine bottles.

Legacy magazines worry about an ageing profile of readers. Does *Decanter*?

We're not concerned at all. We have so many different audiences and demographic profiles, this mix is great. By default, the digital channels attract a younger audience. Off the top of my head, at least ten years younger. The events also bring in a different audience. For example, Fine Wine Encounters at the Landmark Hotel in London might attract 1000 quite affluent older people, but equally, we could be doing a South American event with an outside steak barbecue and dance music filled with new world producers and younger people. In many parts of the world wine is a family business, so new ideas and people come through.

Four 'mixed mode' implications for innovation

Magazines need to be authentic in the age of inauthenticity

Despite the headline decline in the volume of magazines published, publishing theorists from different fields such as media economics (Jim Bilton), design (Jeremy Leslie) and journalism (Megan Le Masurier and Kevin Baker) have all pointed to a more nuanced picture of the digital challenge magazine publishing faces. This is one where the core strengths of being 'expert', 'authentic' and very specialist is the medium's strength in an era where content is so abundant, free and socially mediated. Magazines like *Decanter* are an authority in their field, but at the same time, the Instagram blogger followed by tens of thousands arguably has the same 'reach'. Magazine brands must therefore capitalise on their history, their 'evergreen' archives of content to be digitised (think about the value of 10 or 20 years of content on motoring, cycling, fashion or fishing) while at the same time provide a 'vehicle' to the new vanguard of bloggers and social influencers. Authenticity, seen this way, therefore needs to be platform agnostic – a desire echoed by the CEO of TI Media referring to print, online, digital downloads and social media as the 'verticals' of each magazine brand (Rich, 2020).

Magazines have to protect the value of their specialist content

Jim Bilton describes magazines as having been 'relatively sheltered' from digital disruption compared to sectors such as the music business, as they observed with trepidation the changes experienced elsewhere in the decade after the millennium (Bilton 2014). The arrival of the internet saw newspaper publishers, for example releasing much of their content online with no access tariff or 'paywall'. Having opened Pandora's box, news publishers have spent the last few years trying to claw-back subscriptions, fees and paywalls for premium content. By contrast, the magazine world's *"cautious response"* (Bilton 2014, p. 230) to giving away free content online led to the industry's recent experimentation with magazines as mobile apps and digital editions. Content is an expensive commodity, if done well. Many news publishers such as *BuzzFeed* and magazine-turned video channel *Vice* have felt the economic pain of attempting to do expensive lifestyle and investigative journalism without a paywall. Magazines must continue to watch and learn from this and balance the 'free' versus 'premium' economics carefully. On the one hand, magazines need to maintain visibility of search optimisation and social media, but at the same time provide a genuine reason for readers to regularly pay a premium for value-added content or services such as specialist content, b2b data and events or memberships. Luxury lifestyle magazines such as *Monocle* have long pioneered what could be called a membership model, where being a subscriber doesn't just mean receiving well-edited and designed reading material – it opens-up a global elite world of benefits, offers and occasions outside of the pages of the magazine.

Magazines must replace advertising revenues with other revenues

Circulations were once the strict (and audited) basis of magazines' advertising display sales ratecard: the more magazines sold, the higher the advertising rates based on 'reach' and cost per thousand. According to the Advertising Association (2018) by 2017, UK advertising spend online had risen to around 50% of the total spend by all brands, leaving magazines a meagre 2% share of all advertising spend. An industry that relied heavily on this revenue source (see Chapter 5), the effect of this can be clearly seen in the amount of magazine closures in recent years. In the period between 2006 and 2010, the total number of consumer magazines published in the UK fell from 3445 to 3004, according to Cox and Mowatt (2014, p. 165). Since 2010, print closures have continued in some mainstream genres of consumer magazines that relied on advertising, for example men's and women's lifestyle magazines: these included cessation of *FHM*, *Nuts*, *Zoo* and *Maxim* and recently *ShortList* and also women's lifestyle titles *Look*, *Glamour* (Condé Nast) and the iconic women's fashion monthly *Marie Claire* (TI Media) to name a few. In certain cases, the publisher may opt to maintain a digital only presence.

Advertising in the digital era needs to be 'reconfigured' to include branded content (advertorial), paying for the co-creation of bespoke content where advertisers receive something different from the powerful programmatic 'reach' through Google Ads or Facebook. As the debate about the changing role of the magazine editor has shown (Das, 2016), editors and managing editors today need to be the first people that brand managers go to when creating, not placing, advertising content. Examples of such new forms of advertising moves-on the process of 'dropping in' ads into fixed boxes, into new semi-editorial and consultancy modes of developing sponsored sections, features, videos and other 'assets' that not only have a commercial value to a brand, but also allow access, insights and value to a magazine's central and peripheral audience. Where magazines are concerned about the 'Church versus State' division between advertising and the field of journalism (and the implied need for keeping them impartially separate), some independent lifestyle magazine publishers (more examples of which are provided in Chapter 8) have employed what can be called a 'studio model', where advertisers approach content creators and creatives in their specialist magazine field as 'embedded' journalists and multi-media content creators for brand messages, PR and marketing outside of their own titles. Publishers such as *Hole & Corner*, and TCO London's *Little White Lies* and *Huck* magazines, have all created such forms of branded content and even entire magazines for clients – without necessarily placing them within the pages and platforms of their own magazine titles.

Accept that being niche doesn't mean being unprofitable

The underpinning concept behind management theories of businesses as 'lean', 'agile', 'start-up' or even 'pop-up, is that small is controllable, efficient and dynamic. Such businesses are said to be the perfect breeding ground for disruptive thinking, one discussed above. While the economic scale of magazine publishing shows a clear contraction in the number of people working in the sector (from 300,000 in 1997 to fewer than 200,000 in publishing as a whole, according to Oliver 2017), the digital 'shift' to being smaller has left the industry arguably more 'match-fit' for 2020 and beyond. In John Oliver's (2017) macro-economic data analysis of creative industry economics and sector productivity in the UK, he concludes: "the U.K. publishing industry has been more 'dynamically capable' at adapting and reconfiguring their human resources than their peer creative industries" (Oliver 2017, p. 86). Niche magazines, independent magazines and consumer magazines that know their area well epitomise such dynamism. A publisher (that publishes a single title or even a hundred titles) can aptly change, modify and be creative in what they do in response to demand better, if they are not running a juggernaut.

In Kevin Baker's (2018) case study analysis of three US-based niche magazines, he examines titles that are not general-interest consumer titles, but ones that are often local and niche, and appear not to be battling digital challenge, but instead "doing well" and in many cases profitable (Baker, 2018, p. 407). The reasons for this, he proffers, boils down to creating a magazine brand with a dedicated following, providing attention to detail, creating a small but well-managed subscriptions models, and more ways to engage with brands via social media and mobile apps.

In the example cases of Baker's American regional specialist hobby magazines and a luxury titles, he notes the challenge and opportunity for magazines is to be "an authority" in an era where readers enjoy multiple free digital sources for information (Baker, 2018, p. 415). A similarity of the case examined in *Decanter*, the drive for innovation in being niche is aligned to the digital era's value for leveraging *influence* – a voice, a community and its knowledge – and not necessarily about the more twentieth-century quantitative value in media sales, audience, circulation or even 'hits' online.

References

Advertising Association (2018), *Advertising Expenditure Report*. Available at https://magnetic. media/insight/market-overview-insight (accessed: 10.01. 2020)

Aguilar, F. J. (1967), *Scanning the Business Environment*, New York: Macmillan.

Allworth, J. (2011), 'Steve Jobs solved the innovator's dilemma', *Harvard Business Review*, 24 October. Available at https://hbr.org/2011/10/steve-jobs-solved-the-innovato (accessed 20.02.2020)

Anderson, C. (2006), *The Long Tail: Why the Future of Business Is Selling Less of More*, New York: Hyperion

Anderson, C. (2009), *Free: The Future of a Radical Price*, New York: Hyperion

Baker, K. (2018), 'How niche magazine survive and thrive through an industry in turmoil', *Publishing Research Quarterly*, vol. 34 no. 3, pp. 407–416

Bilton, J. (2014), 'Publishing in the digital age', in D. Stam & A. Scott, *Inside Magazine Publishing*, Oxford: Routledge, pp. 226–247

Birch, I (2018), *Uncovered: Revolutionary Magazine Covers*, London: Octopus Publishing

Castells, M. (2000), *The Rise of The Network Society: The Information Age: Economy, Society and Culture*, London: John Wiley.

Castells, M (2005), 'The network society: from knowledge to policy', in Castells, M. & Cardoso, G., *The Network Society: From Knowledge to Policy*, Washington, DC: Johns Hopkins Center for Transatlantic Relations, pp. 3–23

Christensen, C. M. (1997), *The Innovator's Dilemma: When New Technologies Cause Great Firms to Fail*, Boston, MA: Harvard Business School Press

Christensen, C., Raynor, M, Mc Donald, R. (2015), 'What is disruptive innovation?' *Harvard Business Review*, vol. 93 no.12, pp. 44–53

Click, J. & Baird, R (1994), *Magazine Editing and Production*, McGraw-Hill: New York

Cox, H. & Mowatt, S. (2014), *Revolutions from Grub Street*, Oxford: Oxford University Press

Das, S. (2016), 'Magazine publishing innovation: two case studies on managing creativity', *Publications*, vol. 4 no. 15

Dennis, F. (2004), 'The four horsemen', *British Journalism Review*, vol. 15 no. 3, pp. 45–50

Florida, R. (2004), *The Rise of the Creative Class… and How It's Transforming Work, Leisure, Community and Everyday Life*, New York: Basic Books.

Gauntlett, D. (2011), *Making Is Connecting: The Social Meaning of Creativity, from DIY and Knitting to YouTube and Web 2.0*, London: Polity Press

Hewes, J. (2020), FIPP *Insider Podcast Season 1*. [podcast] March 2020. Available at www.fipp. com/news/features/fipp-launches-insider-podcast (accessed 21.03.2020)

Keen, A. (2007), *The Cult of the Amateur: How Today's Internet is Killing Our Culture*, London: Random House.

Key Note (2004), *Consumer Magazines*, Hampton, Middlesex: Key Note Publications

Küng, L. (2018) *Digital Transformation. The Organisational Challenge – Creating a Roadmap for Change* Journalism Report V. *Innovation and Transition.* Available at www.lucykung.com/wp-content/uploads/2018/03/Digital_Transformation_organisational_challenge.pdf (accessed 2.08.2020)

Le Masurier, M (2012), 'Independent magazines and the rejuvenation of print' *International Journal of Cultural Studies, vol.* 15 no. 4, pp. 383–398

Leslie, J. (2013), *The Modern Magazine* 1st edition, London: Laurence King Publishing.

Losowsky, A. (2007), *We Love Magazines,* Luxembourg: Editions Mike Koedinger SA

Losowsky, A. (2009), *We Make Magazines,* Berlin: Die Gestalten Verlag

Mintel (2019), *Magazines UK December 2019 Executive Summary Report.* London: Mintel Group Ltd. Available at www.mintel.com (accessed 02.01 2020)

O'Sullivan, D. & Dooley, L. (2009a), 'Defining innovation' in O'Sullivan, D. & Dooley, L. (2009) *Applying Innovation,* Thousand Oaks: Sage, pp. 3–32

O'Sullivan, D. & Dooley, L. (2009b), 'Managing innovation' in O'Sullivan, D. & Dooley, L. (2009) *Applying Innovation,* Thousand Oaks: Sage, pp. 33–56

Oliver, J. (2017), 'Exploring industry level capabilities in the U.K. creative industries', *Creative Industries Journal,* vol. 10 no.1, pp. 75–88

Prior-Miller, M. (2015), '*Magazine typology*', in Abrahamson, D., Prior-Miller, M. and Emott, B. *The Routledge Handbook of Magazine Research, The Future of the Magazine Form,* London: Routledge, pp. 22–50

Rich, M. (2020), Personal interview with Marcus Rich, CEO of TI Media, February 2020

Stam, D. & Scott, A. (2014), *Inside Magazine Publishing.* Oxford: Routledge.

Sumner, D. (2001), 'Who pays for magazines – advertisers of magazines? *Journal of Advertising Research,* vol. 41 no.6, pp. 61–67

2

A SHORT HISTORY OF BRITISH CONSUMER MAGAZINE PUBLISHING

Christine Stam

This chapter is updated from Inside Magazine Publishing *edited by David Stam and Andrew Scott and published by Routledge in 2014.*

In the early years of the twenty-first century, colourful magazines are everywhere. We see them in newsagents, in supermarkets, on buses, trains, aeroplanes and anywhere readers have spare time to enjoy them. They entertain us, enlighten us, challenge us (occasionally), sometimes anger and frustrate us. Printed weeklies, monthlies and quarterlies make a popular contribution to the culture of Britain today; many would argue that a world without print-on-paper magazines would be a dull place indeed, whatever the trend towards digital editions might bring.

King William III and his wife Mary were on the throne in 1693 when *The Ladies Mercury*, the very first weekly 'periodical' aimed specifically at women was introduced. Printed in London on two sides of a single sheet of paper, it promised to address the issues of "love, marriage, behaviour, dress and humour of the female sex, whether virgins, wives, or widows." It lasted four weeks but began an industry that expanded rapidly in the nineteenth century, thrived in the twentieth century, then began its diversification in the twenty-first century.

This chapter investigates the evolution of magazines during the eighteenth–twenty-first centuries and aims to show how such an inexpensive, everyday item affected the sociocultural makeup of a nation. In turn, magazines themselves are heavily influenced by the society of the day. It will show how a publication which starts to become out-of-date as soon as it leaves the printing press, by necessity, must foreground the social and cultural ethos of the moment. We will see how the development of transport and communication systems impacted on distribution channels and how technological developments have consistently affected the industry.

In the beginning (1731–1838)

Although various forms of printing onto paper and material have been around for thousands of years, the German Johannes Gutenberg is credited with the invention of the first workable, movable type, printing press in the 1440s. William Caxton brought the technology to England in 1476, setting up a printing press in Westminster and producing the first mass copies of books such as Chaucer's *Canterbury Tales*. It took a further 250 years, however, before the first printed magazine appeared. *The Gentleman's Magazine* was founded in London by Edward Cave in 1731, surviving for almost 200 years, until it finally closed in 1922. Cave coined the nomenclature 'magazine' for his publication after the French *magasin,* meaning 'warehouse' (originating from the Arabic *makhazan*) and, unknowingly,

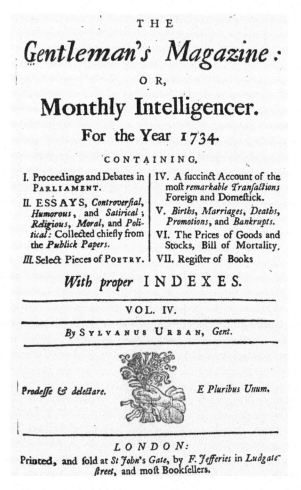

THE

Gentleman's Magazine :

O R,

Monthly Intelligencer.

For the Year 1734.

CONTAINING,

I. Proceedings and Debates in PARLIAMENT.

II. ESSAYS, *Controversial, Humorous,* and *Satirical ; Religious, Moral,* and *Political :* Collected chiefly from the *Publick Papers.*

III. Select Pieces of POETRY.

IV. A succinct Account of the most *remarkable Transactions* Foreign and Domestick.

V. *Births, Marriages, Deaths, Promotions,* and *Bankrupts.*

VI. The Prices of Goods and Stocks, Bill of Mortality.

VII. Register of Books

With proper INDEXES.

VOL. IV.

By SYLVANUS URBAN, *Gent.*

Prodesse & delectare.   *E Pluribus Unum.*

LONDON:

Printed, and sold at *St John's Gate*, by *F. Jefferies* in *Ludgate street*, and most Booksellers.

PHOTO 2.1 Edward Cave's eighteenth century *The Gentleman's Magazine* was the first printed publication to use the term 'magazine'.

generated the modern industry of today. His was a monthly digest of commentary and news on any topic in which the educated public might be interested: from Parliamentary debates to 'select Pieces of Poetry'. Prior to his innovative and perhaps accidental introduction, specialised journals and transitory periodicals, such as *The Ladies Mercury* had existed but had failed to capture the imaginations of the public at large.

Other examples of the deep-rooted historical nature of the magazine industry may be seen in the titles introduced in the eighteenth century. In 1709, Richard Steele founded a literary and society journal, calling it *The Tatler*. Two years later, after the closure of this enterprise, Steele went on to co-found another periodical, *The Spectator*, which catered to the emerging middle-classes. While neither of these august publications are the direct ancestors of today's titles through uninterrupted lineage, they are good examples of how magazines decline and die, only to metamorphose and evolve in future generations. Publication re-commenced in 1828 and *The Spectator* is now the oldest continuously published magazine in the English language having celebrated its 10,000th issue in April 2020.

During this period, one of the most significant advances in printing technology became available. Lithography was developed in Germany by Alois Senefelder in 1796 and the basic principles of this 200-year-old method are still used today in the production of most magazines.

THE SPECTATOR

- Co-founded by Richard Steele and Joseph Addison, the first title by that name appeared in 1711. Published six days a week (excluding Sunday), it offered comment and opinion on matters of the day. It ran for 555 issues until December 1712. Each copy was about 2,500 words and it had a print run of approximately 3,000 but a readership in the region of 60,000, due to its popularity in the London coffee houses. (Today's online blog, *Coffee House*, harks back to the early history of the magazine.) The magazine was aimed mainly to the interests of England's tradesmen and merchants. While claiming to be politically neutral, it did, in fact, espouse Whig (predecessors of the Liberal Party) values.
- The title was revived for six months in 1714.
- On 5 December 1828 Robert Rintoul, a liberal-radical, launched the modern *The Spectator* insisting, as editor, on having total power over its content. Thus began the tradition of the paper's editor and proprietor being one and the same person; an arrangement that lasted into the twentieth century.
- *The Spectator* is now the oldest continuously published magazine in the English language. It is published weekly and has a worldwide circulation in both print and digital formats of over 90,000.

- Over the years, the political leaning of the magazine has been influenced by the editor/proprietor. In the latter half of the nineteenth century, it gradually became more conservative; then reverted to liberalism in the early twentieth century. Editors in the latter half of the twentieth century indicate the political direction the magazine took: Ian Gilmour (1954–59), Ian Macleod (1963–65), Nigel Lawson (1966–70), Boris Johnson (1999–2005), all prominent Conservative Members of Parliament during their careers; the latter of course becoming British Prime Minister in 2019.

The early Victorians (1838–55)

One of the most notable controversies expounded in the early days of *The Spectator* magazine occurred, when it included a hostile review of Charles Dickens's *Bleak House*. In 1853, the magazine held the popular author in contempt; the anonymous contributor commented that the novel "would be a heavy book to read through at once … But we … found it dull and wearisome as a serial" (Brimley, 1853, p. 924). This observation highlighted the unusual method by which the novels of Charles Dickens reached the general public at the time. The journals that serialised most of his works, such as *Bentley's Miscellany* (*Oliver Twist*), *Master Humphrey's Clock* (*The Old Curiosity Shop* and *Barnaby Rudge*) and *Household Words* (*Hard Times*) are long forgotten. In the mid-nineteenth century, however, these weekly and monthly magazines, containing the author's latest episodes, were widely anticipated by his adoring public. Dickens was the master of the 'cliff-hanger' at the end of each episode; a technique employed regularly today in television serials and soap operas. Publishing his stories in instalments in magazines brought his works to a wider audience, especially to those who could ill afford to buy the novel in its expensive book format. It was also a genius stroke of self-marketing; a precursor of today's celebrity techniques as Dickens himself was the owner, editor and chief contributor of the journals.

As the British Empire expanded in the nineteenth century, magazines aimed at the male reader flooded the market: advertising in many such publications clearly defined the target audience as masculine. Most of these magazines were relatively short-lived but *Punch* (1841), *The Economist* (1843) and *The Field* (1853) are three titles that have stood the test of time. Indeed, *The Field* can claim to be the world's longest established field sports magazine, never being out of production since its introduction in the mid-nineteenth century.

For women, perhaps the most significant introduction was made by Samuel Beeton (husband of the ubiquitous Mrs Beeton) in 1852. The content of magazines of the 1830s had predominantly consisted of romantic fiction, providing women with an alternative to the unsuitably 'serious' content of the daily newspapers. By the 1850s, women's magazines had become more practical in content and even, in some cases edged towards the political. Samuel Beeton's *The Englishwoman's Domestic Magazine* (1852–77) was the title that did most to change the attitudes

THE FIELD
THE COUNTRY NEWSPAPER

VOL. CLXXIV. NO. 4524.   SATURDAY, SEPTEMBER 9. 1939

THE MAN WHO FOUGHT FOR PEACE

PHOTO 2.2 Neville Chamberlain appears on the front cover of the 9 September 1939 issue of *The Field*.

and social aspirations of a generation of women. Aimed at the middle-class, with a cover price of only twopence (2d), it included recipes (Mrs Beeton's), an 'agony column', the first paper dress patterns, gardening hints and practical tips on such topics as how to destroy bed bugs. The fiction was relevant and the political commentary treated the reader as an intelligent member of society. The magazine was a phenomenal success, recording monthly sales of 50,000 copies within its first three years (Braithewaite, 1995, p. 12). The era of the woman's magazine as we know it today had begun.

Two closely related events that probably had more impact on the exponential growth of magazine readership in the nineteenth century had nothing to do with the printing processes, the editorial policy or, indeed, the fame of magazine contributors. The expansion of the railways in mid-century and, more importantly, the placing of bookstalls on the platforms by an equally expansive and innovative company known as WH Smith, may claim to be the catalysts that facilitated the explosion. The rapid development of the railway network throughout Britain meant that newspapers and magazines could reach the provincial cities swiftly and reliably, opening up new markets for their publishers. In addition, passengers needed entertainment on their journeys, and who better to fulfil this need than a provider of suitable reading material? Having taken advantage of the public's new-found mania for railway travel, WH Smith went on to build a distribution network that included warehouses in Dublin, Liverpool, Manchester and Birmingham. Today, WH Smith is one of the UK's top retailers.

The growth in magazine sales during the mid-nineteenth century was further compounded by the abolition of the crippling Stamp Duty in 1855; a tax that had been levied on printed newspapers and periodicals since 1712. At the same time, the prohibitive cost of paper, previously manufactured using an ever-diminishing supply of rags, was reduced significantly by the transfer to production using wood pulp. These factors, combined with an increase in capital investment and the beginning of the technological revolution that characterised the second half of the nineteenth century, precipitated the boom years of magazine production and readership. From a high base level – several cheap newspapers and periodicals could already claim readerships in excess of 100,000 before 1855 – the second half of the nineteenth century saw circulation figures comparable to today's top sellers. In 1858, sales of three fiction magazines (*The Family Herald*, *The London Journal* and *Cassell's Family Papers*) totalled 895,000 copies with an estimated readership of at least three million people (Altick, 1998, p. 357).

PHOTO 2.3 Blackpool North Railway Station WH Smith Bookstall, 1896.

The Victorian boom years (1856–1901)

In 1861, the Parliamentary Act demanding high levels of excise duty payments on paper was finally repealed, significantly reducing the cost of this vital element of magazine production. In addition, the print process itself took several dramatic leaps forward during the latter decades of the century, with the introduction of the high speed rotary printing presses (printing on huge rolls of paper rather than single sheets) and the development of the mechanical typesetting process. Photography was also making huge technical advances, allowing the use of illustrations and reproductions that were unimagined by a previous generation.

These innovations heralded the true beginning of the production of cheap, mass-circulation magazines and created opportunities for publishers to tap into the vast numbers that made up the lower and middle classes. In addition, the Elementary Education Act of 1870 and subsequent extensions over the next few years brought basic schooling to the lower classes, and thus improved literacy for generations to come. Magazine publishers happily exploited this new market of customers, dropping their cover prices and providing suitable content to appeal to the masses.

For the first time, the sales potential of the growing numbers of literate children was also recognised. The Religious Tract Society introduced a penny weekly for boys in 1879, following in 1880 with a similar paper for girls. While these story papers were intended to encourage children to read and to instil Christian morals, they became hugely successful, lasting well into the second half of the twentieth century. *Boys Own Paper* and *Girls Own Paper* probably averaged sales in the region of 200,000 copies each every week during the latter decades of the nineteenth century (Drotner, 1988, p. 115), demonstrating the massive potential of this market. Indeed, Alfred Harmsworth introduced the first comic book in 1890, costing only a halfpenny. *Comic Cuts was* initially aimed at adults but was rapidly taken up by youngsters and was soon selling 300,000 copies a week. It is claimed that by the first decade of the twentieth century, this had risen to half a million (Reed, 1987, p. 92).

In the first half of the nineteenth century, cover prices for magazines were high, as they were aimed at the upper classes who could easily afford a shilling (5p) a copy. By the middle of the century, the less sophisticated but far more popular magazines were selling for one-sixth of the price (2d.) While *Punch* (aimed at the upper- and middle-class reader) sold 40,000 copies, *London Journal*, with its mass appeal, sold almost half a million copies. In 1873 alone, 630 different consumer magazines were published in the UK (Altick, 1998, p. 361).

Three men emerged during this period who were to revolutionise the publishing world in Britain: George Newnes, Alfred Harmsworth (later Lord Northcliffe) and Arthur Pearson. All were connected at some stage with *Tit-Bits* (1881–1984) which typified the direction in which many of the new magazines were heading. It was filled with snippets of interesting facts, odd stories, anecdotes, jokes and material that required little concentration from the reader, accompanied by plentiful illustrations. This was described as "…reading matter … to keep their eyes busy while their brains took a rest" (Altick, 1998, p. 364). By the end of the nineteenth century, Newnes was claiming circulation figures of 600,000 copies a week for *Tit-Bits* (Reed, 1987, p. 91). (George Newnes was the progenitor of the company that was to become part of the large IPC Media empire, now integrated into Future plc. Alfred Harmsworth became one of the most successful newspaper publishers in the history of the British press, founding the *Daily Mirror* and the *Daily Mail*. Arthur Pearson became a newspaper magnate, most noted for founding the *Daily Express*.)

Magazines, however, were not aimed exclusively at mass audiences; two highly successful introductions were made towards the end of the nineteenth century which were designed to satisfy the aspirations of the more well-heeled members of society. In 1897, George Newnes launched a limited circulation, highly pictorial quality magazine which celebrated the rural homes and pastimes of Britain's upper classes. Known initially as *Country Life Illustrated* this lucrative publication initially focused on sports such as golf and horse racing but dropped the 'Illustrated' from its masthead in later years to become one of the iconic brands of luxury lifestyle publishing which still thrives today.

A few years before, in 1885, Thomas Gibson Bowles founded a women's magazine that was intended to be practical, while enjoyable to read. He named it *The Lady*. Priced at sixpence, it attracted a limited audience until 1894 when a new, female editor introduced classified advertisements for nannies, domestic staff, holiday lets and similar into its pages. Aimed at intelligent women, it captured the imagination of the growing numbers of 'New Women'. *The Lady* went on to become Britain's longest surviving magazine for women. With a current circulation of 23,280 (ABC, Jan–Dec 2019) it remains to this day in private hands.

Towards the end of the century, the potential of a new mass audience began to be suspected and capitalised upon. As the population became more mobile with the expansion of the railways, both nationally and with the opening of the London Underground system, so the novel concept of suburban living was born. As men found work at a distance from their homes, their wives remained more and more within the domestic sphere. In the last two decades of the nineteenth century, no fewer than 48 new titles for women were introduced (White, 1970, p. 58). Magazines that cost only a penny and were full of practical advice for the home-loving housewife were soon selling 200,000 copies each, becoming the precursors of today's *Woman* and *Woman's Own*. This new army of middle-class housewives were the willing target of advertising on a grand scale, as the range of consumer goods escalated.

Although newspapers and periodicals had contained advertisements for hundreds of years, the real growth in the advertising industry began towards the end of the nineteenth century. As the numbers and circulation figures of magazines escalated, so did the manufacturing and distribution costs. Just as in the present day, the sales price did not cover the final costs of production. Advertising subsidised each issue and ultimately made magazines highly profitable for publishers. By the end of the century advertisements had become the life blood of publishers.

PHOTO 2.4 First issue of *Country Life*, January 1897.

Into the twentieth century

After the revolutionary social changes of the nineteenth century, the magazine-reading habits of the twentieth century settled into a pattern. That is not to say that startling events and radical advances did not take place during the century, merely that these were, in the main, continuations of trends already in place during the Victorian era. Cheap, domestic women's weeklies, established in the 1890s, formed the dominant market by 1910 and remained the most important genre of magazines in terms of sales throughout the twentieth century.

Pre-war (1910s)

In 1910, the small, family-run publisher DC Thomson introduced a magazine for women called *My Weekly*. Having successfully acquired *The People's Friend* (1869–), a family weekly paper with a predominantly working-class readership, the Dundee firm became one of the least likely publishing giants of the time. *My Weekly* was aimed specifically for the working class and it became a phenomenon, creating the mould for popular women's magazines. Appealing directly to its audience (hence the *My* in the title), the editorial was cosy and gossipy with editorial largely remaining defined within the domestic sphere.

Where *My Weekly* differed from its rival penny papers was in its deliberate policy to appear old-fashioned and conservative. It contained few illustrations and certainly no fashion-plates, eschewing any attempt to include features on fashion, appearance or social aspirations. The editor (ironically, a man for the introductory issues) spoke directly to readers, appealing to a brand of femininity that would have appalled the suffragettes. Indeed, the aggressive campaign for womens' suffrage that took place in Britain during the early years of the twentieth century had little impact upon the magazine publishing industry. Even at its height, few articles advocating a woman's right to vote appeared, except in the short-lived journals specifically printed by organisations dedicated to the cause, such as *Votes for Women* (1907–18) and *The Suffragette* (1912–15).

Most editors and publishers ignored the social unrest generated by the feminists and maintained their hegemonic stranglehold on their readers' expectations of their magazines. Even those papers specifically aimed at the suffragettes, written and published by militant organisations such as the Womens' Social and Political Union, still pandered to the feminine aspirations of their readers and employed commercial journalistic techniques. Articles were lively, pictures were included and advertising, such as that for hair dye, copies of Paris fashions and Debenham and Freebody's sale bargains, helped to fund the publication. On the political front, perhaps the most significant introduction came in 1913 with the launch of *New Statesman* by Sidney and Beatrice Webb. Working with Bernard Shaw and other members of the Fabian Society, it aimed to indoctrinate educated and influential people (men) with socialist ideology. From an initial circulation in 1913 of about 3,000 it now boasts weekly sales figures close to 40,000 and maintains its centre-left political stance.

As so often is the case when a highly successful magazine such as *My Weekly* is launched, a rival publisher will introduce a 'lookalike' within a matter of months. In 1911, Alfred Harmsworth launched *Woman's Weekly* and was claiming sales of half a million for the first issue (Braithewaite, 1995, p. 26). Both magazines went on to survive two world wars and intense competition from glossy rivals and publish to this day.

As war broke out in Europe in 1914, there were about 50 women's magazines on the newsstands in Britain (Braithewaite & Barrell, 1979, pp. 10–11). Many of these failed to survive the conflict and the austere social climate of war years would seem an inappropriate time for the launch of a luxury glossy magazine. Against all the odds, however, Condé Nast, an American publisher, chose to introduce *Vogue* to the British market in 1916. Priced at one shilling, its 120 glossy pages of high fashion, society news, literary and cultural articles boosted the morale of those that could afford to read it. Today, *Vogue* remains the archetypical glossy, high fashion magazine

PHOTO 2.5 The first issue of *Woman's Weekly* in 1911 sold approximately half a million copies.

with a circulation in excess of 190,000. As such, it was able to take advantage of the significant improvements to the quality of reproduction afforded by the 'new' rotogravure printing process.

While the three major technological developments of the nineteenth century (automation of composition, increased mechanisation of printing and new graphical techniques) represented huge advances, the practical implementation of the gravure process in the early twentieth century marked a further quantum leap. Although expensive to set up initially, the process allows high speed printing onto less expensive paper with superior image reproduction. Throughout the twentieth century, gravure has been the printing method of choice for high circulation titles such as women's weeklies, TV listings and newspaper supplements.

Post-war (1920s)

The radical economic and social changes brought about by the First World War had an enormous impact on the magazine industry. Society changed beyond recognition: many of the upper class families lost their wealth, while those in the lower classes had become more affluent, resulting in an expanding new social class in the 'middle'. The excess of single women, no longer content to remain in domestic service, added to the realignment of the social classes during the 1920s. This, together with the first radio transmission in Britain by the British Broadcasting Company (BBC) in 1922, heralded a watershed in the cultural evolution of the country. Publishers responded accordingly, launching magazines that catered for the burgeoning middle and lower-middle classes. Many of these journals became household names and remain in print today and include the monthlies *Homes and Gardens* (1919), *Ideal Home* (1920), *Good Housekeeping* (1922) and *Woman and Home* (1926). Advertisers adopted the new, middle-class magazines with enthusiasm, realising that the collective buying power of these readers was greater than those of the expensive glossies.

Surprisingly, the potential for comics deliberately aimed at children was not realised until well into the twentieth century, when James Henderson & Sons (later part of Arthur Harmsworth's Amalgamated Press) launched *The Rainbow* (1914–56). In the 1920s, DC Thomson became aware of the untapped market of schoolboys aged 9–12 and launched their first juvenile magazine *Adventure* (1921–61). Its success generated other boys' storypaper launches including *Rover* and *Hotspur*.

Launches for girls followed some decades later: *Bunty* (1958–2001), *Judy* (1960–91), *Mandy* (1967–91) and *Twinkle* (1968–99). As cartoon strips became increasingly popular, DC Thomson introduced their highly successful and iconic *The Dandy* (1937–2012) and *The Beano* (1938–) comics. Today, only *The Beano* remains in print and published its 4,000th issue in 2019. The cultural importance of this market should not be underestimated as it often proved an entry point for younger readers to embrace the world of magazines.

Only one other significant magazine launch took place in the 1920s, but it was one of overwhelming importance and happened almost by accident. Aggrieved by the demands of the Newspaper Publishers' Association for a large fee to allow radio listings in their publications and the subsequent embargo, the then director-general of the BBC, John Reith, decided to publish his own listings magazine. *The Radio Times* was born. The first edition, 'the official organ of the BBC', reached the newsstands on 28 September 1923. By the end of the 1920s, published weekly and costing just twopence (2d), *The Radio Times* had the second highest circulation of all magazines in the UK. (Only *John Bull* outstripped it during this decade.) By the 1930s, it was selling nearly two million copies a week and in the 1940s, this leapt to just under two and a half million (Reed, 1987, p. 187). By 1950, the *Radio Times* was selling eight million copies a week; the highest audited circulation in the world. With sales still over half a million copies and despite the deregulation of TV listings in 1991, *The Radio Times* remains one of the all-time success stories of the magazine publishing industry.

The war years and the dawn of celebrity watching (1930–60)

Pre-war (1930s)

The 1930s saw the significant impact of the gravure process of printing on the magazine market. Apart from *Vogue,* almost all other magazines had historically been printed using letterpress with its associated dull and colourless appearance. In 1937, Odham's Press launched its weekly magazine *Woman* as a rival to the highly successful *Woman's Own* (1932, George Newnes Ltd.) and *Woman's Illustrated* (1936, Amalgamated Press). By printing the entire magazine using the rotogravure process, at a stroke, *Woman* introduced vibrant colours, together with superior quality printing in a twopenny magazine aimed at lower middle-class readers. Its competitors could only follow suit and, together, they captured the market and sounded the death knell for those that could not keep up with their technological advance. To maintain their viability, however, they had to attract massive circulation figures and advertising revenue on a major scale. The gamble paid off: advertisers were attracted by the high volume print runs and the quality of the colour printing. While the glossy shilling monthlies bemoaned the impertinence of domestic servants and the difficulty in finding good staff, the almost-as-glossy weeklies, selling at a fraction of the price, included articles on cookery, knitting, babycare, problem pages and true-to-life fiction. *Woman* and *Woman's Own* became the publishing phenomena of the twentieth century, going on to achieve enormous circulation figures and massive profits for their publishers. (By 1939, *Woman* was selling more than three-quarters of a million copies every week; in the 1950s, this rose to more than three and a half million; White, 1970, p. 97).

These magazines contributed little to the feminist cause, appealing openly to the traditional homemaking values of women within the domestic sphere. It was almost as if the advances made by women during the war years had been annihilated in favour of a return to Victorian patriarchy. Indeed, attempts made by the editor of *Woman* to include articles concerning social problems were met with a downturn in sales of 30% and the experiment was soon abandoned (White, 1970, p. 112). It took another war before women began to yield sufficient social influence to affect the content of their reading matter.

War and post-war (1939–59)

The Second World War was a watershed in British magazine development. Titles that had endured for decades failed to survive the harsh reality of a changing society, while others took advantage of the high demand for pictorial exposition and expanded rapidly. Coverage of the events of the war both at home and overseas was provided by the newly introduced picture paper, *Picture Post* (1938–57, Hulton

PHOTO 2.6 First issue of *Woman* magazine, 5 June 1937.

Press). With its emphasis on high quality journalism and photography, the first issue sold out almost immediately and circulation figures of nearly two million a week were commonplace.

Perhaps the most significant factor for magazine publishers during the war was paper rationing, forcing them to cut the size of their editions in both page content and, in some cases in physical dimension as well. (*Good Housekeeping* changed its format three times during the war and eventually became pocket-sized in order to maintain a substantial number of pages; Braithewaite, 1995, p. 58). There was little spare room for advertisements as space was at a premium if readers' insatiable demands for entertainment, news and gossip were to be satisfied. Reading material was scarce and every magazine flew off the newsagents' shelves as soon as it appeared, to be read over and over by several different people. Priority was given to Government advertising campaigns leading to the ironic situation of advertisements demanding readers should use less of a product, not more. Many magazines closed and there was no opportunity for new ones as they were not eligible for any paper allocation. When paper rationing finally ended for magazines in 1950, *Woman's Own* celebrated by doubling the issue size from the highly restricted 24 pages to a luxurious 48.

After the war, the ever-expanding publishing conglomerates thrived by providing what the reading public, and in particular women, wanted. By the 1950s, readers had become more sophisticated and demanding, expecting quality products for their money. These were the boom days of Prime Minister Harold Macmillan's 'never had it so good' era; rationing had ended and consumer goods were flooding the markets. Advertisers responded to the expanding buying power of women by dramatically increasing their spend on magazines, further fuelling the profits of the large publishing houses. Colourful photographs began to replace line drawings and advertisements became more appealing to readers. As White observed:

> Before the war, money had been short while goods were plentiful. After it, people had money to spend but the shops were empty. Now, for the first time, production matched spending power, and manufacturers and consumers were eager to make contact through the medium of advertising.
>
> *White, 1970, p. 157*

In the ever-expanding world of media, the introduction of commercial television in 1955 brought with it golden opportunities for both advertisers and the broadcasting companies. Prior to this date, the BBC had held a monopoly on television viewing and the *Radio Times* had exclusive rights for television and radio listings. Now, a new magazine was needed to inform the public of what was available to view on the Independent Television (ITV) channel broadcasting in their region of the country. In September 1955, the new television companies launched *TV Times* which, by 1960, was selling nearly four million copies a week, compared with *Radio Times* at about seven million (Reed, 1987, p. 223).

One other important social event had significant impact on the cultural development of Britain in the post-war period: in 1947, Princess Elizabeth married Prince Philip of Greece, an event that, above all others, marked the dawn of the age of celebrity-watching as we know it. Brian Braithewaite, a contemporary observer commented:

> The wedding, and the birth of the children, began the popular magazines' love affair with the royals. A new industry was created, and it saturated the magazines for decades with photographs and text about every aspect of the royal family. Both editors and readers had an insatiable appetite for the subject.
>
> *Braithewaite, 1995, p. 63*

The years of sexual and technological revolution (1960–2000)

The decade of vibrant change (1960s)

With its emphasis on high circulation numbers in order to satisfy the economic demands of the advertisers and print shops, it was inevitable that the fragmented magazine industry would have to consolidate in order to survive. By 1963, thanks to amalgamations, takeovers and closures at the end of the previous decade, many of the major players had been united to form the International Publishing Corporation (IPC). Most of the long-established houses were no more: gone were

PHOTO 2.7 One of many 'royal' covers of the 1950s.

Odhams, Amalgamated Press (Fleetway), George Newnes and Hultons, all folded into the IPC empire. The other major magazine publishing groups of the time were Condé Nast, the National Magazines Company (a UK subsidiary of the American Hearst Corporation), the Canadian-owned Thomson Publication (UK) and, not to be confused, the Scottish DC Thomson publishing house. Waiting in the wings, however, was the East Midland Allied Press (EMAP), a company successfully producing several local newspapers. In 1953, the printing presses in Peterborough lay idle for part of the week and the decision was taken to start a magazine division and to buy a weekly fishing publication, *Angling Times*. This was quickly followed in 1956 by the purchase of *Motor Cycle News*. These specialist magazines were to form the foundation of a highly competitive publishing business that lasted into the twenty-first century.

The 1960s was the decade that the 'teenager', if not actually invented, was at least recognised and became the magazine publisher's dream with a market of over seven million people. Publishers queued up to make the most of this opportunity with magazines such as *Honey* (1960–86, Fleetway), *Jackie* (1962–93, DC Thomson), *Petticoat* (1966–75, IPC) and *19* (1968–2004, IPC). Their era was relatively short-lived, although the reasons attributed to the decline in sales are complicated and often speculative. Teen magazines have come and gone, since their initial heyday in the 1960s and 70s but almost certainly, inconsistency in the market can be put down in part to the fickleness of the age group, the advent of digital media and the trend for children to grow up, with associated expectations, at a far earlier age than perhaps they did a generation before.

The 'swinging sixties' was a decade that also saw the rise of satire generally and in the magazine world in particular: conventional news and current affairs journalism was subverted when *Private Eye* launched in 1961. Events of the time, such as the Profumo scandal, lent themselves to this irreverent style of reporting, which captured the *zeitgeist* at the tired end of the Macmillan years. The recently developed offset-lithography printing method facilitated the introduction of 'specialist' magazines for publishers who couldn't afford the high costs of set-up involved with the other processes available at the time. *Private Eye,* a small-scale, predominantly black-and-white paper, was the first real competitor to the long-established *Punch* (1841–2002) magazine. Begun by a group of undergraduates from Oxford University as an extended 'in-house magazine', the original schoolboy humour soon hardened into the uncompromising satire with which we are familiar today. Edited until 1986 by Richard Ingrams and since then by Ian Hislop, *Private Eye's* irreverent approach to the world through controversial and combative journalism has led to numerous libel cases. Perhaps the most famous were those brought by Sir James Goldsmith in the 1970s and Robert Maxwell in the 1980s. The magazine continues to thrive on controversy to this day and enjoys sales of over 240,000 every fortnight.

The *Cosmo* era (1970s)

In the magazine world, the 1970s will be remembered for an event that was to make an impact on a huge scale. In March 1972, National Magazines launched the first international version of *Cosmopolitan* in the UK, a title that had been published in the USA since 1886.

Across the Atlantic, Hearst Magazines decided to take a risk and, in 1965, handed the editorship of their ailing family magazine, *Cosmopolitan* over to the enthusiastic and charismatic Helen Gurley Brown (1922–2012). Already a published author with her (then) risqué and controversial book, *Sex and the Single Girl,* Brown almost singlehandedly reversed the fortunes of the magazine and created a worldwide, iconic brand. As Braithewaite (the launch publisher of *Cosmopolitan* UK) observed:

> Hearst saw a golden opportunity. Here was a bright, articulate, exciting new editor with celebrity status and a bestselling book to back her ideas.... The overwelming success of the magazine was undoubtedly due to the persona of Helen Gurley Brown and her dedicated belief that 'out there' were millions of girls looking for self-improvement, self-confidence, interesting employment, good relations with a man and a better sex life.
>
> *Braithewaite, 1995, pp. 96–7*

Cosmopolitan became the jewel in Hearst's crown and it wasn't long before they were looking to other countries to exploit their success. National Magazines (their UK subsidiary) had already demonstrated expertise in transferring US titles such as *Harper's Bazaar* and *Good Housekeeping* to the UK market and British *Cosmopolitan* was launched with great fanfare in 1972.

The timing of the launch could not have been better. The 1960s had been a decade of increasingly liberal attitudes; the Pill was available, abortion and homosexuality were legalised in 1967 and in 1969, divorce became easier to achieve. The women's magazine market was relatively static in the early 1970s and National Magazines judged that it was ripe for this new, brash title that had already taken the US by storm. The UK launch was arguably the most sensational and successful magazine introduction ever: Saatchi & Saatchi, a newly formed advertising agency, took on the television advertising campaign which contributed in no small measure to the overwhelming success of the magazine in its early days. The 45-second commercial and 16-sheet posters in the London Underground were regarded as extravagant for the time, but the initial print run of 350,000 sold out by lunchtime on the first day, justifying the expenditure. The second issue, thanks in part to its attendant publicity generating rumours (not fulfilled) of a full-frontal male nude featuring within its pages, sold all 450,000 copies within two days. Ironically, the highly effective PR campaign for *Cosmopolitan* served to regenerate interest in women's magazines generally and its competitors benefitted substantially from its efforts.

The introduction was a considerable success, despite the fact that National Magazines had got their market research (the little they did) completely wrong. *Cosmopolitan* in the US was aimed at middle-class women aged 25–40 and the company had assumed that the UK version would appeal to a similar class and age group. In reality, the readership turned out to be single women with the peak reading age of just 18, with class and level of education being less significant than marital status. What made *Cosmopolitan* such a phenomenon was its blatant approach to all matters sexual and its open-handed treatment of the subject. As one researcher commented:

> *Cosmopolitan* put female sexuality right out there on the front page, where everyone could see it at the grocery store ... People could no longer pretend that it didn't exist.
>
> *Kim & Ward, 2004*

Encouraged by its incredible achievement, National Magazines took the brave decision to launch a new title that, to all intents and purposes, appeared to compete directly with their own blockbuster. In 1978, they launched *Company*, with similar fanfare and an even larger advertising expenditure, profiling it directly at the 18–24 female market but with careful editorial distinctions. The first issue sold 300,000 copies and National Magazines dominated this market sector in such a way that their publishing rivals gave up any attempts to compete.

PHOTO 2.8 The UK launch issue, March 1972, now a collectors' item.

Domestic expansion and foreign invaders (1980s)

The 1980s may be regarded as the decade that saw a huge number of new magazines come and go. On the domestic front, East Midland Allied Press were building on their expertise in the specialist magazine market with the launch of titles aimed at younger readers. Their introduction of *Smash Hits* in 1978 had taken the youth market by storm and encouraged the company to expand within specific sectors. In 1986, now renamed EMAP, it published 38 consumer magazines in 3 main markets: youth, hobbies and outdoor pursuits as well as 53 business publications.

Until 1986, the British market had been satisfied with home-grown magazines or by anglicised versions of glossies from across the Atlantic such as *Vogue, Good Housekeeping* and *Cosmopolitan*. This complacent attitude, with its associated assumptions, was shattered when a powerhouse of magazine publishing from Germany, Gruner + Jahr, decided to enter the British market. The launch of *Prima* in September 1986 was explosive, expensive and took the British publishers completely by surprise. On paper, such a launch looked commercial suicide: the domestic market was already saturated and women were supposedly flocking to read magazines such as *Cosmopolitan* which rejected the cosy image of family and home. How could a foreign magazine full of recipes, articles about childcare, health and beauty and gardening, which even included a paper pattern in every issue, possibly hope to survive in such a climate?

The launch campaign included television commercials that emphasised, and did not disguise, the homely nature of the product. The free paper pattern (worth more than the cover price of the magazine itself) was an instant success and the first two issues sold out completely with print runs well in excess of half a million. (Much has been made of the novelty of the free paper pattern and its contribution to attracting purchasers; commentators forget that Samuel Beeton had used this sales tactic 134 years earlier in *The Englishwoman's Domestic Magazine*, proving once again that there is seldom anything truly innovative in marketing.) A year after launch, *Prima* broke the million copies a month barrier and in August 1987 Gruner + Jahr added to their success with the launch of *Best,* a weekly magazine that profiled itself as a lightweight, chatty magazine that was classless, fun and cheap at only 35 pence. Within a year, it too was selling over a million copies a week (Braithewaite, 1995, p. 136).

While publishers, traditionally, had taken at least six months to arrange the launch of a new magazine, Gruner + Jahr gave their advertisers and the news trade only two weeks' notice before introducing *Best*. These surprise tactics were also used by their own German rival, Bauer when they launched a direct competitor *Bella,* in the same year, undercutting *Best*'s price by six pence. Soon, Bauer were claiming sales of a million copies a week for their own title and the British (in the shape of IPC) felt obliged to react to the German invasion of their home territory. In February 1988, *Essentials* was launched with an introductory budget of a staggering £2.5 million, directly challenging *Prima* for readers. The new monthly was moderately successful and was soon selling in the region of 750,000 copies. The traditional complacency of IPC was no longer appropriate in this climate of aggressive competition; in the 1980s, IPC was finally forced to change its commercial practices and, with it, its culture. Sale or return was offered to retail newsagents and there was an increased focus on new title development. In the early 1990s, the company ceased collective bargaining with the National Union of Journalists.

In May 1988, the Spanish followed in the footsteps of their German counterparts when, by launching *Hello!*, they threatened the British market still further. Once again, the likelihood of success seemed improbable for such a venture at that time: the Spanish version, *Hola!*, was owned by a private family company without the enormous publicity budgets of the Germans or of IPC, the magazine itself was weekly and priced at 75 pence and, worst of all, it was set to appeal to the voyeuristic nature of celebrity- and royal-watchers. Nothing in this profile was to suggest that *Hello!* would be anything but a niche product. How wrong. Weekly sales soared to over 400,000 by 1993 and the reticent, respectful image of the British stereotype was shattered. Braithewaite describes the phenomenon:

The over-the-top voyeurism of the rich, famous and infamous captured an immediate and passionately devoted readership in this country. *Hello!* is a feast for the curious and the prying, a banquet for armchair peeping-toms.

Braithewaite, 1995, p. 140

Hello! thrived for nearly five years without any real competition until Northern and Shell, launched *OK!* in 1993 and EMAP launched *Heat* in 1999.

Encouraged by the success of other Europeans, finally the French decided to try their hand at attacking the British market. More cautious than their predecessors, Group Marie Claire chose to form a partnership with IPC for the UK launch in September 1988 of its highly successful French women's monthly, *Marie Claire*. The first issue of the British version was a staggering 252 pages of glossy fashion and beauty. By the early 1990s, it was rivalling *Cosmopolitan* as the top woman's monthly. Indeed, the magazine has probably received more awards and prizes for its editorial and content than any other similar product until the publisher surprised the industry in 2019 by announcing the closure of its print version.

PHOTO 2.9 A stylish cover from *Marie Claire*.

The challenges laid down by the European invaders in the mid-1980s was perhaps one of the most significant occurrences in the UK women's magazine market in the twentieth century. The Germans, French and Spanish publishers stirred a flaccid industry into directions it would not otherwise have considered. This was good for the market, for readers, advertisers and newsagents and gave a number of companies, particularly IPC, the much needed jolt that would stimulate them into actions that were rewarded with ever-greater profits.

The decade of TV listings, lads' mags and customer magazines (1990s)

On 1 March 1991, the overall monopoly for printing seven-day programme guides enjoyed by *Radio Times* and *TV Times* came to an end and many new titles flooded the highly lucrative TV listings market. As deregulation took place, the large publishing houses lined up to launch new magazines that would attack the stranglehold of these two, well-established titles. First on the scene in March 1991 were IPC, the publishers of *TV Times*, with *What's on TV* and Bauer followed with *TV Choice* in 1999, to rival IPC's highly successful title at the budget end of the market.

As will be discussed in both Chapters 3 and 4, the 1990s was also the era of customer publishing. Magazines distributed specifically to patrons of, for example a particular store, manufacturer or travel company was not a new phenomenon in the 1990s. British Airways had given their passengers an in-flight magazine, *High Life* (Premier magazines; Cedar Communications) since 1973. Indeed, Harrods and Selfridges had sold copies of their own magazines (free to account customers), while the National Trust had sent copies of their newssheet to subscribers since 1932. Agencies such as Cedar and Redwood exploited this niche market for publications and became extremely successful outside the giant publishing houses.

What changed in the 1990s was the extraordinary success supermarkets' own brand of magazine experienced. Placed conveniently by check-outs and often given away free or competitively priced, these glossy magazines looked like their expensive counterparts in the newsagents with high quality journalism and features. The overt promotion for its own brands and suppliers was an acceptable face of the publication in the eyes of consumers. Sainsbury's launched *The Magazine* (now *Sainsbury's Magazine*) in 1994 and in the twenty-first century almost every significant retail outlet has followed suit. Circulation figures in 2012 are remarkable: Tesco and Asda gave away nearly two million copies of every issue of their magazines. These are massive numbers for print magazines and, needless to say, all are backed up with skilful digital and social media offering. As will be discussed later in this textbook, the traditional print magazine medium remains a key part of the modern day offering by (the now named) content marketing publishers or agencies.

As this chapter has shown, the development of magazine publishing in the last three centuries has been a series of significant events, both socially and technologically, each followed by periods of evolution and expansion. For every significant introduction, imitators jump into the fray to capture their own share of the market.

Women's magazines probably started the trend three centuries ago but throughout that time, the publication of magazines aimed specifically at men has been a relative failure. Right up until the 1990s, the idea of general interest men's magazines was regarded, at best, as niche and at worst a recipe for disaster. The market for men's magazines consisted of specialist titles devoted to masculine pursuits such as cars or football and mainstream pornography, the latter titles being banished to the top shelves in newsagents. By the mid-1980s, however, the concept of a 'lifestyle' magazine for the growing numbers of 'new men' who were seen to be expressing interest in fashion, grooming and relationships, was being explored. Born in the 60s and 70s, these young people were the first cohort to grow up alongside new digital technology. Stereotyped as 'Generation X' (the name popularised by Douglas Coupland's 1991 novel), the potential for these readers was even more appealing as men stayed single longer and had more cash in their pockets than ever before.

The major publishers remained sceptical and it was Nick Logan's small company, Wagadon who took the brave step in 1986 of launching *Arena* (1986–2008). Building on his experiences with *The Face*, the style magazine for the under-25s he had introduced in 1980, Logan turned his attention to older male readers. With little introductory fanfare, *Arena* was soon selling 65,000 copies a month and others sat up and took note. Condé Nast launched GQ in 1989 and National Magazines followed with *Esquire* in 1991. Editorial on all of these titles was carefully curated to avoid being perceived as either pornographic or gay and issues seldom featured women on their covers. The aim was to have newsagents place them alongside upmarket, political journals such as *The Spectator* and *The Economist*.

What followed in May 1994 was to turn the traditional processes of magazine launches on their head – at least in the short term. From out of nowhere, a whole new genre of magazines was created when IPC launched *Loaded,* aimed at young, heterosexual males. Gill defined them as "pursuing women, alcohol and football … Anti-aspirational, inept, optimistic and self-deprecating" (Gill, 2003, p. 51) and as the editor, James Brown put it in the first issue: "the man who believes he can do anything, if only he wasn't hungover." Seen variously as a backlash against feminism and the *Cosmo* ethos of women or as a rebellion against the male stereotype of 'breadwinner' and family man, the laddish culture seemed to provide escapism for those who really didn't care for traditional male responsibilities or image. The era of the lads' mags had arrived and others soon jumped on this bandwagon. Within a year, EMAP had revamped their recently acquired men's fashion title *For Him,* and relaunched it as *FHM* and Dennis Publishing introduced *Maxim* in 1995. By the end of the century, these three titles contributed three-quarters of the men's market by sales, having expanded this sector from a total of a mere 250,000 copies in 1990 to nearly five times that number in 1998. As the market became increasingly competitive, the titles became more sexually blatant in the quest to chase sales, moving away from the initial *Loaded* concept as a lifestyle magazine. Developments of this sector in the twenty-first century were both controversial and dynamic, with the launch of similar weekly magazines such as *Nuts* (2003; IPC) and *Zoo* (2004; EMAP now Bauer).

None of these titles remain, in either print or digital form. The market for male titles has presented itself as more fickle and more open to digital competition than titles aimed at women. Few would dispute, however, that the launch of *Loaded* was one of the influential publishing events of the last quarter of the twentieth century.

The new century

As is discussed throughout this textbook, the twenty-first century saw the magazine publishing worldwide square up to two major challenges; a cyclical advertising recession driven by a downturn in the world economy and a seismic shift towards digital media. As publishers' development and launch budgets were rapidly funnelled towards digital innovations, there were few print launches worthy of note. Largely due to an unhappy investment in the United States, EMAP was broken up and divisions sold off – the consumer titles principally to Bauer. IPC went through a period of private equity ownership to be acquired by Time Inc and latterly by Future plc. and BBC publishing assets became part of Immediate Media. Current pen pictures of these companies are painted by David Stam in Chapter 3.

As the cost of consumer launches rose and circulation expectations dwindled, an interesting supply chain innovation became increasingly important – large-scale free consumer magazines. Free distribution had always been part of the magazine scene but titles were invariably small circulation and funded by a major sponsor (customer magazines) or by classified advertising. The year 2007 saw a team led by entrepreneur Mike Soutar, a publisher with experience in men's magazine, launch the male title *Shortlist*. This was followed two years later by *Stylist*, which was aimed at a female audience. With circulations in excess of 400,000, these titles were given away free in major cities at transport hubs, hotels and leisure centres. Product quality was compatible to paid-for titles and advertisers welcomed their mass circulation appeal. The word 'freemium' was coined to describe the blend of quality content for free. *Shortlist* closed in 2018 by which time London listings title *TimeOut* had also changed its model to free distribution. Distribution switches from being a revenue to a cost and titles are exclusively funded by advertising and sponsorship. Given the decline in consumer magazine advertising revenues and distribution uncertainties driven by the coronavirus crisis of 2020, the longevity of this sector in print has to be considered as a tough business model.

The two sharp winds of recession and technological change also helped a new genre to blossom – that of the independent magazine. The rise of these new types of magazines is discussed at length by David Stam in Chapter 8. 'Independent' magazines are more than the mere term suggests; yes, they are largely owned and run by private companies and entrepreneurs, but the hallmark of their large and growing number is editorial passion and understanding of the served community. There are no large-scale advertisement or circulation departments providing commercial support. These audiences are, by definition, often niche and can encompass titles related to a range of topics such as gender, sexuality, ethnicity, art and design, lifestyle choices, travel or sport. The medium of choice is print, more often than not adopting high-end paper selection and print quality making the magazines highly desirable and collectable. The sector has been compared to the rise of vinyl records in the music streaming age.

Social media is hugely important for this sector. It allows for these niche communities worldwide to connect with the magazine brand as the focal point or hub. It gives editors the opportunity to source contributors of both words and pictures and offer sales through e-commerce. Business models vary from title to title, some commentators will argue that many independent magazines do not have a business model, yet their number increases month by month. Worthy of note are UK title *Delayed Gratification* and Danish *Kinfolk*. The former delights in the long-form articles and graphics featuring events after the initial hue and cry of the original news story has died down; the latter title encourages simple and relaxed living spending time with friends and family.

Our walk though consumer magazine history has now reached the present. Political, economic, sociocultural and technological changes have largely been kind to the magazine business from Victorian society to the society that spawned both the Cosmo Girl and the Loaded Lad. In the early years of the twenty-first century, magazine publishing worldwide was genuinely at the crossroads. Sleepless nights were had: how on earth are we going to survive this advertisement recession and what can we do to adapt to the enormous challenge of new media?

The industry has been incredibly resourceful on both fronts to ensure survival. It is smaller but considerably more fleet of foot. Innovation and creativity have been the keys and that is the theme of the rest of this book.

References

ABC (2019), *Circulation Release*, Jan to Dec.

Altick, R. D. (1998), *The English Common Reader: A Social History of the Mass Reading Public, 1800–1900*. Ohio: Ohio State University Press.

Braithewaite, B. (1995), *Women's Magazines: The First 300 Years*. London: Peter Owen.

Braithewaite, B. (2009), *The Press Book: Adventures and Misadventures in Print Media*. London: Peter Owen Publishers.

Braithewaite, B. & Barrell, J. (1979), *The Business of Women's Magazines*. London: Associated Business Press.

Brimley, G. (1853), *The Spectator*, 24 September, pp. 923–5.

Drotner, K. (1988), *English Children and their Magazines, 1751–1945*. London: Yale University Press.

Gill, R. (2003), 'Power and the production of subjects: a genealogy of the New Man and the New Lad', in B. Benwell, ed. *Masculinity and Men's Lifestyle Magazines*. Oxford: Blackwell Publishing.

Kim, J. L. & Ward, L. M. (2004), 'Pleasure reading: associations between young women's sexual attitudes and their reading of contemporary women's magazines', *Psychology of Women Quarterly*, Vol. 28, pp. 48–58.

Reed, D. (1987), *The Popular Magazine in Britain and the United States of America 1880–1960*, Toronto: University of Toronto Press.

White, C. (1970), *Women's Magazines, 1693–1968*. London: Joseph.

3

UK MAGAZINE PUBLISHING

Innovation as necessity

David Stam

This chapter is designed to give a panorama of the magazine industry in the UK, the home country of the editors. It will examine how the traditional dual business model of reader and advertiser revenues has had to change – and change quickly. Three areas of publishing will be explored: mainstream consumer, customer publishing or content marketing and independent magazines. The increasing interest of venture capital houses in the sector will be examined, as will the growth of new digital providers for magazines. The chapter will conclude with some brief observations on what the future might hold.

Magazine readers in the United Kingdom spend nearly 40 minutes per day enjoying their chosen titles in print. This time commitment is largely unchanged since 2017 and is expected to remain the same in the early 2020s. It is longer than time spent with a daily newspaper but considerably shorter than hours spent watching TV or using the internet on the various devices available (Wessenden 201, 2019, p. 15). Whilst the overall size of the magazine market is smaller than it was five years ago, the format continues to satisfy media appetites by informing, explaining and inspiring ideas and lifestyles; the role it has fulfilled since the early magazines of the eighteenth century.

To get the bad news out of the way first. In 2013, the author estimated the total sales of magazines at retail or through subscription sales to be £1.8 billion. For 2018, it was estimated to be a shade less than £1.2 billion – a fall of one-third. Print launches of any scale, for years the lifeblood of the industry, are rare. The picture for traditional magazine advertising sales is also gloomy. In 2013, magazine publishers sold £668 million of print advertising sales – in 2018, the number was £380 million (Zenith Media, June 2019). To counter these trends, as the central theme of this book shows, magazine publishers have been creative and innovative in their efforts to replace revenue losses.

Taxonomy and business models

The term taxonomy can be loosely, if a little cheekily, borrowed from science and applied to attempts to arrange and categorise the thousands of magazines available to the consumer in the UK today. What makes the fashion titles *Stylist* and *Grazia* different to each other? Likewise, what differentiates movie titles *Empire* and *Little White Lies*? The answer can be many faceted: it can lie in the market served, the distribution channel, publishing frequency, main source of revenue or even ownership. Debates about which 'pots' to put magazines into predate the digital era. To magazine outsiders, taxonomy may seem a little irrelevant but to magazine practitioners and researchers, it is important as it allows companies to prioritise revenue streams and evaluate where competitive dangers lurk.

It is important to remember that magazines, like other media forms, have a duality of purpose; their primary role is to attract readers or purchasers. By quantifying these readers and presenting their influence and importance as a community, the publisher will attract advertisers, who in turn pay to reach this audience. Increasingly, as traditional advertisement sales have tumbled, the publisher has had to look further afield to attempt to maintain revenue streams.

The importance of this duality is largely reflected in the manner that the media world categorises magazines. There are four main groupings and often subdivisions within each grouping.

PHOTO 3.1 Movie title *Little White Lies* is published by TCO London.

- **Consumer magazines.** These can be subdivided into titles which have a **mass** appeal, such as Bauer Media's *Take A Break* or Future plc's *What's on TV*, and titles which have a more **specialist** appeal such as *Country Walking*. Additionally, the market tends to categorise by frequency of publication, the distribution routes of paid for and free titles and the platforms of print and digital 'bundle' or 'pure play' digital only. *Stylist* is free to readers, *Grazia* is not but both would consider themselves to be reaching a mass of consumers – in this case, fashion conscious young women.

- **Content marketing.** This growing sector was formerly known as contract or customer publishing and has developed into an important part of the burgeoning content marketing industry. Simply put, if you pick up a free magazine at the supermarket or are mailed a glossy because you own a certain marque of car – you have seen a content marketing title. If you are a member of a trade union, support a major charity or subscribe to the UK's huge National Trust, you will be almost certainly receive a publication in some form. Such titles are produced mainly by agency-type publishers to deliver a bespoke marketing brief. Briefs can be as diverse as devising inspiring recipes to strengthen supermarket branding to membership drives for a union or political party. This sector is supported by a variety of funding models.

- **Independent magazines.** Market consolidation has ensured that the vast majority of mass consumer and specialist consumer titles are owned by the UK's major publishers. The last ten years, however, has seen an explosion in the number of magazines published by small teams, initially operating on limited resources. It is important to recognise that the tag of 'independent' goes far beyond ownership. Independent titles are also defined by tackling subject matter considered too niche or perhaps too sensitive for the main players, by relatively small circulations and (often) incredibly high production standards. Movie title *Little White Lies* considers itself to be a commercially successful independent title covering movies, whereas *Empire* (another cinema title) is published by the largest magazine house in the UK. This emerging genre will be discussed in detail in Chapter 8.

- **Business to business magazines.** This sector, known as B2B, was an enormously profitable print sector for UK publishers in the last quarter of the twentieth century. It is a hugely diverse sector. Every profession, every trade or form of commerce has at least one brand supporting and communicating with it. This sector, however, has seen a major shift away from print. Many B2B publishers now primarily view themselves as providers of business information, business event organisers or data providers.

Within magazine types there are some curious and interesting countertrends in play. General consumer magazines are in decline, but major retailers and consumer brands are increasingly turning to the magazine medium to support marketing objectives. At the same time, the independent end of the publishing market expands at a pace. Reasons for these contrasting moves will be explored later in this chapter.

Magazine taxonomy is also heavily influenced by the business model that an individual magazine has, as every single title in the marketplace will have a unique mix of revenues and costs.

What is a business model?

The term 'business model' describes how an organisation creates and delivers value for its customers, shareholders and employees in a systematic and sustainable manner. As such, it can be considered a structure or template for financial success. Primarily, the focus will be on customer types and where revenues are derived from; but hand in hand with revenue generation, of course, go costs. In a highly simplistic example, the main revenues of a traditional print magazine will be circulation revenues and advertising sales – the main costs print, paper and people. Consistency is generated by the frequency of the title, weekly or monthly. There are other factors to consider in order to ensure that a business model is ongoing or sustainable. Good quality marketing, another key cost variable, is needed to generate circulation sales. It has been necessary for successful magazine companies to invest heavily in new technology to support digital platforms. As well as this investment continuing to require significant levels of capital, it has created an ongoing need for trained staff to produce platform-neutral content, sell it to would be advertisers and provide essential technical support. Training in new skills remains an important item on every publisher's To Do List.

As media consultant Jim Bilton states in a major 2019 report and survey (Bilton, 2019), every business model is unique. For example, *Which? Magazine* is the magazine of the UK Consumers' Association. It prides itself on independent product reviews and carries no advertising – the majority of revenue originating from member subscriptions. At the opposite end of the spectrum is London listings title *TimeOut*. Distributed free, the weekly is dependent on advertisement sales revenues.

In their 2014 textbook *Inside Magazine Publishing*, Stam and Scott demonstrate that two major changes affected the worldwide magazine industry from 2008 onwards. First, a cyclical change as all revenues, particularly advertising sales, were seriously hit by the financial crisis of that period. Secondly, and ultimately more profoundly, an array of structural changes delivered by consumers rapidly moving to new digital technologies and social media platforms for their media consumption. Magazine business models have had to change rapidly to adapt to the new landscape. Two examples of this innovation are summarised here.

Two magazine business model innovations

Bundle it up

When it comes to the magazine supply chain, the UK and the USA markets are the mirror image of each other. In the USA, approximately 75 per cent of magazines are sold via postal subscriptions, while the remaining 25 per cent is made up of retail sales. The UK sees the reverse: 25 per cent of sales are direct subscriptions. That number is a general industry average; niche and specialist titles are far more likely to have a subscription dependence than their larger mass consumer competitors which are widely available and have much stronger sales in stores. For example, music, computing, country pursuits and news and current affairs titles all have models, whereby subscriptions make up over 50 per cent of circulation (Enders Analysis, 2018, p. 8). Within the overall decline in circulation revenues noted at the start of this chapter, there is a gradual but definite move from retail to subscriptions throughout the industry.

The sale of a 'sub', as opposed to a copy purchased at a newsagent, benefits publishers in a number of ways. They have captured a loyal reader who will see every issue; what is more they know who that reader is and his or her data profile. Most subs sales are paid in advance which gives very useful cash flow advantages. Almost all consumer publishers make available digital versions of their print products. This can be as simple as a basic pdf copy, through to a complete service which offers digital and print platforms combined in a one-price bundle. The news and current affairs magazine market in the UK has benefited from political and social uncertainty worldwide. *The Economist* has been highly skilful in leveraging this with a brilliant content offering aimed at an informed readership. On their website, their best value offer is flagged as a bundle, a weekly print copy, access to two apps, a detailed website and a daily newsletter.

Pursuing a bundle subscription strategy has been one of the levers to help *The Economist* to become a major player in the market for serious political and business

PHOTO 3.2 Magazine postal subscriptions are growing. Photo Alexander Spatari.

information. The title now boasts a worldwide circulation of 1,657,935 (ABC, July to Dec 2019). Of these sales, 909,000 are print and 748,000 are digital copies. However, and this is important to note, 470,000 of the digital copies are bundle sales. That sizeable 63 per cent portion of their digital readership will receive both print and online editions. Readers have the freedom of how, when and where they access. Giving readers this access to print and digital bundles has allowed the publisher to maintain a healthy subscription price – in this case £215 per year in July 2020 – and has skilfully enabled them to protect the print circulation by offering digital enhancements. Bundle sales have been vital for the well-being of publisher business models as solo digital sales (where the purchase is not part of a package) are tiny and estimated at around 3 per cent of circulation volumes (Wessenden 203, 2019, p. 18) It is likely that this number will have increased during the 2020 pandemic.

Extend the brand

As magazine publishers continue to see severe falls in their traditional sources of revenue – and particularly in advertising sales – they have been both innovative and inventive in leveraging two key hallmarks of the medium. These are magazine brand strengths and the reader relationship. As Guy Consterdine demonstrates in a key 2005 report, magazine readers have a unique relationship of trust with their chosen publication (Consterdine, 2005). Forays beyond traditional weekly and monthly journal publishing are numerous. They can create new revenue opportunities from readers, advertisers, exhibitors and sponsors. Amongst the more popular and successful innovations are the following:

- *Exhibitions and events.* These can be as diverse as the *BBC Good Food Shows,* which attract 175,000 visitors interacting with 900 exhibitors and sponsors, to more niche events. These include guest lectures and debates hosted by news magazines attracting attendances in the hundreds. Clearly, this area of revenue was halted in 2020 by the pandemic but will surely return.
- *Books and bookazines.* Tie-ups between magazine publishers and their book counterparts are not new. For example, *Private Eye The First 50 Years* was a highly successful history of the satirical magazine presented in book form. A larger and more recent market is the bookazine. These will normally be large format, glossy cover, paperback titles retailing at sums significantly higher than monthly magazines. Subject matter is diverse but one of the most popular categories is computing. The retailer WH Smith has a strong market share in the bookazine market as do international retailers.
- *Subscriber clubs.* Investment in customer relationship management systems has given publishers the wherewithal to anticipate their readers' needs and to understand their purchasing habits. On the back of this, magazine and newspaper subscriber clubs have flourished; subscription customers can be automatically enrolled in a club or loyalty scheme. Popular incentives will be discounted

wine or travel offers. One of the largest in the UK is *Times +*, run by the daily *Times* and weekly *Sunday Times*.

- *Podcasts.* According to Ofcom, 7 million adults in the UK listen to a podcast every week. Podcasts are developing into a successful medium for magazine publishers, they attract sponsorship revenue and are cost-effective to produce and run. Although best recorded in a dedicated sound studio they do not have to be. Magazine contributors, particularly celebrity ones, often make lively and interesting podcasters. A wide variety of magazine brands now offer podcasts to readers, free of charge and easily available through the main podcast apps. They will often be funded via sponsorship, providing useful revenue enhancement to publishers suffering from traditional advertising downturns.

PODCASTS – AUTHENTIC BUT NOT AMATEUR BY CHRISTOPHER PHIN

Apart from porn, no media industry is more intimate than podcasting. There is literally no way to get closer to someone than with a podcast; if – as most do – you listen on headphones, then the sound of a podcaster's voice appears to emanate from the centre of your skull. I'm literally inside your head.

And so for publishers of all sizes – from multinationals to one-person indies to cruiserweights like my own company, DC Thomson Media – podcasting should be an important component in how brands engage with their audiences.

Print brings authority and experiential reading; the web brings massive scale; social brings engagement; and podcasting brings *authenticity*. And if you're able to pull stakeholders' attention together to marshal different departments' will and resource, each can, should and must promote and support the other in sensitive and appropriate ways. That goes double when you're thinking about providing advertising and other commercial opportunities to clients.

Podcasts provide, for news brands especially, a way for journalists to put themselves in front of the audiences they serve in a way that shows them to be three-dimensional people rather than an abstract byline, and allows them to show how you can marry erudition and objectivity with uncertainty, curiosity and emotion.

They can help brands reach new audiences. Typically what we mean when we say that is that for print-centric publishers who have often struggled to instil the habit of picking up a daily paper or a monthly magazine into younger audiences, podcasts are a way of taking the existing, well-honed storytelling abilities the organisation has, and use them to make stuff that younger audiences already have the habit of consuming.

An example: one of the podcasts we produce is called *Pass It On*, associated to one of our newspapers, *The Sunday Post*. I can see in my producer dash-board in Spotify – and so it's important to caveat this by reminding you that what follows only applies to those who listen via Spotify – that the biggest demographic chunk is men aged 45–59 years. Unsurprising, given industry norms. What's more surprising, though, is that only a few percentage points behind that is women aged from 23 to 27 and that in part, an outcome of a deliberate decision of mine to put a 21-year-old woman in place as the host of that show.

It's not just about finding younger audiences, though. It could be about reaching beyond your borders. Catering for niches that can't be sustained with other media. Hooking in casual readers.

That engagement is key. We can see that the average listener to some of our football podcasts, for example spends nine times longer listening to podcasts in a month than does the average user of the associated news websites spends reading about football in a month. Important caveat: there are far more people doing the latter than the former, and so understanding the strength of each is vital, not just for us but in messaging to commercial partners looking to us for guidance in how their marketing budgets can be best used.

But that point really does bear repeating. People who listen to podcasts tend to spend a long time with them. Indeed, one of the world's biggest, *The Joe Rogan Experience*, usually runs to a couple of hours, and is often longer than three.

That provides an unparalleled opportunity for publishers to draw their audiences – whether established or newly acquired – closer to their bosom. One of my favourite things about podcasts, as a listener long before I was a producer, is that they turn onerous activities into fun. How marvellous if you can be the entity that means someone think "Yay, I've got a new episode of my favourite podcast to listen to!" as they step out their front door in the morning rather than "Oh, hell, another hour stuck on the Tube." All that engenders trust in and affection for the brand, trust and affection which can be parlayed into commercial gain.

It's common in podcasting for shows to be sponsored, and for the hosts themselves to read out sponsor messages – with varying degrees of scripting, slickness and conviction – and if you've had someone listening to your show for months or years, it's likely they'll be well-disposed to the message since you've built up a relationship with the host's voice.

Increasingly common too as podcasts grow up are dynamically inserted ads, where you'll mark your podcast with timestamps where ads can be inserted, and an ad network like Acast or DAX will cut in ads based on set criteria – and give you an amount of money based on how many thousand times that ad is run. This, though, needs huge scale to return significant revenue.

There is a middle-ground between the host-read ads you hear from indie and bedroom podcasters and the more 'radio ad'-style drop-ins. Our gardening and allotment show, *The Dirt*, was sponsored from its first episode by an organic gardening catalogue, and they not only got 'in association with' branding at the top of the show and in supporting marketing collateral, and a host-read puff at the end of the show, but the opportunity to have their ambassador give a single short tip as part of a practical section of the show, as a piece of highly valuable and tightly integrated native content.

There is a problem with advertising in podcasts however. Most people listen while doing something else, and there's no fundamental mechanism between going from hearing an ad for mattresses to buying one – in effect, there is no button to click. You are also usually otherwise occupied, so there is no obvious or direct way to correlate advertising conversions outside of the slightly clunky process of coupon redemption codes.

Podcast advertising has to be part of an advertiser's brand-building rather than direct sales driving activity. That's another reason why publishers should consider it as an integral part of the suite of opportunities they can offer commercial partners, usually as part of a bundle sell across different platforms.

Ultimately too, one of the reasons publishers love podcasts – or will come to, when they wake up to their advantages – is because they can be very low-touch and deliverable. A modest investment in kit and training – and putting in place sympathetic workflows – can yield really good results. Some of our shows can be live within 10 minutes of recording. Others get more care lavished on them – in part an artefact of them being more complex, and in part if the teams require more editing.

There's a mantra I adopted from an old colleague, Grant Bremner: **authentic but not amateur.** You're (probably) not making Radio 4 documentaries here. Encourage warmth. Don't edit out all the ums. Get to a not-embarrassing level of polish on the audio – a combination of decent kit and some templates in your editing software – and then let the content be just a little scrappy. Find your way – with your audience's involvement. A good podcast needs a good topic, a good structure to serve it (supported by judicious editing to get it to conform to that) and good hosts to do it justice. There is, of course, scope to screw this all up, but don't let the perfect be the enemy of the good. Better to get something out and iterate and improve, than to tie yourself in knots or invest far beyond what the return might be.

Just remember: authentic, but not amateur. And having failed to resist writing a juvenile and provocative opening sentence to this box-out, I am at least going to resist drawing a parallel with it now.

Christopher Phin is Head of Podcasts, DC Thomson Media
@chrisphin chrisphin.com

UK consumer magazine companies – brands, markets and platforms

Paid circulation market share of the main UK consumer publishers in terms of number of copies is shown in Figure 3.1. Six publishers are responsible for two-thirds of all magazines sold.

TABLE 3.1 Volume market share by leading publisher.

Publisher	Market share (%)
Bauer	20
Future plc	16
Immediate Media	12
Hearst	12
Condé Nast	4
DC Thomson	3
Others	33

Source. Compiled by Marketforce (UK) Ltd based on ABC figures for 2019.

Future plc includes titles formerly published by TI Media.

Publishers' websites reveal a clear focus on the three strands which make up the offer to both consumers and advertisers for the modern-day media company: brands, markets and platforms.

- **Brands**. A key unique selling point of the magazine medium is that consumers identify with and feel loyalty towards titles. This is key to building and maintaining circulation in both print and digital.
- **Markets**. Whether the audience is mass or niche, targeted to young or old or the rich or those less well-off, magazines continue to do the job of delivering well-targeted and audited communities to advertisers in a cost-effective way.
- **Platforms**. Advertisers increasingly require an array of media platforms to reach their chosen markets. Publishers respond by creating opportunities to leverage their titles across both print and digital, through exhibitions, awards, events, podcasts and a raft of brand extensions. These will be explored throughout this book.

Portfolios and circulations can and do change but the message of strong brand, vibrant lucrative market and choice of platform invariably shines through. Readers are advised to consult websites for up-to-date information and data but this is a brief pen picture of six leading UK publishers.

Bauer Media Group

With a volume market share of 20 per cent, the UK titles of the privately owned Bauer Media Group make up the single largest magazine publisher in the UK today. Bauer covers both mass markets and more specialist targets. Comprising many of the nation's largest sellers, such as *TV Choice* and *Take A Break*, the company is also strong in the celebrity sector with *Closer* and *Heat*. The portfolio has been a successful merger of the high volume weekly titles of the original H. Bauer group with the more specialist titles sold by the former EMAP company in 2007. These brands include *Trout and Salmon* and *Motorcycle News*, must have reads for fly fisherman and leather clad enthusiasts alike. Bauer also own substantial radio station assets. These include *Magic*, *Kiss* and a number of regional broadcasters. This gives the company the ability to sell across platform packages to advertisers focussing on audience reach as Bauer states that their brands cover 25 million UK consumers. Bauer are also majority partners (shareholders) in the newstrade distributors Frontline and Seymour, giving their titles significant presence in WH Smith, supermarkets and neighbourhood newsagents, as well as earning useful revenue from other publishers with whom they are contracted to provide distribution services.

Future plc

In the summer of 2020, Future plc acquired TI Media, making it the largest publisher in the UK by number of brands and with a volume market share of 16 per cent. The original Future Publishing was launched during the home computer boom of the 1980s by entrepreneur Chris Anderson, who today runs TED Talks from the USA. In the early 2000s, Future was particularly strong in the computer gaming market and to this day is at the forefront of publishing brands connected to technology and IT. Future plc now incorporates TI Media, which in turn was formerly known as IPC Media and was part of the US-based Time Inc. group until 2017. The publisher has strong positions in the TV Listings sector and the traditional women's weeklies with *Woman*, *Woman's Own* and *Woman's Weekly*. The rest of the former TI portfolio tends to be split into one of two groupings: home interest and general women's monthlies sit alongside specialist tiles – a number of which compete with Bauer. They proudly publish the iconic *Country Life*, originally launched in 1897. The distributor Marketforce is part of the company, again providing the titles with significant leverage in the retail marketplace.

Immediate Media Company

Immediate has been one of the most exciting developments in the mainstream industry in the last ten years. Currently with a 12 per cent share of the market, the business was created in 2011 with the purchase of some of the most iconic names on the newsstand from the publishing arm of the BBC. These included *Radio Times*, *BBC Good Food* and *Top Gear*. The company incorporated smaller publishers Origin and Magicalia and in 2014 purchased a range of craft and special interest titles from Future plc. Immediate's relationship with the BBC gives them access to superb content for children from the BBC channel CBeebies. Immediate claim to be the number one publisher of children's magazines in the UK. Kids is an important and sometimes overlooked sector of the overall magazine market at retail. Traditionally known as comics, popular characters come and go creating opportunities for new titles whilst other market sectors struggle to launch. Moreover, parents are very happy to subscribe to print products as they see print as a good thing and a springboard into more serious book reading. Immediate sell 11 million magazines to children or their parents, creating £36 million at retail annually. Their titles include *CBeebies Specials*, *Hey Duggee* and *Match of The Day*. In the ABC release of July to December 2019, *CBeebies Magazine* chalked up an enviable circulation of 47,485, all fully paid at £2.99. On a digital platform, they have the parenting advice and review site *MadeForMums*.

Hearst

As described in Chapter 2, American publishing tycoon Randolph Hearst brought his company to the shores of the UK in 1922 with the magazine *Good Housekeeping*. This publishing house still bears his name and that founding brand remains one of its best sellers. Hearst's prime focus is on markets for communities of women through a range of titles, including the iconic *Cosmopolitan*, *Elle* and *Elle Decoration*. The acquisition of US publisher Rodale has also given them a strong presence in the health and fitness market with *Men's Health*, *Women's Health* and *Runner's World*. Importantly, the publisher owns the entertainment website *Digital Spy*. According to Google Analytics 2019, this site has 28 million monthly users worldwide, giving it competitive clout to attract advertisers in that digital marketplace.

Condé Nast

Condé Nast's relatively small market share by volume downplays the importance of this publisher of quality brands and its role in the UK marketplace. Arriving in the UK in the early years of the twentieth century, this media owner has developed a clear strategy of attracting up-market and influential audiences with high production value titles. Stand out amongst them are the fashion bible *Vogue*, leading men's title *GQ* and its large live brand extension *Men of the Year*. These sit alongside *Vanity Fair*, *Tatler* and *Condé Nast Traveller* – with an interesting brand development ownership of the famous *Johannsen's* hotel guide. The overall business model of Condé Nast remains advertisement driven, with its affluent communities acting as magnets for advertisers and sponsors. To continue to maximise revenues in the new commercial landscape, their digital division offers content marketing solutions for partners across print, digital, video and social media.

DC Thomson

Scottish publisher DC Thomson has a proud history, as traced in Chapter 2 of this textbook. Still in private hands, with family members working in the business, the company has an excellent track record in acquisition, innovation and diversification. The traditional magazine media business boasts brands for adults and children such as *My Weekly*, *People's Friend* and the famous *Beano* comic. These sit alongside sister companies Puzzler Media, the UK market leader in the attractive puzzle market, and niche-magazine publisher Aceville. They also own the major free distribution magazine, *Stylist*. DC Thomson's private company status, presided over by a tight management team of decision makers, has enabled it to innovate and diversify its media asset base. It is one of the few UK publishers who still own a printer, working for third-party contracted publishers as well as its own brands. They own *Brightsolid*, an IT and cloud solutions company and *Findmypast*, a leading genealogy and family history research online research service and finder.

(numerical data for the above section was accessed 13 September 2020)

THE ROLE OF PRIVATE EQUITY

One of the core themes of this textbook is to demonstrate that despite core traditional revenues of the magazine business being in decline, publishers are responding with innovations. Observers of the scene will have noted that private equity firms (PE) have shown significant interest in the sector by acquiring magazine houses in the last 15 years. The trend started back in 1998 when private equity company Cinven acquired IPC Media in one of the largest acquisitions of a publisher of all time, going on to sell the business to Time Inc in 2001. IPC Media became TI Media and was again briefly in PE hands before being sold to Future plc in 2020.

In 2011, the BBC sold its publishing assets to Exponent, a private equity player with sound experience of publishing deals. These former BBC titles became the backbone of The Immediate Media Company, now owned by Burda of Germany. Also, on the sad death of the energetic and eccentric Felix Dennis in 2014 his trustees elected to exit the world of media and sold Dennis Publishing, again to Exponent.

The basic mechanics of private equity are simple. A business is bought by the PE house, securing finance on the open loans market and as such incurring debt. The PE player and its investors now own the majority of the shares in the acquired firm. Senior management become linked to the success of the investment by buying or being allocated a shareholding at a highly discounted price. Because the purchase of the company has been funded by fixed price debt, any increase in the value of the acquired assets goes straight to the shareholders, including management. Hence profits on resale can be significant – but it needs to be pointed out that the deal is not without risks. Linking the management to the success is absolutely crucial, hence such deals are sometimes popularly known as 'management buyouts'.

So why are hard-nosed PE finance executives attracted to the modern magazine world? Tim Weller, formerly Chair of TI Media helps explain:

> Of course, the purchase price has to be right but magazine assets offer a number of key benefits. Subscription revenues are predictable and, in most cases, made up-front. Contracts with news wholesalers also ensure

that their payments are timely. Both these factors bring benefits to cash flow. Unlike manufacturing, the business has relatively low demands for capital expenditure so the cash generated can be invested to drive innovation and sales.

Weller, 2019

Most of the innovations which publishers develop focus on the two key hallmarks of magazines – strong brand values and reader engagement. Owners from the private equity world are likely to take more risks than traditional media proprietors, or in the case of the BBC, a publicly funded broadcaster. Events and e-commerce seem to top the list of potential innovations. Under PE ownership, Dennis has invested solidly in *buyacar.co.uk*, a car purchase and finance platform closely linked to magazines *Auto Express* and *Carbuyer*. As seen in the previous section, Immediate also saw significant innovation and diversification under the PE ownership of Exponent including the development of *BBC Good Food* live shows.

Private equity investment focuses on adding value to their media assets. Tim Weller continues:

Cash generated in the day to day trading of magazine companies can be used to pay down debt. That means that interest payments on that debt are reduced ensuring not just more profit for shareholders but importantly funds for investing in growth.

Private equity, however, is not without its critics. Some argue it can foster an overzealous focus on cost-cutting and pursuit of profit. Of course, PE investors look for the 'low-hanging fruit' of operational efficiencies not pursued by previous owners but innovation and growth can be the rewards not just for a few individuals but for the industry at large.

Magazines – print or digital brands?

Publishers' websites invariably refer to their titles as brands and where appropriate, stress their multiplatform approach to potential advertisers. The magazine articulation of these brands can of course be either print, digital or both. Media guru Jim Bilton identifies three main formats for the digital magazine or edition. First, PDF replicas are still 'the workhorse' of the type accounting for around two-thirds of digital titles. Second, these PDFs can be enhanced by embedding video, audio and hyperlinks. Finally, ambitious publishers have funded fully interactive bespoke applications but at less than 10 per cent of the digital market, this is still a small number and requires significant investment. Trends suggest this will be forthcoming (Wessenden 202, 2019, p. 18).

So when is a magazine not a magazine? The derivation of the word means warehouse or storehouse and that is reflected in content and design of magazines to this day, with sections for dedicated editorial strands. Art Directors point to the need for good 'signposting' for readers to reach these destinations, a design attribute relevant to both print and digital. Printers require a reasonable standardisation of page size and publishing frequency; this is echoed by their colleagues in distribution. Retailers find it hard to give good display to awkward sized titles. When print and digital is offered to the consumer side by side in a bundle sale, there will almost certainly be great similarities between the platforms. However, if publishers launch a brand purely online or switch off the print edition, these constraints vanish overnight. In what is increasingly becoming known as pure play, there is no need to stick to weekly or monthly cycles or be formatted to a magazine type design. New business opportunities present themselves.

Hence, the success of digital-only brands owned by media firms who once would have called themselves traditional magazine houses. Future plc's *Techradar* offers up-to-date news and reviews on products and gadgets together with price comparisons and purchasing opportunities. Claiming 32 million global unique users per month, the site is clearly of appeal to manufacturers and retailers and states that "*TechRadar* is supported by its audience. When you purchase through links on our site, we may earn an affiliate commission" (Techradar, 2019). This indicates an important shift in the business model towards e-commerce with partners and is surely a trend for other consumer publishers to emulate. So much, so that this innovation has been instrumental in boosting the stock value of Future plc. The *Financial Times* notes – "Future…deploys proprietary software, called Hawk, that scatters live retail prices and 'buy it now' links throughout its online stories. Whenever the consumer clicks though to make a purchase, the company takes a cut" (Elder, 2019).

At times, the lonely transition to purely digital can be seen as an inevitable end point for magazine titles which have fallen on hard times. In October 2017, *Glamour* took the market by surprise by cutting print editions back to all but two specials per year, and November 2019 saw the last print edition of *Marie Claire*. Shorn of print, distribution and some staff costs, a solo digital platform can be a recipe for survival; but one has to question their ability to compete with internet giants for both readers and advertisers.

Content marketing and magazines

In the pre-pandemic world, magazines were everywhere. They filled an important part of media consumption in our daily lives. In a supermarket, you were invited to pick up a free title as was the case in your gym or health club, or when relaxing in a luxury hotel. Surely, these times will return. Through your door, a glossy title packaged by an estate agency chain as a lifestyle magazine will still thud, and supporters of charities or members of a trade union will almost certainly receive a regular frequency title specifically published to communicate with donors or members.

A review of the Audit Bureau of Circulation figures for January to June 2019 shows that 7 of the top 20 magazines in the UK are published or sponsored by large retailers or consumer brands. *Tesco Magazine* and *Good Living* from Asda are in fact the largest distributed offerings in the country with circulations close to 1.9 million copies apiece. Also in this top 20 are magazines from John Lewis, Waitrose and Slimming World; with the lifespan from birth to old age neatly covered by *Emma's Diary Pregnancy Guide* and *Saga Magazine*. There is nothing new about the concept of a magazine designed to support a consumer brand. The first was *High Life,* the in-flight magazine for British Airways. There was no better place or medium for air passengers to dream about and plan future trips than whilst reading in the air or in a passenger lounge. *High Life* became known for its quality travel journalism and striking photography. It was the forerunner of that part of the publishing world known as contract or customer publishing – magazines that were sent out to do the job of promoting a brand. The task of publishing these titles to a dedicated client brief was often seen by the traditional industry as requiring specialist skills and as a result, a group of entrepreneurial 'publishing agency' companies grew to fulfil this need. Cedar are one such firm and have published *High Life* for over 500 issues.

The proliferation of media platforms and ease of generating content in recent years has seen a change in the role of traditional contract or customer publishers. These now see themselves as an integral part of the growing content marketing industry.

What is content marketing?

The trade association for the 50 plus content marketers in the UK is very clear. "Content marketing is the discipline of creating quality branded editorial content across all media channels and platforms to deliver engaging relationships, consumer value and measurable success for brands," states their website (Content Marketing Association, 2019). It is a growing industry which is claimed to be worth around £5 billion in the UK alone.

Good quality branded content can help to retain existing loyal customers as well as increasing sales. As a marketing tool, it can have huge value if a brand is to be relaunched or repositioned to attract a new target market. Its value should be seen as long-term rather than a quick sales fix, the latter being more appropriate for a traditional advertising campaign. The business culture and day-to-day practices of a modern content marketing company are likely to have more in common with a client-facing advertising agency than a traditional publisher – although it is important to note that trained journalists have key roles to play. Practitioners create branded material for a whole host of media platforms with an increasing emphasis on social media, video and podcasts. Moreover, major brands themselves are becoming recognised as content creators in their own right: Red Bull is becoming as recognised for its quality video production as it is as an energy drink (see Chapter 5).

Magazines as part of the content marketing mix

At a time when traditional consumer publishing is under revenue pressure, magazines as a medium remain an important part of the content marketing mix, punching their weight against newer media platforms in the fight for budget and client resources. The unique characteristics of magazines to connect with the reader, to inspire, inform and entertain is still highly valued by this growing band of marketers.

The agency Dialogue represents the equestrian sport of eventing in the UK. This sport, known for its spills and thrills, wished to attract new participants and to raise the skills and participation of existing riders. To this end, Dialogue has relaunched the magazine *British Eventing Life* and added a new video platform streaming training videos as well as interviews with the sport's stars. It is possible for traditional magazine companies to succeed in the competitive agency world of content marketing. Immediate Media publish *BBC Wildlife* and their Branded Content arm looks after the publishing interest of the World Wildlife Fund (WWF). They publish three titles, *Action, Impact* and *Go Wild* – the latter aimed at children – and bring to this charity's publications editorial and design expertise, as well as working closely with the WWF membership department to enhance the titles through quality research.

Funding models for magazines within the content marketing arena will vary and there is a degree of confidentiality attached to them. Where possible, advertisements will be sold and this will be a useful source of revenue for retail focused titles with a supplier base who can be persuaded to pay for space. The client themselves may fund a title in part or fully. With membership titles, a part of the annual subscription may be channelled off to create a magazine publishing budget. If the brand is strong enough and the magazine well established, it may be possible to migrate to a paid for model. *Sainsbury Magazine* has an audited circulation of 128,133 (ABC, July to Dec 2019) with an annual subscription price of £32 whilst being available in store for £3. This paid for status, however, will restrict circulation, making it less available than its main supermarket rivals.

Content marketing – the future

As customer publishers have metamorphosised into newer and trendier content marketing firms, they have carried their publishing contracts with them, offering refreshed titles with digital platform extensions. There remains a clear commitment to the medium but there are potential clouds on the horizon for magazines within the content marketing industry.

Print publishing is timely and expensive. Print slots have to be negotiated and paper purchased. Distribution, far from being a significant revenue stream, becomes a cost. As has already been noted, tight schedules have to be adhered to. As annual budgets are reviewed and agency contracts renegotiated, it is an easy if possibly simplistic choice for the team to say "let's go digital only and stop the print version".

Writing this in September 2020, it must also be noted that the pandemic makes physical distribution of copies considerably harder due to health concerns. Initially, digital titles may have the look and frequency of their print alternatives but over time, these characteristics can slip away. In so doing, the traditional hallmarks of credibility and trust can be eroded. It is therefore important to stress continually the benefits and virtues of the magazine medium. Technology allows for content to be produced in many different working environments and on the surface, the journalistic or curation role may look easier than it is. Will there be a temptation for the brand company itself to take control of creativity from the publishing agency or the host magazine itself – and does that matter in the long term? Will Editors be replaced by the corporate Chief Content Officer?

In terms of effectiveness of communication, this matters. Magazine making is storytelling with words and pictures. It is a skill, be it print or digital, text or design. Developing that all-important reader trust is a slow burn and does not happen overnight. Magazine professionals put flesh on the bones of creative ideas and visions, bringing them to life in a way that readers relate to. History and experience show that this is best done within a magazine publisher or publishing agency type environment, by trained teams who have learnt their craft in college or on the job working across a portfolio of titles. An open environment where they can spark off each other is an asset. Content marketing agencies employ publishing professionals and will continue to do so and are currently an important source of employment for graduates.

DID THE PANDEMIC SPEED UP GOODWOOD?

One luxury brand that has made the move from print to digital magazine is *Goodwood Magazine*, and its first online edition demonstrates the importance of experienced magazine curation and storytelling. The Goodwood sporting estate is spectacular. Settled in the beautiful South Downs close to the historic cathedral city of Chichester, it has been home to the Dukes of Richmond since 1697, and is renowned for its thrilling motorsport and horseracing events, including the Festival of Speed, the Qatar Goodwood Festival and the Goodwood Revival. Members can also enjoy two golf courses, four restaurants and a private health club. Should they wish, they can land at a private aerodrome to avoid the stress of driving through country lanes. Since 2010, the estate has produced a high quality quarterly print magazine for its 18,000 members but as the UK emerged from its COVID hibernation in the summer of 2020, the title turned digital in a highly innovative way.

The digital edition provides a fully immersive experience where the reader interacts with a wide range of moving and still images, rich sound-bites, intriguing rub 'n reveals, as well as traditional magazine articles. The publisher believes that the new format and free *Goodwood Magazine* celebrates everything that makes Goodwood unique with topics ranging from motorsport and aviation to fashion and vintage, art and design, food and drink, horse racing and country life. This bespoke digital platform is fully dynamic, providing readers with the familiarity, enjoyment and benefit of their traditional print magazine, while enhancing their experience. It also allows Goodwood and its partners to access real-time insights to drive future business and editorial decisions. Contributors include Stephen Bayley, Hannah Betts and Lucia van der Post, while advertisers include Hermès, Chanel and Rolex.

Curation, design and production is shared between the agency Uncommonly and e-Mersion Media. John Iliopoulos of e-Mersion Media states "we have developed a dynamic platform to 'Bring Magazines to Life', moving from the constraints of print to digital's creative freedom, yet keeping the authority, beauty and engagement of a superbly produced magazine such as Goodwood's" (Goodwood, 2020). Importantly, the agency responsible for content has a strong magazine background with its founders having come from the tough publishing environment of Times Newspapers. When questioned about the pandemic of 2020, the publishing team stated that they had been considering new media platforms for a couple of years, but the crisis of 2020 created both the environment and the opportunity to make digital happen, with issues of cost, sustainability all coming to the fore.

This app is highly polished, innovative and well curated. There is little doubt that some traditional readers, used to a quality print title, will take time to become acquainted, comfortable and familiar with it – but it is likely that this fusion of magazine skills and new technology will shape content marketing in the post-COVID world.

Independent magazines

Magazines are holding their own as a weapon of choice in the commercial and highly competitive content marketing world. At the opposite end of the business spectrum, the medium is also buzzing – and that is independent magazines. Independent magazines are just that – owned by private individuals or groups without the backing of a mainstream publisher in the disciplines of distribution or advertisement sales. Launch may have been funded by savings, investments from friends and family or possibly crowdfunding.

The definition of the genre, however, goes far beyond the name over the door. Independent magazines represent a newfound love of print, with titles usually printed to exacting and high-quality production standards, more often than not on superior paper stock. Publishers are rarely constrained by the height of a traditional newsagent's shelf so formats can be large or unusually packaged. Quality is an important characteristic of differentiation against 'zines' as is discussed in an important paper by Megan Le Masurier in the *International Journal of Cultural Studies* (Le Masurier, 2012). It is extremely difficult to quantify the market for independent magazines; a general consensus would be around 3,000 titles. Industry readership and audit data are not available. Many titles consider themselves international with London, as ever, one of the important publishing centres. Cover prices tend to be higher than mainstream magazines; the lowest this author found was £6 and prices are often well over £10.

The hallmarks of independent magazines are innovation and community, served with a high degree of empathy and understanding of the chosen topic. Le Masurier describes many of the microbusinesses which make up this sector as 'asset poor and imagination rich' (Le Masurier, 2012, p. 386). In the excellent and superbly illustrated book *Print is Dead Long Live Print*, Ruth Jamieson argues that independent editors approach their topic "as readers first, publishers second, these creatives have a love of and curiosity about magazines" (Jamieson, 2015, p. 8). They can take an idea or an interest – almost certainly too niche for major publishers – and explore and push the boundaries issue by issue, many being themed. Subject matter is diverse and often too niche for mainstream publishers to concern themselves with. To see the bandwidth of this sector, readers are encouraged to read Jamieson's text. She categorises nine main areas of interest ranging from art and culture, though gender, to sport.

Why are independent magazines thriving?

What has been the business and technological environment that has given momentum to this small but important part of today's magazine market? This will be explored in detail in Chapter 8, but is summarised here. The consolidation of market share amongst a handful of major publishers, coupled with the focus of those publishers to invest launch funds in the digital world, has caused a backlash of frustration amongst those editors and designers with a love of print. In times gone by, an experienced and persuasive editor may well have been awarded some launch funds to test out a new idea – in the harsh post-2008 world, this was unlikely to happen. For niche markets to prosper in print, an alternative funding and ownership model needed to be found.

If the expression of the independent marketplace is largely through high quality print publications, there is no double that technology has been an important enabler and has removed a number of the traditional barriers to magazine creation. Apple Mac computers and Adobe InDesign have simplified editing and design and enabled the tasks to be carried out anytime, anywhere. In his discussion of Long Tail economics, this is the process which Anderson calls the democratisation of the tools of production (Anderson, 2006). Despite their devotion to print, niche publishers find louder voices through social media and file sharing networks. Online communities be they ethnic, gender specific, niche sport, photographers or designers now have the ability to create worldwide networks and share thoughts and artefacts globally. Embracing social media enables independent print publishers to source and test new ideas, find content and contributors and promote their print on paper titles. It is slightly ironic that a genre which had its roots as at times being digitally averse now relies upon the new media world for its growth.

Kinfolk magazine was founded in Denmark and now sells in 100 countries including the UK. This quarterly title focuses on developing a quality of life through more simple living and spending time with family and friends. It has a gallery and exhibition space in Copenhagen and is also a book publisher. Connecting with fellow creatives worldwide is key and the title has a social media following on Facebook of over 350,000 and on Instagram of 114,000. *Burnt Roti* is a magazine launched, with some assistance from crowdfunding, in 2016 to give South Asians a platform for showcasing their talents. Their community is clearly enhanced by a Facebook following of over 3000, an Instagram following of 13,000 and a YouTube channel which regularly showcases bespoke videos.

Is there an independent magazine business model?

It is important to understand that independent magazines make up a wide spectrum of commercial acumen. Not all are hand-to-mouth microbusinesses; a number have developed unusual business models. However, there are two tough nuts to crack.

Retail distribution is particularly hard. The combination of long publishing frequency with small sales to niche markets make many independent titles unattractive to high street retailers. Most countries have seen a consolidation of magazine distributors and wholesalers, making it harder for the independent to find a route to market. Moreover, in-store retail promotions with chain outlets are invariably beyond budgets. Ironically, as the ease of production a magazine has improved, the ability to achieve distribution of print editions has become harder. Specialist magazine stores such as London's magCulture can help to fill the gap,

PHOTO 3.3 The magCulture store in London features 500 titles to browse.

but such outlets are few and far between. The solution will almost certainly lie in the independent sector taking a more focused approach to selling subscriptions and by embracing a greater use of digital marketing – skills rapidly being learnt by the mainstream.

The focused and niche nature of content, together with small and unaudited circulations, puts constraints upon the number of traditional advertisement pages an independent publisher can sell. Elsewhere in this book, we can see how the overall magazine advertisement take is in sharp decline. Some titles have no interest or ability to sell ads and focus on a reader-funded model. But there are notable exceptions. Jamieson states that some titles, whilst crafting their magazines as labours of love, can see them as calling cards "used to gain more lucrative side projects" (Jamieson, 2015, p. 8). An excellent demonstration of this is publisher TCO London. As well as being the proud publishers of *Huck* and *Little White Lies*, they offer a content marketing arm producing branded material across a range of platforms for blue chip clients. *Rouleur* magazine – a premium cycling title – hosts exhibition events in both London and Australia attracting sponsorship and reader revenue. Penny Martin, Editor of *The Gentlewoman* magazine, points to the strong relationship her title has with advertisers who are attracted by its tactile print quality (Matthews, 2018). Chapter 8 will examine in depth business models for the independent world.

Supply chain innovations

The traditional supply chain for print as mapped out in Chapter 6 of Stam and Scott has changed little since 2014, although the market has seen significant consolidation of both distributors and wholesalers (Stam & Scott, 2014). The annual decline in print circulation revenues from the mainstream market does not go unnoticed by retail buyers – particularly supermarkets – and there is growing concern amongst circulation directors that this is causing shelf space devoted to the medium to shrink.

Buying a digital edition has become easier and can be done in a number of ways. Unsurprisingly, the publisher will wish to trade with the consumer direct; this maximises the revenue take and also gives access to useful demographic and usage data. Preferences, however move on. The way in which consumers receive digital media has seen considerable innovation with the development of 'all-you-can read' subscription based models as with music (Spotify) and film and TV (Netflix). Two such companies will be examined here – Readly and Cafeyn – and they operate in similar ways. After a short, discounted trial period, subscribers pay (in 2020) £7.99 per month for access to a large array of digital magazines. Readly offers 5000 titles, Cafeyn over 1600. (Cafeyn has French roots so a number of these titles are French.) Paid up customers have unlimited access to all titles which can be downloaded, so easily read offline on flights or train journeys. Cafeyn claim that the average member reads 20 titles per month in 20 sessions of reading (Wessenden 203, 2019, p. 13). Statistics from Readly show that an average consumer will dip into 33 titles per month with some dwell sessions for niche or specialist titles up to 45 minutes.

Moreover 40 per cent of customers check into Readly every day (Hogarth & Hill, 2019). The average user will spend seven hours per month on Readly and worldwide, the top three interest categories are celebrity, lifestyle and automobile (Readly, 2019).

Both companies are in the process of making their delivery more targeted and curated. Readly now offer curated articles based on downloads and reading experiences, allowing the consumer to read a theme across a range of journals. From the point of view of a consumer, these services offer a huge range of leading magazines for a fantastic price; the monthly subscription being little more than a single quality print monthly. The download capacity is a real plus for travelling readers and the app is especially useful for international customers who wish to see a range of titles that just cannot be purchased in print locally. Satisfaction levels seem positive – in July 2020, both services had App Store satisfaction ratings well above 4.

How do publishers see these services? Whilst noting an initial certain ambivalence towards them, there is now a growing acceptance. Both websites show that large titles are available, although they can withdraw at the end of contract. At this point, comparisons with Spotify part. Bands and record companies had to start doing business with legitimate and recognised digital music providers or risk seeing their sales become eroded by illegal or pirate downloads. Pre-pandemic, money from gigs and merchandising also improved for bands making them less dependent upon traditional album sales. Spotify generates millions of streams or downloads and so a tiny sum from each customer adds up. The Managing Director of Readly UK, Ranj Begley, states that in the early days of the business it was tough to get existing publishers to sign up to a pricing model some considered to be disruptive. But there is little evidence to show that Readly will cannibalise existing readership; Ms Begley claims that overlap is less than 1 per cent. She continues: "Now that we have an established platform we are in a fortunate position and have publishers coming to us" (Hogarth & Hill, 2019).

A key benefit for publishers in allowing digital business such as Readly and Cafeyn to market their titles digitally is data provision. These platforms enable a huge amount of very valuable analytics to be harvested. This enables editors to see the popularity – or not – of certain features and articles in both current and back issues; who is reading, when they are reading and which issues get the most hits. Taking this knowledge and spinning it out across the whole operation, print as well as online, allows for better targeting, editorial choice and curation.

It is relatively early days for businesses such as Readly and Cafeyn but they clearly have a model which can be readily rolled out to many markets geographically. Publishers with large subscription enrolment machines may decide to stay outside as they remain of the view that they can disrupt sales, but time will tell. Data provision is definitely assisting to allay such concerns. These digital providers, however, may have to take the route of curation and selection cautiously as this may provoke concerns from the owners of strong brands that an element of brand equity could be damaged.

PHOTO 3.4 The Readly app offering consumers a large range of titles.

What the future holds

Before attempting to make predictions for the medium-term future, it is interesting to speculate on what has *not* happened to the UK magazine business since the dual onslaught of declining advertisement revenues and new media challenges. Mainstream consumer publishers have stopped launching magazines on anything like the scale of activity of the 1990s. An analysis of the top 50 titles for the period January to June 2019 shows that the youngest brand is *Stylist*, the free distribution title launched in 2009, followed by the Bauer title *Closer* in 2005. There are niche launches, there are specials, there are countless new independent titles – and the children's market by necessity has to reinvent itself on a frequent basis to keep up to date with TV and cinema franchises – but there are no new titles aimed at a mass audience. The majority of paid for titles in that ABC analysis were launched in the last quarter of the last century. Looking after legacy brands can only ever be half a strategy. Yes, it is important to freshen up and reinvest in the cash cows of the famed Boston Consulting Group matrix, but a business which fails to bring new customers to its core products will gradually wither. Retailers cannot reasonably be expected to support such lack of innovation with significant promotions and shelf space. Try and think of another sector of commerce where there are no new brands in a rank of top 50 sellers.

If mainstream houses have had their eye off the ball regarding new print launches, on balance they must be applauded for grit and determination to tackle a hostile commercial environment with their existing brands. This textbook has demonstrated a range of innovations, in the guise of product, market and platform developments or extensions, which have taken publishers into commercial activities which would have been considered off limits 20 years ago. Not all have been successful but many – particularly events, exhibitions, bundle sales, radio and podcasts – have provided new and welcome flows of revenue from readers, advertisers and sponsors. The model has started to change to one whereby editors are asking those readers to pay for more of these brand enhancements. An example of this is *Rouleur* cycling magazine which invites readers to its Classic live events. For brand extensions to be successful, the core brand needs to be strong, well-written, edited, designed and marketed. Additional activities need to be in complete harmony with the magazine's image. Communities or audiences of core customers or readers must be placed centre stage with any new development designed to strengthen their loyalty, trust and goodwill towards the magazine.

To develop their brand-based businesses, publishers must continue the positive trend already started and search outside of their traditional networks when forming teams. In the early part of this author's publishing career, outsiders coming into the magazine publishing business were viewed with caution or scepticism. One colleague was known to call them 'tourists' on the basis that a short spell steeped in the strange ways of publishing would see them off! And with many of them it did. Luckily such times have changed. Now, one sees subscriptions departments staffed with digital direct marketing experts from a range of industries, events departments staffed with professional exhibition organisers and direct retail and customer service more often or not contracted out to specialists. Publishers are increasingly being realistic about what they are good at and where they need new blood and increasingly seeing their skills base as a key asset of the business.

Finally, what of the physical format? Notwithstanding the huge problems generated by the 2020 pandemic, this traditional method of communication, which has been around since the eighteenth century, is still in demand. People like it. Magazines continue to inspire, entertain and inform. Commercial executives of the content marketing world recommend customer magazines to their clients. There is a myriad of independent titles out there, the majority crafted beautifully, all waiting to find adoring readers through that elusive distribution model. As the UK business moves into the difficult third decade of the twenty-first century, the verdict has to be that this sector has innovated, by necessity, to survive.

Useful web resources

Professional Publishers Association – www.ppa.org.uk
Audit Bureau of Circulation – www.abc.org.uk
magCulture – www.magculture.com
Content Marketing Association – www.the-cma.com
In Publishing Magazine – www.inpublishing.com
Zenith Advertising Agency – www.zenithmedia.com
Boston Consulting Group – www.bcg.com

Readly – www.readly.com
Cafeyn – www.cafeyn.co.uk
Wessenden Marketing – www.wessenden.com

References

ABC (2019), *Circulation Release* July to Dec 2019, UK: Audit Bureau of Circulation.
Anderson, C., 2006, *The Long Tail,* London: Random House.
Bilton, J., 2019, *Media Futures, Benchmarking the Business of Media,* Godalming: Wessenden.
Consterdine, G., 2005, *How Magazine Advertising Works*, 5th Edition, London: PPA.
Content Marketing Association (2019), *Home.* [Online] Available at: www.the-cma.com [accessed 5.11.2019].
Elder, (2019), 'London's top stock suggests magazines are the future' *Financial Times,* 1 November.
Enders Analysis (2018), *Consumer Magazine Publishing-Quality not Quantity,* London: Enders Analysis.
Goodwood (2020), *Goodwood Members Magazine Goes Digital.* [Online] Available at: www. goodwood.com/media-centre/goodwood-members-magazine-goes-digital-with-fully-e-mersive-experience/ (accessed 8.08.2020).
Hogarth, M. & Hill, S., (2019), *How to Maximise Revenue for Digital Content.* Available at: www.whatsnewinpublishing.com (accessed 14.01.2020).
Jamieson, R. (2015), *Print is Dead. Long Live Print,* Munich: Prestel
Le Masurier, M. (2012), 'Independent magazines and the rejuvenation of print'. *International Journal of Cultural Studies,* Vol. 15 no. 4, pp. 383–398.
Matthews, L. I. (2018), *How Do Independent Magazines Make Money?* Available at: www. businessoffashion.com (accessed 6.01.2020)
Readly (2019), *The Readly Report.* Available at: www.corporate.readly.com (accessed 2.08.2020)
Stam, D. & Scott, A. (2014), *Inside Magazine Publishing,* Oxford: Routledge
Techradar (2019), Advertise with Us, Available at: www.techradar.com (accessed 22.10. 2019)
Weller, T. (2019), *TI Media* (personal interview (25.09.2019)).
Wessenden 201 (2019), *Wessenden Briefing,* Godalming: Wessenden Marketing.
Wessenden 202 (2019), *Wessenden Briefing,* Godalming: Wessenden Marketing.
Wessenden 203 (2019), *Wessenden Briefing,* Godalming: Wessenden Marketing.
Zenith Media, (2019) *Advertising Expenditure Forecast, June* London: s.n.

4

MANAGING INNOVATION

The three 'Ps' of creativity and commercialisation

Simon Das

If the previous chapters are focused around 'the what' of innovation (its drivers, historic and contemporary examples), this chapter aims to look at 'the how' of this subject – and to consider innovation in a holistic way through working with recent research on media management in magazines. By employing a model based around the author's research on creativity in magazine media, a '3Ps' methodology in this chapter is presented for examining insights in managing innovation in magazines, specifically by looking at qualitative data on magazine publishers' *products, people* and *processes.*

Using a varied sample of magazine innovation case studies from a study of managing creativity in magazine publishing (Das, 2019), interview data from UK-based magazine editors and publishers over the last five years are analysed. Developing empirically driven analysis of magazine *Products* (print and digital 'vertical' channels), *People* (creativity, skills and talent) and *Process* (journalism, content creation and media management), the chapter concludes with insights into magazine publishing *innovation* and its contribution to a theory of managing *creativity* by considering it against a 'missing middle' of cultural industry study that favours outputs over processes.

Innovation management theory

The field of innovation management has been traditionally dominated by considering either *product* innovation (design, research and development or R&D) or *process* innovation (around organisational structure and strategy) in its theorising of the way companies can manage innovation, as a reaction to external forces, markets and drivers. O'Sullivan & Dooley (2009a), for example discuss new product development (NPD), as incremental and radical design changes and process that starts with ideation, and works through to development testing (sometimes known as UX design or 'user experience' in the tech sphere) before considering the steps involved in a market launch. Innovation management *process,* on the other hand refers to 'how' a company goes about all their business, including such NPD, in that it means examining "process that relate to all operational activities designed to transform inputs into a specified output for the customer" (O'Sullivan & Dooley, 2009a, p. 18).

Using a framework to encompass these *product* and *process* viewpoints, the inclusion of another perspective, P for *people*, towards innovation, is seen as important for the study of innovation management in media. Although the field of *people* management (human resource management) is large, there is relatively little research about people and innovation with regards to managing creativity – despite creativity being regarded as important for a number of cultural and media industries (Bilton, 2007).

Based on Schumpeterian ideas of creative destruction (Schumpeter, 1949), creativity has historically been positioned as an oppositional chaotic force against the rationality of management (Dwyer, 2016). In examining new 'P for *people*' modes of working and organisational cultures and structures within magazine publishing, the enduring myth that 'heroic creativity' (Bilton, 2010) is better aligned to entrepreneurship and not management, will be challenged. Rising to the challenge laid down by media management theorists such as Lucy Küng (2007, 2010, 2018), the argument made here positions people's creativity as central to innovation in media industries, especially as magazines are businesses with creativity embedded within many functions, compared to traditional R&D process of other sectors.

In the discussion below of a framework of '3 Ps' of innovation in magazine publishing, we shall see, the P for *people* relationship between innovation and creativity is a strong one, despite the fact that management theory (and practice) has historically regarded creativity as unmanageable (Dwyer, 2016).

What is innovation in magazines: the three Ps of products, process and people

P for products: defining a magazine

New product innovation in magazines is a fluid area. There have been so many magazine innovations in the past (from innovations in colour, content, format and feel, freesheets, premium and luxury products), through to innovations in recent years on the digital side (apps, electronic editions and social feeds), that magazine innovation is perhaps today arguably hard to recognise, given the changing media landscape.

Traditionally, magazines have always been hard to define. Click and Baird's definition of a magazine is more "of an approach than a format" (Click & Baird, 1994, p. 5). A magazine can be both a consumer product and a business to business (B2B) service – having a duality of a customer focus, but an advertiser who pays for it. In addition, a magazine today, is also more likely to be a customer magazine (in the

UK, they are the highest circulating titles), and one entirely based on paid-client relationships. But whether customer or consumer magazines other dualities in purpose exists for magazines. Quoting America's 'Mr Magazine' author and blogger Samir Husni, magazines are "both fixed (in concept) and in flux (in content)" Losowsky (2007, p. 12), explaining that a magazine is therefore "both ephemeral and long lasting" Losowsky (2009, p. 7).

Magazines demonstrate both consistency and surprise: places where experimentation should meet regularity. A magazine is not about a type of platform, physical product or format – it is an approach to content delivery where ultimately both originality and familiarity are balanced against each other. This balance in Marcia Prior-Miller's formal 'taxonomy of magazines' (Prior-Miller, 2015) is described better as a 'dichotomy', as whatever the process, the publisher or platform – the 'general-specialised' nature of magazines means they are simultaneously broad collections of articles, while having a need to be narrow in editorial focus and content.

According to Mintel (2019), despite the downward trend in print magazine sales across the UK, "nearly seven in 10 people have read a magazine in the last six months." Such a magazine might get to a reader via a newsstand, but equally, as a free magazine, as a customer of another service (a contract or customer magazine, for example the giants of *Tesco* or *Asda* magazines), a website (such as *TimeOut* or *The UpComing*), a free magazine in a metropolitan transport hub or station (like Women's fashion weekly *Stylist*), a digitally downloaded magazine app (such as the widely downloaded and interactive edition of *Wired*) or via an enhanced PDF or e-Pub format of publisher's printed title, through a subscription service, such Amazon Kindle's magazine section, Magzster, Apple News+ or Readly – a service alone that boasts hosting around 5000 magazine titles.

P for process: service levels in media

Innovation management theory is heavily influenced by 1980s scholarly studies of Japanese and American management practices that lead to efficiency and marginal gains, often in relatively stable and internationalised consumer markets. Management theories that developed in the 1980s around Total Quality Management (TQM) and Just-in-Time Logistics (from Crosby, 1979) focus on efficiency from inputs of raw materials through to distribution to consumers: they theorise innovation by removing organisational barriers and improving efficiency and productivity. An example of this *process* innovation in retail, for example is TK Maxx – a retail chain that has no innovative products *per se*. They gain competitive advantage in the budget fashion market by offering designer garments cheaply, easily and quickly to high street consumers. Intelligent purchasing of surplus stock from high fashion brands as 'seconds' and out of season garments, they make huge efficiencies in their speed to market, by their method of low cost 'pile it high' retailing (no fuss, no boutique style service) and the scale economies in shop rental by having a huge retail presence in many high streets and city centres.

This type of process innovation, however, is often based on the premise of stable consumer goods, and *post facto* product innovation – innovation that has already happened in fixed products – not more 'fluid' services. In digitally disruptive media markets, process innovation could be the main innovative attribute of a service itself: the way a media company curates, connects, advises and takes-on feedback. According to O'Sullivan and Dooley, a key attribute of service innovation is a very high level of customer interaction where "the customer is often unable to separate the service from the person delivering the service" (O'Sullivan & Dooley, 2009a, p. 20). Quality assumptions therefore of media products can be in levels of customer service or what tech companies might call 'user experience'. In magazine markets, where brands lead taste making, specialist interest leadership (hobbies, sports, pastimes), dissemination of news and consumer information or even entertainment (lifestyle magazines), a new alternative has been created slowly but surely. This alternative is the disruption of social media-led choice, a service level of endless channels, and selectable 'verticals' of taste and consumption suggestions.

The new digital media companies of the last decade (namely the giants in Facebook, Twitter, Netflix, Google, Amazon and Apple) have gained global audiences who consume content, of whatever type, whenever they want and wherever they want to consume it. This is echoed by Marcus Rich, CEO of the UK's magazine giant, TI Media as the digital tech giants are explained as providing a level of customer service innovation through their IT systems and its interface with social media that legacy magazine publishers just can't match:

> Traditionally we're not great at seeing the data, the links, doing the follow-up processes and making the opportunities to connect with our readers. We need to be more like Facebook and Amazon, and not like businesses that simply makes great content that gets distributed without any direct ownership or control by us.
>
> *Rich, 2020*

In recent years, however, the mainstream magazine industry has been adapting to this challenge. There is clear evidence of it reorganising itself, creating new agile roles, changing editing and content curation processes, especially those around the repurposing of content across platforms. Publishers have also integrated its sales divisions across print and digital, and changed the very entrenched roles that people in magazines used to occupy; for example the current head of *Decanter* magazine is listed as 'managing director' and not managing editor.

P for people: managing creativity

Bilton's (2010) concept of 'heroic creativity' in the media and cultural industries, is one taken from the work on eminent creativity and 'myths' of creativity by Weisberg (1993). This heroic view (linked to Big C creativity narratives of extraordinary things by extraordinary people), is said to underpin what he describes as a mythical 'X Factor' or talent management view of creativity in cultural industries. As unmanageable ingredients for innovation, the default position of managing creativity is, therefore, simply the 'procurement' of creative people – the hiring (and firing) of talent.

Something not to be discounted for its efficacy, the recruitment of talent, and different 'types' of expertise, has been by far the most significant way that creativity is practically managed in the media industries. Discussed by Das (2019), it is important to note that unique 'characters' have often played a significant role in some of the historically innovative magazine launches of the past from *Smash Hits*, through to larger recent launches of free magazines such as *ShortList* and *Stylist* magazines. If innovation does equate to "creativity + exploitation" (O'Sullivan and Dooley, 2009a, p. 8), the magazine industry may provide unique P for *People* insights about the dichotomy between the freedom of *creativity* (in the hiring of mavericks or providing freedom to magazine employees) versus management's need to control resources and costs in *exploitation* during times of economic challenge.

Creativity theorists widely agree on a definition of products that are both 'novel and appropriate' as being creative (Amabile, 1983, 1996) – innovations can be seen as these products turned commercially successful. Although innovation theorists' definitions have long accepted a close relationship between ideation, product invention and its exploitation, especially in technological settings (e.g. Roberts, 1988; Martin 1994), the relationship to creativity is one made explicit more recently by O'Sullivan and Dooley, expressing "*innovation = creativity + exploitation*" (2009a, p. 8). Creativity in this conceptualisation is seen as fundamental to the more concrete and product-related innovation process in service and technological areas. Seen this way, innovation may not require any full formed 'inventions' *per se*. Instead, organisations (especially applicable in media) can develop a creative concept, work an idea into a treatment or in the service sense, just formulate an initiative that might be a management process and not even a prototype or working product at all.

As a way to exploit the commercial or even reputational benefit of a person's or people's collective creativity, managing creativity is therefore not something to be left to happen on its own, thereby fixating on just the exploitation side of the innovation equation alone. To quote the editors of the international magazine trade body, FIPP (the international federation of periodical publishers), in a recent 'Innovations in Magazines' report, innovation is seen by publishers as 'creativity with its sleeves rolled up' (Señor et al., 2014). This 'rolling up of the sleeves' is something that has been examined by creativity theorists for decades. When it comes to what's behind creativity in a person, we know the function of people's skills, fluency of thought and psychological motivations towards tasks (Amabile, 1983, 1996).

However, when it comes to management theory, creativity is a somewhat uneasy friend. Although some of human and organisational behaviour aspects have undoubtedly been considered by management theorists in discussing management as a *process*, the subject of innovation through managing *people* has remained largely elusive to management scholars, with the exception of improving creative environments, so as to not to 'kill creativity' (Amabile, 1998). In her model, Amabile concedes creativity cannot be effectively managed for innovation, but merely aided through improving aspects in her model for creativity (Amabile 1983) that deal with intrinsic motivation.

Such environmental concepts were first widely disseminated into the field of organisational theory by management gurus such as Charles Handy (1985), where types of corporate culture included a 'person culture' where relationships between skilled people requires maintaining the intrinsic motivation in freedom. This theory might work well in the management of a small firm of architects, for example but as David Hesmondhalgh points out (Hesmondhalgh & Baker 2011), in media work (and its associated gig economy), not everybody has this type of professional power and skill base. Management through creative freedom in media, according to Dwyer (2016), still remains largely antithetical to the core Weberian traditions of management as centralising and performative through hierarchical relationships.

In an emerging field of media management theory, however, Lucy Küng's insistence of the 'centrality of creativity' in media businesses (Küng 2007, p. 25) has reignited the debate about innovation and creativity in creative work. Media companies, including magazine publishers, are content creators who are said to be distinct to other industries. Not requiring one 'killer' concept or product a year, media industries (and especially magazine publishers) are hungry for a constant supply of smaller ones. Creativity theorists have termed this 'Small C' creativity (everyday creativity), versus Big C' (or domain changing creativity).

A renewed emphasis on managing creativity by improving this 'Small C' creativity through improving what Lucy Küng calls a 'microclimate' (Küng 2010) for creativity, it is theorised as ultimately improving 'Big C' or commercially innovative creativity: a sort of secondary 'effect'. In various media case studies, Küng provides examples of where this has worked, for example in the management practices of autonomy (long-term contracts for key creatives) at HBO, as well as advocating the collaborative leadership seen at the top of Pixar, Disney and Apple during key periods. This focus by Küng, and Amabile before her, on the one key area of improving intrinsic motivation, is critiqued by Paul Dwyer (2016), who argues that it ignores the 'harder' facets or components of creativity (given in established psychological models of creativity by Amabile, 1983) as 'expertise' or domain knowledge and 'creativity skills', such as divergent thinking ability.

Research methods: 3 PS data on *products, people and process*

Data set around 'Ps' of innovation and creativity

Data from primary qualitative interviews were employed from a PhD thesis on managing creativity in magazines (Das, 2019). In this study, interpretative insights were gathered from respondents (at least three per case) for each publishing entity in three functions: publishing, editorial or sales and marketing between 2012 and 2017. The qualitative interview data used were collated and tabulated from semi-structured interview processes led by a semi-embedded researcher (interviewer as researcher and also industry 'insider'), structured around conversation to reveal management insights around *people, process* and the *products* produced by each publisher. In Das (2019), the inclusion of another 'P' (P for *Place)*, examined organisational and contextual factors for assessing environments for creativity. These P for *Place* insights have been combined here with P for *Process* insights in publishing for this chapter, as many related to generalisable phenomena about organisational process despite the heterogeneous nature of the industry.

Although Das (2019) examined themes emerging against justified 'proximal measures' for creativity (and not innovation *per se)*, the methodology and procedure derived for the research around creativity generated tabulated analysis rich in industrial insight about what is concluded about creativity causes (e.g. around character 'types' backgrounds of *people* and specific editing and commercial *processes)*. These can be seen as approximating dependent variables, against the 'Big C' creativity of new *products* and services generated, seen as an independent variable. This theoretical framework and methodology can be seen as compatible with O'Sullivan and Dooley's definition of product innovation (discussed above) where, "*innovation = creativity + exploitation*" (2009a, p. 8), given much of the structured summaries of data gave insights of creative expression, talent, skill and experience, but also commercial and organisational processes and marketing specific to their publishing entities.

A 'cross-section' sample across magazine publishing

Five magazine 'cases' from Das (2019) were purposefully identified for their individuality and variation from one another. According to case study methodology theorists such as Yin (2002), a case study is designed for examining "a contemporary phenomenon within its real life context, especially when the boundaries between a phenomenon and context are not clear and the researcher has little control over the phenomenon and context" (ibid., p. 13). Given the variation in phenomena explored here (types of innovation, creativity etc) and context (changing structure of the publishing industry), a maximum variation choice in case examples from Das (2019) was identified on the basis of publishers being as heterogeneous as possible in terms of: (i) type of organisation (mainstream or independent), (ii) type of audience (customer, consumer or other) and (iii) company size (number of people in each magazine publishing team).

The five interview-based cases from Das (2019) examined here are:

Case 1: *Cycling Weekly*. The longest running specialist cycling magazine, the weekly title is published by the largest UK 'legacy' publisher, TI Media, formerly IPC Media, a company that owns over 40 well-known magazines brands in the UK

PHOTO 4.1 *Cycling Weekly* was first published by Future Publishing's legacy company IPC Media in 1970.

Case 2: *Rouleur*. A relatively newly launched specialist cycling magazine, it is a luxury quarterly magazine, featuring special collection covers and events. It is published by an independent publisher from its own premises in London

Case 3: *Stylist*. The UK's largest circulating specialist mass media national and international 'freesheet' or 'freemium' magazine publisher. Published by ShortList Media, they form part of the larger DC Thomson group.

Case 4: *ASOS* magazine. Published by the UK's best-known online high street fashion retailer between 2009 and 2019, the magazine was published in-house as a quarterly glossy customer magazine.

Case 5: *Hole & Corner* magazine. A small independent publisher of a specialist lifestyle and craft quarterly 'bookazine'

PHOTO 4.2 First published by cycling fashion brand Rapha, *Rouleur* combines sport, fashion and heritage.

PHOTO 4.3 Free magazine *Stylist* being distributed (pre-2020) in a metropolitan area. Photo Ken Moreton.

PHOTO 4.4 Despite its claim as the most widely read fashion magazine, ASOS closed its magazine in 2019. Photo: Getty Images.

Procedure

Employing the summary analyses in Das (2019, pp. 157–202) P for *Product*, *Process* and *People* from the five chosen case studies, two key 'quotes' are identified from interview qualitative data sets that support data analysis. The sample quotes, which are derived from over 15 interviews with publishers, editors, journalists or marketing professionals in each case, have been highlighted from the narrative data to 'reinforce' a specific 'P' related to magazine *innovation*. The following coding for an interpretative narrative analysis was used to select examples quotes from all the data sets that aided the interpretation of the summary analysis in Tables 4.1–4.3 below.

> Code 1: Explanation of *Products*: innovation in magazine genres, print, platform, service, content marketing, clubs, events or provision of premium services.
>
> Code 2: Detail about *Process*: management and information systems, processes that include ways of editing, news gathering, marketing and PR.
>
> Code 3: Descriptions *People*: information regarding creativity, talent, background, recruitment of skills and experience.

PHOTO 4.5 Independent quarterly *Hole & Corner* espouses 'slow living' through craft and artisanal work.

Data analysis

TABLE 4.1 P for products: what is a magazine?

Magazine title/Brand	P for products
Cycling Weekly **Summary from Das** (2019): A 'super brand' in cycling. Platforms include daily online and social media, weekly magazine, quarterlies and one-shots	**Key Quote 1** *[events] used to be a brand building exercise. We just don't make enough money out of the magazines. It's now how do put on events to support the magazine.* **Key Quote 2** *Branded content is more and more important. Really interesting to see where it goes.*
Rouleur Magazine **Summary from Das** (2019): Premium coffee table 'bookazine' that bridges sport, lifestyle and fashion	**Key Quote 1** *Cycling magazines tend to be cheap throwaway [this] is timeless. There should never be a feeling when you pick up one of these that it is out of date* **Key Quote 2** *…the original issue, goes for £200.00 on e-bay, and there is hardly anything in it. There just was absolutely nothing like this magazine at the time.*
Stylist **Summary from Das** (2019): 'Freemium' innovation as a 'glossy'. Edited to be social media fuelling	**Key Quote 1** *What's at the heart of what we've done? Innovation 1 it's free. Innovation 2 it's distributed where people want it: the working demographic who don't go to the newsagents any more.* **Key Quote 2** *People don't associate free with low quality. Especially in the digital age. People don't reject FB because it's free or watch Sky Sports instead of Match of the Day because it's paid for.*
ASOS magazine **Summary from Das** (2019): Customer fashion magazine that is much more than a catalogue. Reverse publishing: digital to print for a 20 something audience	**Key Quote 1** *We go way beyond producing a catalogue with picture of what we sell online. We write about fashion trends, beauty how-to, even getting interviews with A-list celebrities.* **Key Quote 2** *[ASOS magazine is about] excellent fashion pieces, selected from information gathered about latest trends, and what types of fashion they like from the website registrations. And the way we reach customers.*

(continued)

TABLE 4.1 Cont.

Magazine title/Brand	P for products
Hole & Corner	**Key Quote 1**
Summary from Das (2019): Independent niche magazine as example of forming 'tight' community	*It is about people who spend more time doing than talking, for whom content is more important than style; whose work is their life. It's about stories of dedication* **Key Quote 2** *…now we are having clients coming to us and taking those same themes those stories and making it into a brand.*

TABLE 4.2 P for process: new 'ways' of doing magazines.

Magazine title/Brand	P for process
Cycling Weekly	**Key Quote 1**
Summary from Das (2019): Content and data analytics driven. Processes for consistency, coverage and repurposing of content	*The success of this isn't to do with innovation, it's more about consistency* **Key Quote 2** *we're recruiting from younger and different backgrounds*
Rouleur Magazine	**Key Quote 1**
Summary from Das (2019): Structured way of 'doing things' from editors. Thinking in 'inventive' ways encouraged within parameters	*Creative freedom? I think there is a massive amount of it. I am not going to tell you what I am looking for. It is more like when you get it right that is when I go: "great, right, yes."* **Key quote 2** *There are some pitching meetings but usually [senior editors] have an idea of things aligned which then get assigned. We are quite hierarchal in that sense. This makes a great way of doing a quality control*
Stylist	**Key Quote 1**
Summary from Das (2019): Established processes for launches. Brainstorming for day to day creativity	*New ideas for magazines is not rocket science. It's having a few people with good ideas, testing them, learning and having the confidence to throw them away if they're are cr★★.* **Key Quote 2** *I think in big idea generation we have a quite a set process that sits within the business. But on a daily and weekly basis the idea is generated though smaller processes, like brainstorming sessions.*

TABLE 4.2 Cont.

Magazine title/Brand	P for process
ASOS magazine **Summary from Das** (2019): Emphasis on strong leaders facilitating team work. Investment in skills, training and mentoring	**Key Quote 1** *What we do here at ASOS is quite unique, the ideas get iterated continuously and it is a very fluid work environment. It is a circular evolution process: back and forth from team to team or from teams to directors.* **Key Quote 2** *Nimbleness, resilience and adaptation are key characters of the people and also the business..*
Hole & Corner **Summary from Das** (2019): Supportive and social environment with staff and people featured. Ideas allowed to compete with each other from all directions	**Key Quote 1** *…you can introduce something that is extraordinary and it will not be pushed to the side. Just a few minutes ago we had a meeting in which everyone presented something they are interested in.* **Key Quote 2** *it is such a great thing to be able to talk about things beyond work and the interests we have – it is a healthy way of doing work.*

TABLE 4.3 Three Ps for people: creativity and backgrounds

Magazine title/Brand	P for people
Cycling Weekly **Summary from Das** (2019): Analytical editors, driven by data and not 'taste' in cycling. Young people with multiplatform skills	**Key Quote 1** *The editor and me (head of Digital Content) – we're on the same level…* **Key Quote 2** *That's now why we have a digital team, because there are places we want to go online that we don't want to go in print. Either you do that, or you give up and say, let's let other publishers have those places e.g. commuting.*
Rouleur Magazine **Summary from Das** (2019): Intrinsic love of subject matter by all staff. Team have experience in different fields	**Key Quote 1** *I consider myself a cyclist and journalist* **Key Quote 2** *tap into what we have done in cars…because cycling as a sport belongs to nostalgia.*

(continued)

TABLE 4.3 Cont.

Magazine title/Brand	P for people
Stylist **Summary from Das** (2019): Experienced launch experts. High profile magazine editorial and art team	**Key Quote 1** *The publishers learned this stuff, and in the end built specialist units: [former art director and editorial director at IPC] editorial and design people, and people who would do some maths in the background. By the mid '90s, we learned to do this quickly as a team. Out of that came a lot of ideas.* **Key Quote 2** *The great thing about digital – is a few kids can do amazing things. You used to be able to do things quickly before, but it would still cost thousands to launch a student magazine. Young people do a lot more experimentation.*
ASOS magazine **Summary from Das** (2019): Content people with a strong marketing background. Creatives compliant to corporate strategic needs	**Key Quote 1** *People here are creative – but also follow the guidelines…* **Key Quote 2** *When it comes to creative freedom, I guess the main aspect is the space to use your own creativity, having an input in the process and coming up with new proposals. We are considered the 'specialists' of the area we work on. So I guess the individual freedom is what makes you feel appreciated.*
Hole & Corner **Summary from Das** (2019): Experienced fashion and lifestyle people seeking new creative challenge. Media and design student talent attracted by style and ethos in 'craft'	**Key Quote 1** *…we were literally just fed up with [mainstream publishing] industry, we had good jobs in terms of the money but they were not fulfilling. We used to do this on the weekends and around our day jobs at first.* **Key Quote 2** *we were thinking it would be nice to sort of have all the photographers and journalists that we know to come here with their creative portfolios.*

Findings: the three Ps of managing innovation in magazines

P for products

Evidence in Table 4.1 shows us that innovations in magazines can be 'superbrands' with heritage and a large multiplatform 'verticals'. In print, there were both mass circulation and specialist 'luxury' niche products.

(i) *Print as premium or 'luxury' product*

Magazine innovation in print products in the sample are more 'premium' and less transitory. Magazines as luxury type products, shows emphasis on periodicity as quarterly and bi-annuals (what some term 'bookazines'), customer loyalty vehicles (a form of 'gift' in the case of ASOS) and less on the immediacy of information being monthly or weekly. Even in the case of *Stylist*, the most disposable magazine in the five case studies, it is presented as a keep-able weekly magazine, not a daily newspaper.

(ii) *Established brands as digital 'verticals'*

Magazine innovation in non-print platforms has become as important for mainstream publishers as their printed product business – if not more so. For established specialist consumer brands, such as *Cycling Weekly*, they firmly assert being a 'magazine' but the increasing importance of digital channels, social media and importantly events is clear, as is the need to commercialise content (branded content), given the changing economics of traditional display advertising.

(iii) *Independent magazines as voices of authenticity experts*

Independent magazines in the case data, such as *Rouleur* and *Hole & Corner*, although often assumed to be less innovative in the 'tech' sense, are innovators by their approach or 'philosophy' towards their content. In building a very close relationship with a relatively small number of readers, their 'post-digital' authenticity leads to community creation and cult following. The journalistic and creative content in these magazines, and their physical and design aesthetics in print, have made their brands influential. This influence can be seen as the economic value it has in innovations such as design and brand consultancy.

P for process

Evidence in Table 4.2 shows a varied array of processes to edit and publish innovatively. The sample shows evidence of changing roles and functions of being an editor or 'editing', and that different approaches are evident in different genres. Factors such as: the importance of content consistency (not just 'news' or creating shared viral stories) in the consumer specialist titles; the established model of freesheet innovation based on focused demographic advertising' formal management and training processes in the customer publishing sector (more aligned to brand messages) and the importance of creative freedom, sharing ideas and the organisational model of an informal tight-knit culture in the independent magazines.

(i) *Data-driven customer service*

The case of *Cycling Weekly* and *ASOS* shows the importance of customer-related data, previous sales history, consumption and taste. The assumption that a good magazine can be edited, published and 'pushed' through unknown distribution channels such as the newstrade has disappeared in the views expressed. The magazines in these cases all demand constant feedback, cited 'consistency' in media message through vertical channels (online, social media and video) and a hierarchy of knowledge about online readers, search engine optimisation, and in the case of the customer magazine title, *ASOS*, ownership and control of this content by a marketing function.

(ii) Independent magazines: creative freedom versus management 'control'

The renaissance in independent magazine publishing in the digital era (described widely in Le Masurier, 2012 and Leslie, 2013) – celebrates a form of counter-intuitive innovation process – print-first, digital-second processes. Formed in the digital era, the two independent magazines in the case studies represent forms of 'reverse publishing', going from digital culture into printed media. The data used in this study align with a conclusion in the wider study by Das (2019), that processes for innovation in 'indies' requires tight-knit teams, creative freedom and forms of informal or hidden training and 'apprenticeship' of inexperienced staff by the experienced. Independent magazines are discussed by David Stam in Chapter 8.

P for people

Unsurprisingly, when it comes to Table 4.3 and *People*, this breadth shows a requirement for creative talent and a diversity of people, some with both traditional background and skills in editing, and also increasingly 'new blood' and creativity from other fields and possibly derived from a younger 'digitally native' mindset.

(i) Recruitment and background experience

Data-driven younger Millennials instead of experienced 'journalists' can be said from the data to be driving some of the digital changes. Delving further into the supporting narrative data, it is interesting to recognise that some of the content creators working under experienced editors in these magazines did not have the training in local news journalism or even in publishing, but came from other backgrounds, such as marketing or PR, or even digital content and blogging (e.g. in *Cycling Weekly*). When it comes to the independent magazines, recruitment seems based not so much on 'talent' but on an intrinsic interest in the content, philosophy and culture of the magazine itself.

(ii) Experience and knowledge sharing

While the recruitment of younger more digitally focused skills is increasingly important, the core role of magazine experience seemed at the heart of the five cases explored. In the freesheet magazine, a closely defined process for launches (conducted across the world) defined the business model and the experienced high profile 'generalist' editors needed.

(iii) *Independent magazine 'creatives'*

It's clear from the data analysis that the long-described relationship between creativity and intrinsic motivation seems to hold true for independent magazines such as *Hole & Corner* and *Rouleur*. In each case, a love for the magazine's subject matter and content drives the people working there. In order to manage creatives in these settings, staff need to be 'living' within a specific culture – and that might be one defined by a leader or founding editor publisher.

Discussion

What innovation 'looks like' in magazine publishing: P for products

The data in Tables 4.1–4.3 show a cross-sectional snapshot of huge variation of what innovation looks like as a 'magazine'. This is seen as part of a historical relationship of redefining what a magazine is (format, periodicity, genre), with examples in the case studies examined in Das (2019) highlighting the role of magazines as not magazines *per se*, but 'verticals'. A reader of a well-known title may not buy the magazine, or subscribe, but simply 'like' their content on their social media feed or, if more commercially focused, pay to come to a yearly event.

The case studies also showed the role of magazine brands as trusted sources of information – something aligned to debates about news, fake news and serendipitous content discovery. When it comes to the traditional 300-year-old format of printed magazines, this research shows, like many others, that it is alive, but being reinvented as both a premium product and one that is less mass media and consumerist in its periodicity. Successful independent magazines and customer magazines (such as *ASOS*) are more and more like 'bookazines', published infrequently, they need to be sought out, read and collected. This increasing reliance for magazines to be niche to survive the digital challenge is echoed by recent case study research on niche magazines in America (Baker, 2018).

Industry insights: a management challenge for publishers

The case study research taken from Das (2019) shows a snapshot of magazine publishers who have responded to the existential threat of digital media in number of distinct ways. These changes constitute nothing short of a reinvention of the magazine business in the last decade by thinking about magazine products as platform-agnostic 'verticals', through the provision of community building and events (previously, the domain of service industries), and also in the repositioning of print to a 'luxury' or collectable niche format. The magazine as a format has also become, for good or bad, a premium customer communication vehicle for a number of brands, mainly in retailing.

In the last two decades, the overall industrial structure, reacting to 'digital' drivers of change discussed here, shows an industrial pattern of fragmentation of markets (and with it, a growth in the number of new independent magazines), but simultaneously huge consolidation in what might be called the mainstream or legacy publishing businesses. At the present time, international consolidation of capital in the UK has seen the break-up and sale of larger publishers to venture capitalists (described in Chapter 3). Since the millennium, International companies purchased the largest two magazine publishers in the UK (formerly EMAP sold to German Bauer Media and IPC to the American Time Inc group). Subsequently, IPC Media was rebranded TI Media and (after returning to private equity for a short spell) was in 2020 sold to Future plc, a company whose success is driven by the scale gained from success in US markets and its strategy around publishing for technology markets and video content.

It's undoubtedly true that magazine publishers and their managers, at whatever level, will be overseeing more print magazine closures in the coming years. There is little doubt that the economic impact of COVID-19 will have accelerated some of these closures by the time this is published – but they will be magazines in traditional markets, with traditional readers and distribution methods. This, of course, does not predict the death of magazines *per se*, but merely another transition marker point in a long process of reinvention discussed in Chapter 1 as having taken place over the last decade.

As the case studies show, a complex challenge within this reinvention of magazine media is its management. Many aspects of magazine publishing – such as managing journalism – might become very different in the future. Evidenced in a recent sector-wide analysis by the National Council for the Training of Journalists (Spilsbury, 2018) 70 per cent of all 'journalists' work outside of journalism, the report citing roles we have seen in the case study data here of multiplatform content creation, PR and brand communications, search engine optimisation and even customer events. Given the backdrop of the economic climate, not only have magazine publishers had to manage such varied and intertwined functions of content creation, journalism, marketing and production functions – they have had to do it all for 'less', as the PEST analysis in Chapter 1 shows us, the powerful combinative effect of technological and socioeconomic shifts, relaxed global competition and the post-2008 recession.

While there is a clear underlying management drive towards efficiency by multiplatforming and repurposing content, leading to a contraction in the number of people working in the wider publishing sector in the UK from around 300,000 in 1997 to fewer than 200,000, according to Oliver (2017), the digital 'shift' has at least left publishing more 'match-fit' for 2020 and beyond. In his analysis of media economics in the UK, John Oliver states that "the UK publishing industry has been more 'dynamically capable' at adapting and reconfiguring their human resources than their peer creative industries" (Oliver, 2017, p. 86).

The macroeconomic data suggest that magazine workers have, during the digital era, become some of the most productive in the creative industries: and the microeconomic qualitative data in this study show this dynamism reflected in the new *products, processes* and *people* case evidence examined – factors that will define the industry's future resilience to change and disruption. While there is no doubt that people love to read magazines, and to publish them – the future challenge will be significant. As former editor of *Smash Hits*, Ian Birch, warns in his book about magazine publishing's iconic cultural status: "the technological barriers to producing a magazine have never been lower, those to achieving success have never been higher" (Birch, 2018, p. 20).

Towards a theory: the 'missing middle' of managing creativity

Creative industry research is said to be skewed towards creative outputs or on marketing these outputs (exploitation), avoiding the examination of the people or the processes that leads to it. This argument of a so-called missing middle in creative industry research (Warhurst, 2010) describes a lure of media content (treatments, new magazines, TV series or pieces of music), while marginalising the study of less exciting processes that helps media work become innovative. This blinding by the cultural value of artefacts, like magazines, obscures knowledge about production, management and its link to innovation.

Much of innovation theory is based around focusing on either product or process innovation. In the age of the digitally disruptive, research and practice has been focused on replicating 'tech' companies and their business practices. The theory of disruption (Christensen et al., 2015) shows us that replication is not enough as an innovation 'strategy' and radical innovation therefore demands the management of the unusual, the out of the ordinary and possibly the maverick idea makers themselves. Although magazine publishing has fallen foul of disruptive forces in media and 'tech', even less radical 'sustaining' innovations require at least genuine novelty and new offerings, even to loyal consumers.

Accepting innovation management theorists O'Sullivan & Dooley's (2009b) conception that *innovation = creativity + exploitation*, we have discussed the theory and practice of managing creativity being one that is deeply problematic: there is an enduring legacy of seeing creativity as unmanageable. Therefore, pragmatically, it might be only exploitation that has been theorised as managing innovation. By using a differing 'Ps' of innovation in *People* and *Process* leading to *Products*, the case studies of managing creativity and innovation from the work in Das (2019) can be seen as challenging the idea of creativity as unmanageable in commercial contexts by putting a focus onto people and their creative management. A knowledge of field of creativity theory sees both 'Big C' and 'Small C' creativity, after all, as something directly affected by intrinsic motivation, skills and expertise (Amabile, 1998).

The data in Tables 4.1–4.3 suggest that when it comes to managing P for *Process* and P for *People* (those that could be considered types of dependent variable) in different business contexts, magazine publishers manage creativity not just through the recruitment of people with proven creative experience, for example as launch editors for a freesheet like *The Stylist* (as per Bilton's heroic creativity model), but by management through fostering teams' intrinsic interest (through a shared, social culture), and importantly, by developing and supporting less experienced editors, writers, photographers and marketers in their field, for an industry in the midst of dynamic change.

Outside of knowledge about assessing corporate organisational environments by Amabile (1998), the insights here via Das (2019) add to Küng's media management 'microclimate' thesis (2010) by suggesting the management of creativity to be more direct in industries such as magazine publishing in the digital era. Echoing conclusions in Das (2019), it can be said that, unlike the pre-digital 'heyday' of magazines, publishing is perhaps not creative by virtue of the 'heroic' creativity of its editors alone. This is made clear by the difference in the case studies examined here between management within large 'legacy' brands (with their emphasis on data, customer service and recruitment of these digital skills) compared with independent magazines, where the fostering of close-knit cultures and 'apprenticeship' is one that relies on organisational 'looseness' and an intrinsic feel for the content or subject genre of the magazine.

When it comes to managing innovation in magazines today, a conclusion here is perhaps that we cannot neatly separate creativity and commercialisation (or its exploitation) in specific media industry contexts. Creativity, in its purest and most artistic sense, is now less important for an industry striving to find new relevance and compete in a media saturated world. However, in its more practical or useful 'Small C' sense, it is also in huge demand in a world of intense digital media competition, fake news, PR and sometimes inauthentic social media voices. Where real innovation has taken place in publishing – for example in the freelance dominated world of independent magazines – management is conducted both at arm's length for freedom (traditionally considered a form of 'no management'), yet with a closeness of supervision and guidance from seasoned experts – suggesting this type of creativity is more expertly managed in these digital era contexts than most would recognise.

References

Amabile, T. (1983), 'The social psychology of creativity: a componential conceptualization', *Journal of Personality and Social Psychology*, vol. 45 no.2, pp. 357–376.

Amabile, T. (1996), *Creativity in Context*, Boulder: Westview Press

Amabile, T. (1998), 'How to kill creativity', *Harvard Business Review*, vol. 76 no.5, pp. 77–89

Baker, K. (2018), 'How niche magazines survive and thrive through an industry in turmoil', *Publishing Research Quarterly*, vol. 34 no. 3, pp. 407–416

Bilton, C. (2007), *Management & Creativity: From Creative Industries to Creative Management*, Blackwell: Oxford

Bilton, C. (2010), 'Manageable creativity' *International Journal of Cultural Policy*, vol. 16 no. 3, pp. 255–269.

Birch, I (2018), *Uncovered: Revolutionary Magazine Covers*, London: Octopus Publishing

Christensen, C., Raynor, M, Mc Donald, R. (2015), 'What is disruptive innovation?' *Harvard Business Review*, vol. 93 no.12, pp. 44–53.

Click, J. & Baird, R. (1994), *Magazine Editing and Production*, McGraw-Hill: New York

Crosby, P. (1979), *Quality is Free,* New York: McGraw-Hill

Das, S. (2016), 'Magazine publishing innovation: two case studies on managing creativity', *Publications*, vol. 4 no. 2, p. 15.

Das, S. (2019), *Managing Creativity in Magazine Publishing: The 4 Ps of Creativity*, PhD thesis, University of Westminster. Available at https://westminsterresearch.westminster.ac.uk/item/qz985/managing-creativity-in-magazine-publishing-the-4ps-of-creativity

Dwyer, P. (2016), 'Managing creativity in media organisations', in Lowe, G. and Brown, C., *Managing Media Firms and Industries*, London: Springer, pp. 343–365

Eisenhardt, K. (1989), 'Building theories from case study research', *Academy of Management Review,* vol. 14 no.4, pp. 532–50

Gauntlett, D. (2011), *Making Is Connecting: The Social Meaning of Creativity, from DIY and Knitting to YouTube and Web 2.0,* London: Polity Press

Handy, C. (1985), *Understanding Organisations,* London: Penguin

Hesmondhalgh, D & Baker, S (2011), *Creative Labour: Media Work in Three Cultural Industries,* London: Routledge

Key Note (2004), *Consumer Magazines*, Hampton, Middlesex: Key Note Publications

Küng, L. (2007), 'Does media management matter? Establishing the scope, rationale and future research agenda for the discipline', *Journal of Media Business Studies*, vol. 4 no. 1, pp. 21–39

Küng, L. (2010), 'Innovation and creativity in an age of disruption' *Presentation to Columbia Institute for Tele-Information Conference 'Transforming Media Professions', 11th June 2010, New York.* Available at: www.lucykung.com/wpcontent/uploads/2015/07/KüngColumbiaCITI-Final-.pdf (accessed 27.03.2020)

Küng, L. (2018), *Digital Transformation. The Organisational Challenge – Creating a Roadmap for Change.* Oxford: Reuters Institute/Thomson Reuters. Available at https://agency.reuters.com/en/insights/industryreports/going-digital-a-roadmap-for-organizational-transformation.html (accessed 19.04.2020)

Le Masurier, M (2012), 'Independent magazines and the rejuvenation of print' *International Journal of Cultural Studies,* vol. 15 no. 4, pp. 383–398

Leslie, J. (2013), *The Modern Magazine,* 1st edition, London: Laurence King Publishing

Losowsky, A. (2007), *We Love Magazines*, Luxembourg: Editions Mike Koedinger SA

Losowsky, A. (2009), *We Make Magazines*, Berlin: Die Gestalten Verlag

Martin, M. (1994), *Managing Innovation and Entrepreneurship in Technology Based Firms,* New York: Wiley

Mintel (2019) *Magazines UK December 2019 Executive Summary Report,* London: Mintel Group Ltd. Available at www.mintel.com (accessed 2.01.2020)

O'Sullivan, D. & Dooley, L. (2009a), 'Defining innovation' in O'Sullivan, D. & Dooley, L. *Applying Innovation,* Thousand Oaks: Sage, pp. 3–32

O'Sullivan, D. & Dooley, L. (2009b), 'Managing Innovation' in O'Sullivan, D. & Dooley, L. *Applying Innovation,* Thousand Oaks: Sage, pp. 33–56

Oliver, J. (2017), 'Exploring industry level capabilities in the U.K. creative industries', *Creative Industries Journal,* vol. 10 no. 1, pp. 75–88

Prior-Miller, M. (2015), 'Magazine typology', in Abrahamson, D., Prior-Miller, M. and Emott, B. *The Routledge Handbook of Magazine Research, The Future of the Magazine Form,* London: Routledge, pp. 22–50

Rich, M. (2020), Personal interview with Marcus Rich, CEO of TI Media, February 2020

Roberts, E. (1988), 'Managing invention and innovation', *Research Technology Management,* vol. 31 no. 1, pp. 11–29

Schumpeter, J. A. (1949), The historical approach to the analysis of business cycles, in *Essays: On Entrepreneurs, Innovations, Business Cycles, and the Evolution of Capitalism,* New Brunswick, NJ and London: Transaction

Señor, J. Wilpers, J & Giner, J (2014), *Innovations in Magazines 2014 World Report,* 5th edition, London: FIPP.

Spilsbury, M. (2018), *Journalists at Work: Their Views on Training, Recruitment and Conditions.* London: National Council for the Training of Journalists. Available at www.nctj.com/downloadlibrary/JaW%20Report%202018.pdf (accessed 2.05. 2020)

Stam, D. & Scott, A. (2014), *Inside Magazine Publishing,* Oxford: Routledge.

Sumner, D. (2001), 'Who pays for magazines – advertisers of magazines? *Journal of Advertising Research,* vol. 41 no. 6, pp. 61–67

Warhurst, C (2010), 'The missing middle', in Townley, B. and Beech, N. *Managing Creativity: Exploring the Paradox,* Cambridge: Cambridge University Press

Weisberg, R. W. (1993), *Creativity: Beyond the Myth of Genius,* New York: W H Freeman

Yin, R. K. (2002), *Case Study Research: Design and Methods,* Thousand Oaks, CA: Sage

5

THE ADVERTISING REVOLUTION

Past, present and future

Helen Powell

Introduction

With national and global ad spend data evidencing a consistent trend in the decline of investment in magazines in relation to other media choices, the impact this is having on the magazine industry is significant. Titles are folding, and the major players all experienced circulation declines in 2019 according to ABC data. When examining forecasting and trend analysis, the future also remains bleak as all predictions point to a continuous downward slump, exacerbated by economic conditions engendered by the recent pandemic. Since the inception of the magazine, advertising has been an integral part of both its identity and more importantly as a critical income stream. However, the relationship between the magazine and its advertisers is predicated on an unequal balance of power: as part of an overall media plan, the magazine is one choice amongst many. All logic dictates that the magazine will be squeezed to the point of extinction as a media form – and yet, despite all the indicators, there remains hope. For as this chapter explores, there is a distinctive qualitative difference to magazine reading that takes you into an immersive world of escapism and where a willingness to engage with its promotional content becomes an integral part of both the medium and our interactions with it.

The first part of this chapter lays the groundwork by defining what is an advertisement and how magazines make money through the selling of space. It examines how the growth of magazine advertising as a promotional tool is aligned to a broader economic model that measures success based on economic growth underpinned by the ongoing necessity to consume. In order to achieve this goal, magazine advertising positions itself as a necessary resource in guiding consumer choice centred around lifestyle building through close adherence in terms of creative content to a specific set of semiotic principles. The chapter will then examine the key players in the process of crafting and placing an ad and the increasing turn towards the domination of programmatic advertising within the broader scope of media planning.

The second part of the chapter charts the ongoing struggles that magazines are facing to attract advertisers and how they are simultaneously countering this with new promotional formats. Via an examination of the 'attention economy' we can see a new line of attack that the magazine can exploit. The chapter will explore how emphasis is now placed more than ever on the magazine itself as brand, and it is a lack of strong brand identity that is determining winners and losers in who stays around for longest. Brand extensions therefore become lucrative options for a successful magazine allowing for strategic brand partnerships to be built, although the ethical challenges posed here around editorial objectivity are worthy of discussion. It concludes with a short thought piece on the future of magazine advertising with reference to broader industry trends, consumer media engagement and the challenges of external factors, including sustainability and COVID-19.

What is advertising and how does it work?

When we consider what actually constitutes advertising, we should consider its three inter-related elements: as a communications business, centred on **advertising agencies**, increasingly niche and specialised, who work for **clients** to promote their message both creatively and strategically, producing **promotional content** that enters into the public domain and, if effective, into popular consciousness propelling consumers to act on what they see or hear. The modern origins of advertising began with an advertising 'agent' who worked for a newspaper, rather than a modern-day client, selling advertising space for a fee. It was the advertisers themselves who initially produced the copy. Indeed, back in 1710, Joseph Addison of *The Tatler* wrote a piece commenting on the changing nature of language in advertising. Specifically, how it sought to make the ordinary seem extraordinary as a way to get products noticed (Feldwick, 2019). However, with the increase in the number of newspapers the seller recognised the value of independent status and evolved into a 'space broker': buying space from the newspapers and selling it to clients keen to promote their wares on the back of the first industrial wave. In order to add value to this service and give themselves a competitive edge, space brokers began to comment on and then craft the copy, including early illustrations, and also advise on media planning as they began to provide early research data on readership. This led to the first advertising agency model, the full service agency, whereby both the creative and media elements were exercised under one roof. The 1920s and 30s was a significant era of growth for the advertising agency as advertising became recognised as a key tool in crafting a brand reputation. As the brand identity became integral to consumer familiarity, and with it a sense of consumer trust, so the role of creativity was enhanced in building brand value and personality through image and copy.

Good Housekeeping in April 1935 cost one shilling, and on the cover of this edition is a beautiful hand-drawn illustration of two small children in the garden.

Gender stereotypes prevail as a younger sister looks up in awe while her older brother attaches a home-built birdhouse to a tree. Turn over and the inside cover comprises a full page black and white display ad for *Nash's*, a literary and features magazine of the time. This is followed by a further black and white ad for an ESSE heat storage cooker and then a full page ad for Ovaltine featuring the image of the young actress Pearl Hay. The body copy is a testament from the actress's mother who writes:

> My daughter used to get terribly strained nerves through being in the Studio all day. Now that she has a cup of Ovaltine every morning she can stand any amount of work without the slightest strain.
>
> *Good Housekeeping, 1935, p. 5*

In all of these ads copy dominates and functions to reinforce the brand offer. However, what is most interesting here is that the ads stop abruptly after these first three pages: content, free of ads, then dominates until we get to page 83. At this point, the layout shifts drastically so that the remaining 133 pages (61.5 per cent) are filled with advertising and the magazine even carries a categorised advertising index at the back referencing the 250 different brands featured inside. We even get our first hint in this edition of a sense of nascent media planning in a feature called 'The Beauty Clinic' which allows readers to write in with beauty problems. The actual responses are brand neutral but a significant ad for Elizabeth Arden is prevalent on the page. However, a more consolidated, strategic approach to media planning is absent on the majority of the pages as a Daimler car ad shares a page with Larola beauty cream and Carr's table water biscuits.

The number of different brands shown in the index and the idea that a reader would use the magazine to actually seek out an advertiser marks a turning point in the relationship between magazines and a developing promotional culture, with magazines positioning themselves as trusted environments through which consumer choice is mediated. This is reinforced initially through a number of footers that remind the reader: 'Advertised Goods are Good Goods', or 'All advertisements in *Good Housekeeping* are guaranteed' or finally 'Advertising is the consumer's guarantee of merit'. *Good Housekeeping* capitalises upon this building of trust further with the development of its *Good Housekeeping Institute* in London where products are tested, scored and results printed in the magazine. This validation is maintained in current editions where this function of the magazine as the embodiment of consumer trust underlines the identity of the magazine itself. The top right-hand corner of the cover of the May 2020 issue carries the logo "Good Housekeeping Institute: Tried, Tested, Trusted". Each month different product sectors are selected for testing and results printed here can shape and inform readers' decision-making process. This is then taken one step further whereby the *Good Housekeeping* kitemark of trust actually appears on brands' packaging that score highly in these features.

Advertising needs to understand brands and branding so that it can amplify what they stand for and what they can offer the consumer. Such achievements did not come without difficulties as certainly in the United States, the home of modern advertising, agency employees were largely middle-class, Ivy League educated men who were struggling to make contact with the man and woman in the street. This came at a time when magazines really began competing with newspapers and indeed radio in terms of the value of their advertising space due to their increased circulation figures. Interestingly it was the agency J. Walter Thompson or JWT (now Wunderman Thompson) who addressed this problem head on by exploring the content of the confessional *True Story Magazine* to understand its popularity and see what advertising could learn from how it addressed its audience. Firstly, its popularity came out of identifiable content via the "first-person, confessional formula" (Marchand: 1985:54) incorporating dramatic photographs and the use of the close-up to convey emotion. JWT recognised the potential of these readers, the wives of skilled workmen, as a target audience for advertising and with a circulation of two million in 1926 (ibid.). The agency soon began placing ads for Lux, Ponds and Camels in the publication. However, of greatest interest here is the synergies adopted between the style of the ads and the magazine content itself centred around dramatic realism and the confessional style. In one ad for a cereal brand (Wheatena), the headline took the wife's point of view as she claimed "Some wives do it – but I wouldn't dare" only to reach the end of the copy and the realisation that going to work on an empty stomach was not the right way to prepare your husband for the day ahead!

Following the Second World War and the reconstruction of cities and economies, magazines became aware of the kinds of relationships they were building with readers in line with this activity and initially it paid dividends. However, the rise of commercial television in the 1950s saw many major brands adopt this new moving-image promotional format, especially in relation to food and household goods, thus placing the magazine on the back foot. The ability to provide specialist content that would appeal to advertisers functioned as a response not only in relation to the attractiveness of a single magazine, but produced a burgeoning market sector with new titles springing up around all things domestic and leisure. Magazines became lifestyle templates and brands were willing to pay to become an integral part of this process aligning the specialisation of publication to their particular offer. As Das (2016) has argued "this process of mining more targeted readers, and the advertisers who pay for this connection, is one that has extended from the twentieth century well into the twenty-first". This notion of a more targeted, indeed media-savvy, reader has seen a turn since the 1980s in the creative direction of much advertising: from the informational, rational and text heavy ads of the 'hard sell' era to the more emotional appeal of the 'soft sell'. A shift towards selling an idea rather than a product *per se* opened up greater creative potential and ads have become more inter-textual, drawing on a multiplicity of reference points outside the ad in crafting meaning. In this process, meaning-making comes from reference points within the broader sociocultural environment, with the onus on the reader to explore mentally how the product or brands speak to their aspirational and transformational self.

Critical here is the consideration of how readers are receiving advertising. Advertisements in print magazines function metaphorically as though they were Russian dolls: we explore the ad and its brand message, which is enhanced through the associative images of other ads in its orbit, contextualised by the content of the magazine in which it sits and reinforced through the brand identity of the magazine itself. Finally, the reception environment is integral to the degree of attention we pay to what we encounter. This then allows for consideration of the amplification of the message further as we distinguish between circulation and readership: how many copies of a particular publication are distributed and an estimate of how many readers a publication has. This highlights that most publications have more than one reader per copy. The relationship between readership and circulation is known as readers-per-copy. Unlike newspapers, the appearance of magazines in a number of environments associated with waiting, for example, provide increased opportunities to see. With the proliferation of choice in terms of media content, offline and online, the challenge for advertising agencies is about getting their work seen, or rather 'cutting through the clutter'.

The rise of digital and the challenges of convergence culture

Looking back, the magazine's encroachment into the online world encapsulates all that is convergence culture in terms of how it impacts technologies, industries, markets and audiences. It was Henry Jenkins (2008) who popularised the term as he focused attention on the changes happening in the media industries and the content they produced. Its complexity is highlighted by the "dialogic relationship between old and new media, rather than the simple replacement of one by another, although the utilization of these terms and their appropriateness are also made problematic" (Powell, 2013, p. 2). From the 1990s, we see the 'remediation' of media forms, challenging traditional models of how media are produced, distributed and consumed and specifically in this context, how interactivity when placed at the heart of the reader experience, offers new promotional opportunities. Advertising at large repositions a long-standing model of 'push', mass marketing messages interrupting the daily flow, towards a more personalised, customised approach that 'pulls' the reader in, based on a knowingness of their interests and preferences and predicated on the proliferation of digital technologies. Convergence culture also blurs the boundaries between producer and consumer: the democratisation of content creation and distribution channels presents challenges around access to and ownership of culture and the ability to monetise it that previous iterations of the creative industries benefited from. In summary, two challenges arise. To counter this abundance of free content, magazines need to carefully consider where they can add value and produce content accordingly, and secondly to consider a more flexible, 360 degree offer adopting platform technology that via apps serve up a complete digital format whilst their website provides additional and more time-sensitive content to complement the primary edition. These future developments are fundamental to the success of the magazine industry for the media landscape has undergone a seismic shift with correlating ad spend data (the amount of money spent on advertising) forecasting continuing declining investment in magazines.

Therefore, over the past three decades magazines have been adapting to technological change and adopting new formats which has allowed for additional forms of promotional opportunities. Initially, this centred on websites that allowed for content that moved beyond text and still image to include video and sound. As Holmes (2019, p. 194) indicates, a significant sea change came with the introduction of the iPhone and smartphones more widely with website content requiring reconsideration for life on the small screen and a literally mobile consumer. From iPhone to iPad and the introduction of the app: "for a while the iPad was celebrated as the (potential) saviour of the magazine industry, although it has not quite worked out that way" (ibid.). For the challenge, here is somewhat Janus headed: monetising digital space was a plus point but accompanied by a growing recognition that consistently sales and advertising revenue were coming from the traditional print copy.

The rise of digitality in the magazine industry also heralds a textual convergence, with readers moving seamlessly via hypertext links across features and ads both synchronously and asynchronously. As a result, three models have emerged to address the relationship between print and online content. First, standalone magazines, with no print equivalent. Increasingly, this is emerging not out of choice but rather necessity, as in the case of the *NME* (*New Musical Express*) from 2018 onwards. Second, magazines such as *Cosmopolitan* use print plus a range of platforms to deepen and extend audience relationships at a time when its print sales are falling. As former editor-in-chief Farrah Storr (2017, p. 250) stated: "*Cosmopolitan* in print and digital formats are separate entities, united by the same spirit and tone". Whilst the print version carries long-form journalism, digital delivers breaking news. Such an approach is further refined by knowing how the audience wish to be reached, with older audiences preferring the traditional print copy and a younger audience

TABLE 5.1 Growth in global ad spend by media, 2019–2021f (selected markets). Global year-on-year percentage growth at current prices.

	2019a★	*2020f*	*2021f*
Television	-1.8 (-0.1)	0.6 (0.6)	0.0
Newspapers	-8.5 (-7.7)	-7.1 (-6.6)	-10.2
Magazines	-7.4 (-7.4)	-6/3 (-6.0)	-11.5
Radio	-0.3 (1.7)	1.7 (0.6)	0.8
Cinema	9.7 (6.1)	5.0 (5.9)	4.8
Out-Of-Home	1.5 (4.3)	2.4 (3.9)	2.5
Digital	11.2 (11.5)	10.5 (11.0)	9.5

Figures in brackets show previous forecasts from June 2019.
★2019 actuals are based on November 2019 figures.

Source: Dentsu Aegis Network Global Ad Spend Forecasts January 2020

drawn to social platforms such as Instagram and Snapchat. Finally, in the case of *Red* magazine readers can choose between either print or digital, using bonus content for subscribers (guaranteed sales) which through '*Club Red*' partners with brands to offer discounts and deals. However, the notion of relevancy between advertising content and context is key as advertising fatigue online increasingly sets in complemented by total avoidance via ad-blocking software, a point noted later in the exploration of native advertising. On a more positive note, the move online does allow for greater interactivity and the magazine therefore has an opportunity to get to know its readers more effectively, thus producing more on point content that also has specific advertiser appeal.

The magazine business: how magazines make money through the selling of space

All ads that come into an advertising agency begin with a client brief that documents the specific aims and objectives for the campaign. Following research undertaken by an account planner on market sectors and consumer behaviour, these findings are then translated into a creative brief for the art director and copywriter to work on. In some cases, the specific media will be determined by the client at the outset, in other cases it will be media-neutral. If then the agency chooses to include magazines in its media strategy, it is the work of the media planner to develop a media schedule driven by the ability to target the right people in the right place at the right time. Furthermore, it is important to schedule on sale dates rather than cover dates and to consider that it can take four weeks for monthly magazines to reach their intended readership. When the appropriate titles are identified, space within them is negotiated and purchased via media buyers. Where in times gone by each title would have its own sales team, it is now recognised that the publisher–advertiser relationship can be very labour intensive when it comes to the negotiation around the buying and selling of space, coupled with the increased media proliferation. Consequently, the terrain is now occupied by advertising networks and exchanges. Ad networks function as intermediaries working on commission and are responsible for aggregating and curating a publisher's ad inventory and then selling accordingly to advertisers. The ad exchange in contrast is a digital marketplace allowing for direct transactions between media buyers and sellers (publishers). As with other commercial media, magazines function on the basis that they assemble content that appeals both to readers and to advertisers, with creatives crafting dedicated copy for specific titles. Advertising historically has been the lifeblood of magazines due to the fact that the cover price alone does not meet the cost of publishing, before even beginning to consider the notion of profit. For consumer magazines, the ratio of revenue generation of cover price to advertising is roughly 38–62 per cent with business and professional magazines taking as high as 82 per cent from advertising (McKay, 2018, p. 249). The history of advertising commenced with the straightforward selling of space (via space brokers) and it is the value of this space that is integral to the success of any magazine today.

For a space to be perceived as valuable to advertisers, the magazine's content must align with a designated target audience that is also the consumer base (actual or intended) of the brand or service placing the ad. The aim is to achieve maximum coverage or 'reach' (the percentage of your target audience seeing your ad at least once) coupled with optimum frequency (the actual number of times they see it). An effective media strategy is about balancing enough opportunities to see (OTS) to motivate a consumer to purchase but without overexposure and lack of ROI (return on investment). A multiplicity of tools is available to inform planning decisions, including ABC data (abc.org.uk) that documents magazine circulation figures and broader trends; PAMCo (formerly the NRS) the governing body which oversees audience measurement for the published media industry; and TGI consumer data. To make comparative judgments and drive choice of media, the standard measure of CPM (cost per thousand/mille) is used: the total amount an advertiser pays for 1000 impressions on their page. However, this is not always about seeking out the lowest CPM. Rather a qualitative approach might be required whereby a higher CPM delivers readers who can afford to act on what they see, positioning them as more legitimate consumers. The brand value of the magazine itself determines the price of the space and is reflected accordingly in a rate card made available to media buyers. The rate card which forms an integral part of the overall media kit or pack details editorial pillars, profiles readers (demographic and lifestyle data) and captures brand reach. Here the magazine sells its profile, amplifying its attributes to prospective advertisers. As Iain MacRury states

> The reader profile the magazines promise attempt to serve as a shorthand link between editorial policy (what goes in the magazine) and the media sales pitch. By no means a description of actual readers, this 'character' is a hybrid composed to conjoin commercial imperatives with cultural values.
>
> *MacRury, 2009, p. 97*

Using *Vogue* magazine as an example, it is clear that the cost of placing a display ad is predicated on the size of the space an advertiser wishes to occupy and the positioning of the ad within the magazine, with inside front cover and back covers carrying a premium rate, albeit always subject to some negotiation on the final fee. Deconstructing *Vogue UK's* May 2020 edition Libre perfume by Yves Saint Laurent featuring singer Dua Lipa occupies the back cover with the inside gatefold across four pages taken up by Dior. Indeed, two double page ads, then a four page ad followed by five double ads are positioned at the front of the magazine prior to the contents listing on page 23. Indeed, of the 252 pages of the magazine, 50.3 per cent is made up of advertising. The ability to reliably deliver readers is paramount to accruing regular advertising revenue. In contrast to a display ad, predicated on the basis of brand building and the most frequently used format in magazine advertising, is the classified ad, sold by the line or the column centimetre. "Classified ads have little element of branding and are a direct call to action from seller to buyer with a minimum of design and obfuscation" (Scott, 2014, 214).

US Vogue clearly shows that over the past 20 years, the allure of print to attract advertisers is declining. Traditionally, the September issue was a target for the fashion industry to advertise in, a signifier to kick-start new trends and lines. For the competitive world of fashion magazines, when comparing themselves with their competitors then, the more pages a magazine has in September, then the more ads it carries and hence affords a public display of popularity with advertisers. In September 1999, the magazine carried 562 pages of ads; 427 in 2009 and 356 in 2019 (Hays, 2019). However, as McKay indicates (2018, p. 251) there is an alternative reading of these data that has to do with the overall brand value of the magazine, in that a magazine can regulate the number of advertisements it wishes to include and raise the cost of the space accordingly. With fashion magazines as brands in their own right, the impact of association is such that advertisers must meet the requisite standards in terms of production values: high-end shoots, often with legendary photographers. This relationship between magazine content and advertising working together to enhance the value of 'magazine as brand' as well creating an aura around the brands it features was seen in the relaunch edition of *The Face* in 2019.

The Face, a British music, fashion and culture monthly, had an initial run from 1980 to 2004. It relaunched online first in April and then in print in September 2019. Following much press and publicity, it was back with a quarterly publication of some 312 pages and a cover price of £9.95. Multiple covers including Harry Styles of One Direction, now solo and advertising Gucci, spoke to Millennials and Generation Z but the challenge to attract and hold such audiences this time around is potentially harder when this target audience is itself at the heart of their own content curation. So what is *The Face* doing differently now? This is not about nostalgia. Their brand director (Jason Gonsalves), who is ex-Chief Strategy Officer of London creative advertising agency BBH, believes that the magazine's fundamental offer to readers is all about context, positioning itself in the market as an urban style guide gravitating around ideas, behaviours, sport, tech and fashion. This is reinforced through the relationship between content and promotion, working more with brands to highlight the dynamic of its cultural purpose: "It is treating its ad inventory online in a similar way to its quarterly print run with a select number of brands keen to access a taste-maker audience" (Pena-Taylor, 2019). To be part of this advertising will be limited and "high rent" (ibid.). The magazine will work only with a small number of brands that reflect its identity and readership. Examples include Supreme, Palace and Stone Island who will sit alongside Celine, Gucci and then BMW and Sonos. Not just luxury: "I want to have a Carling ad next to Louis Vuitton" (Gonsalves in Pena-Taylor, 2019). Yet, there is already a recognition of the need to monetise beyond advertising with early explorations into TV production, audio and video content and an online store. In their relaunch issue, Gucci dominated with a series of double page ads from the inside cover onwards. This was followed by multiple occupancy of double page spreads from Prada, Saint Laurent and Burberry all seeking to reinforce their brand identity within this cultural moment. From the reader's perspective, it feels like a heavy-weight boxing match of the luxury fashion world and from the ads alone, we would be forgiven in thinking we were actually accessing a high-end fashion magazine. However, the editor's letter frames the subject matter of the magazine positioning it in the broader context noted above. Interestingly, about a quarter in and the ads peter out: it is all about cultural content now. Here, we have an example of curated advertising complementing curated content: reinforcing each other to shape the overall brand identity of the magazine and its lifestyle messaging.

The advertising agency world in 2020 is dominated by global media super agencies, the top five of which are: WPP; Omnicom Group; Interpublic Group; Publicis Groupe and Dentsu (www.warc.com). Their authority emerged out of their international footprint in the 1990s as they embraced the rise of digitality and the quantitative potential of such capabilities to find the right audience for a brand. Media buying and planning has now become a creative exercise in itself compared with previous eras. Formerly reliant on high-level segmentation centred on basic demographic and psychographic information and where in the case of magazines, circulation data appeared at just two points in the year, now we are entering an evolving media landscape driven by internet, social and mobile communication platforms and where ad spend data reflects this shift (see Table 5.1).

Early digital technologies with promotional capacity was encapsulated in the banner ad, the interactive link and the cookie. The cookie was key here as it allowed distinction between whether the same person was returning to a site or was indeed a new user. Later, its value would be that of a trail, allowing for further promotion based on past records, and when the blocking of cookies began this was then replaced by more sophisticated "digital fingerprinting" (Turow, 2011, p. 152). The decline of the banner ad was commensurate with the recognition that audiences would not pay for online content and that a more robust promotional method would be required to counter the lack of payment. Search ('paid' content) comes out of a recognition that you cannot 'buy' space in advance as you do not know any user's online intentions. Furthermore, there are two other competing means of communicating with consumers over and above 'paid' communication: brand 'owned' content accessed via their website, for example or 'earned' or shared content via peers, PR, influencers, ratings and reviews. A more targeted, real-time approach was required and it was Google who spearheaded the sale of digital advertising. Search was born through the marrying of consumer interests with products. An ad appears aligned to search terms used and if the ad is clicked on ('click-through') the viewer is deemed to be engaged. Advertisers pay based on recorded interactions known as a click-through rate (CTR). Google then developed an auction system based on bidding on search words to allow for a higher ranking in a "keyword universe" (Young, 2017:138). So the critical question raised, which Google responded to and capitalised upon, was not just the long-standing issue of how to connect but rather how to connect in real time? Solving this problem has been a lucrative venture and pioneered the emergence of "platform capitalism" with profits arising from advertising without the need to curate accompanying content (Leiss et al., 2018, p. 317).

Whereas paid search centred on paying for a high-ranking position around a keyword or Adword, programmatic advertising delivers more sophisticated layers of targeting through the use of algorithms. In relation to media buying, this results in greater degrees of refinement in terms of who sees your ad. Even though many viewers may be on the same site, sophisticated data analysis drawing on browsing history and profiling refines who exactly the ad is best exposed to. To win that exposure auctioning takes place in real-time bidding (RTB) exchanges.

> The opportunity to serve an ad impression (namely, each time an ad is served) is done by 'auctioning' ad slots in real-time so advertisers (and the software working on their behalf) bid for slots where they would like to place their advertising (judged on the person and the spending parameters set by the advertisers before they bought their campaign).
>
> *McStay, 2018, p. 94*

That is to say, this is all about microtargeting: aligning a profile to a price and believing in the opportunity for greater degrees of interactivity with the ad due to its relevancy. The advertiser sets search parameters and if they do not win the real-time auction, then the metrics can be analysed and refined, for example with an increase in budget required. Programmatic arises in an era of big data which in itself evidences the amount of time we are spending online, allowing known demographic data to work alongside real-time data extracted from current online activity. When you pull both of these sets together you get a 360 degree consumer profile.

The digital age heralds a new media environment and new media strategies for the selling and buying of advertising space (See Table 5.2). Such is the enthusiasm for online and performance marketing that digital ad spend now accounts for around half (54 per cent) of the global market (See Table 5.3).

In summary, no longer do brands simply pay in advance for exposure but also digitised consumers can now be reached by content that is 'earned' through social media coverage and indeed 'owned' by the brand itself. This has impact on the traditional role of the value of advertising space that magazines now need to counter. Furthermore, such initiatives have induced the decline of the organisational relationship between magazine and advertiser in the context of the rise of the global media agency super players and advertising exchanges that are "centralised markets for buying and selling audience impressions," matching ads to consumer profiles based on an "ecosystem" of data (Turow, 2015: 105). From an advertiser's point of view, there is an immediate appeal here: budget friendly, data-driven, a plethora of metrics and a promise of optimisation. However, there is also a drawback as such a quantitative approach towards media planning does not take into account the qualitative nature of reception and more specifically, the relationship between attention levels informed by the accompanying environment.

TABLE 5.2 Taxonomy of Internet Advertising Formats.

Category		Description	Examples
Search		Paid-for listing in search results, such as sponsored or promoted listings	Sponsored links on Google.co.uk web search results
Display	Banner	Advertising shown in standard display units on webpages or in apps – ad content types include images and animations	Banner advertising appearing at the top of pages on FT.com
	Native	Advertising integrated into the surrounding content, predominantly in-feed advertising such as promoted posts in social feeds or paid-for recommendations on webpages	Sponsored product links appearing on an Instagram feed Facebook carousel image ads 'Promoted links from around the web recommended by Outbrain' appearing below articles on The Guardian app
	Sponsored content	Advertiser-sponsored content on a webpage or app such as in ad-features/advertorials	Sponsored articles on Buzzfeed.com
	Out-stream video	Video advertising shown in non-video content	Video advertising appearing in ad units within text articles on Mirror.co.uk
	In-stream video	Video advertising shown before, during or after video content – also known as pre- and post-roll video	30-second video ads show within programming on ITV Player 6-second bumper video ads shown before YouTube videos
Classifieds		Paid listings such as recruitment, property, cars and services	Paid-for listings on Yell.com and Autotrader.com
Other		Audio adverting and lesser-used formats such as solus email, lead generation and mobile SMS/MMS. Emerging online advertising formats, such a virtual reality (VR) and augmented reality (AR)	Audio advertising on Spotify, Jaguar Land Rover ad using AR on mobile ads to show users a car overlaid on their surroundings

Source: Plum Consulting; Digital Advertising January 2019.

TABLE 5.3 Advertising Expenditure Forecasts March 2019

Share of global adspend (%)

Newspapers: 7.0 / 5.1
Magazines: 3.9 / 2.8
Television: 29.1 / 26.0
Radio: 5.5 / 4.9
Cinema: 0.8 / 0.7
Out-of-home: 6.4 / 6.0
Internet display: 26.1 / 28.5
Internet paid search: 17.1 / 22.1
Internet classified: 4.2 / 4.0

■ 2019   ■ 2022

Source: Zenith Media

The magazine fights back: the rise of the attention economy

If attention has now become the holy grail for advertising, what is it and how can it be accrued? The notion of an "attention economy" (Goldhaber, 1997) is an interesting one and gravitates around the concept of rarity of resources shifting from the physical to the intangible. As documented, one of the most significant threats to the magazine industry is the abundance of free digital content but diametrically opposed to this is our inability to engage and focus on all that we see. This is exacerbated by the number of devices optimised, often at the same time. As a result, avoidance becomes an ingrained response. As Rosengren (2016, p. 6) outlines, attention paid to an ad can arise from three causal factors, often inter-related: the creativity of the ad itself; situational factors aligned to its placing in time and space; and the more personal dimension in that it speaks to a particular purchase need. As noted previously, contemporary advertising seeks to 'pull' readers into its orbit and this reframes the notion of attention: away from the concept of managing avoidance towards the generation of direct engagement. As early as 1903, Walter Dill Scott was one of the first academics to not only study the discipline but also to consider the role psychology might play in formulating responses to creative advertising (Feldwick, 2019). If we think about social media, it plays on the notion of instantaneity and immediate gratification, but research from the field of neuromarketing, which uses neuroscience to explore consumer choice and decision-making, evidences that reading magazines taps into a different kind of response. Magazines speak to that which interests us: we choose them due to specific content that has appeal. This then induces particular emotions that arise from an area of the brain discovered in the 1950s entitled "the pleasure centre" (Nobel, 2012), which aligns motivation to act based on how it make us feel and inextricably linked to this, what we are prepared to pay for such feelings.

An example where this effectively plays out is in relation to the '2019 Watch Report', a feature of *Esquire* magazine (July/August 2019). Functioning as a shop window for luxury watch brands and consumers with a passion for watches, the magazine features ads including Cartier, Breitling 1884, Longines and Tag Heuer before we even arrive at the magazine's contents page. Only three-quarters of the way through does the actual report 'The 17 Best Watches of 2019' appear. It is as though the watches are waiting their fate: this is what all this advertising has been leading up to. The positioning of the survey in relation to the advertising and indeed how consumers read ads is the key here. If the survey had been presented much earlier, then readers would be judging the ads through a specific lens of ranking, devaluing their semiotic choices and connotations. By placing the advertisements prior to the survey results, this allows the reader to pass their own judgements or challenge the taste culture that informed the rankings. And the winner? Interestingly, there is no actual 'first place', rather a more neutral alphabetical order is presented starting with an Audemars Piguet Code 11.59 at £37,500. Whether you can afford the watch or not is largely incidental. Rather, the fantasy, or reality, of the world of luxury brands triggers activity in the 'pleasure centre' and the emotions that come with exposure to these aspirational signifiers.

Research between Magnetic, the marketing body for consumer magazines, and Bournemouth University sought to explore the relationship between attention and effectiveness in advertising and to situate this in the context of an ever-changing media landscape. The authors address the issue of attention and make a qualitative distinction when they argue that "attention is routinely measured as time spent" but that this "is not an accurate predictor of 'quality attention' or 'time well spent'" (Denegri-Knott et al., 2018). This introduces the recognition that in the attention economy not all attention is of equal value. Rather attention is disaggregated into two dimensions: intensity (quality) and duration (length). With the advent of a more digital culture, a tension is produced around the fact that whilst there remains a finite number of hours in the day, there is now an exponential number of things to do to fill that time. The experience of time pressure accrues with coping mechanisms arising such as multitasking across screens as a way to manage this new temporal architecture. This then brings us back to problems that can arise out of programmatic advertising in that it "capitalises on poor quality attention that is measured crudely in clicks and impressions…(and)…it denies advertisers opportunities to capitalise on a deeper, more meaningful measure of attention. Attention that can be cultivated over time" (ibid.). In essence, this is of fundamental consideration for media planners when they are mapping out the media mix for a campaign: that is to say, they should not focus specifically on attention for their brand *per se* but rather the "kind of attention they need" (ibid.), recognising that not all media channels deliver quality attention. This point seems to have been embraced by Dentsu Aegis Network (2019) which recognises that "our planning and buying measures need to change, to reflect what we consider to be of most value to clients – a genuine opportunity to communicate with a consumer".

Magnetic launched its first advertising campaign in conjunction with design agency D. Studio on 7 February 2019 under the headline of 'Pay Attention'. It sought to highlight the perceived "mismatch" between magazine effectiveness and advertiser perceptions (Sampson, 2019) and reinforce that magazine advertising offers greater value for money compared with other media when concentrating on the concept of attention. Of particular importance in this campaign is to counter the role of short-term metrics in relation to online advertising and instead place emphasis on the role of magazines in longer-term brand building. To concretise this argument and concentrate the minds of advertising agencies on the role of magazines as a valuable space for brand promotion, Magnetic (2017a) emphasise the value of attention as a scare resource and iterate that "not all reach is equal": that is to say, magazines offer a more focused and immersive environment of reception. As a result, advertisers can pay less for more attention: hence the tagline of the campaign "I pay less for more attention" and which appeared on special coverwraps including the *Radio Times*, *Grazia*, *Cosmopolitan* and *Empire* magazine. The special issues were distributed in media agencies in London and Manchester and directly to marketers. When considering contextual relevancy a Magnetic survey of a 2000 data sample, found that 43 per cent deemed magazine ads to be more relevant to them compared with 27 per cent on social media and 24 per cent on television (Sampson, 2019).

PHOTO 5.1 Magnetic unites magazines in a campaign for media buyers to reappraise the value of print.

Source: Magnetic News and Design DStudio

New forms of promotional content and the ethical challenges posed

One of the principal outcomes of convergence culture is the amount of free content now available and that, this in itself becomes attractive to both audiences and advertisers. As magazines seek to grapple with changes in reading habits in a time-poor, always on, mobile culture, so they must also reconsider how revenue is realised as business models and pathways to profit are re-evaluated. Increasing production costs and decreasing sales require attention on an ongoing strategic basis. "Previously advertising and copy sales were the key streams of a magazine's income, today with falling sales and a decrease in many titles' circulation combined with rising business expenditure this is no longer sufficient to sustain a title" (Hogarth, 2018, 62). For advertising to be effective in the twenty-first century, it must do more than hold attention: it must add value through original, professionally curated content creation that is meaningful to the lifestyle of the reader. Furthermore, the shift from a reliance on the sale of advertising space for revenue generation to more nuanced and sophisticated forms of content marketing impacts the role of the editor, now "both a journalist and a brand manager...a more commercially minded professional who curates and co-creates with agencies, advertisers, and audiences" (Das, 2016). A series of promotional strategies indicative of a "media-marketing convergence" (Hardy, 2018, p. 117) will now be considered, coupled with the ethical challenges posed when greater degrees of synergy arise between the ad itself and the content of the media in which it is situated.

The definition of branded content is contested and takes many forms. In its earliest iteration, branded content emerged out of the *Michelin Guide* (1900), a promotional tool with a purpose centred on brands as generators of their own content. We can also consider soap operas, devised simply to assemble an audience and then advertise to it, and the *Guinness Book of Records* also under this heading. Fast-forward to an era of social media and one of the fundamental challenges that brands face is as custodians of their own identity. Branded content seeks to seize back control but needs to initially ask 'What is good content?' and 'How do you record impact?' Positioned alongside traditional advertising, the nomenclature of branded content is that it is all about investment in brand building rather than the more detractive notion of ad spend. Unlike earlier examples cited, it is now produced by specialist providers who generate meaningful content that targeted readers will want to spend time with. If we take the example of brand publishing, Red Bull's *Bulletin* magazine (produced by Red Bull Media House, a multiplatform media company) offers up an alternative approach as to how a brand can tell stories about itself in alternative ways through 'owned' media. Readers choose to engage as they already have an affiliation with the brand in question. Another example, but this time tapping into the auditory rather than the visual, is Land Rover's podcasts, designed to accompany travellers on car journeys and all about spending time with the brand in the surroundings of the brand itself. In order to 'pull' the reader further into the brand's orbit, content must either inform, educate to entertain or an amalgamation of these, with a view to the messaging adding value to the participant's world. It sparks interest and therefore, in the attention economy, is worthy of time spent. A dynamic example of this is the Net-a-Porter luxury fashion brand. It defines its approach as follows:

> A pioneer of innovation, Net-a-Porter delivers the ultimate curation of product and content through its websites, shopping apps and the world of PORTER, speaking to a monthly audience of over 6 million via a global, multi-channel ecosystem and providing a seamless shopping experience across mobile, tablet and desktop.
>
> *net-a-porter.com*

Integral to this approach is its *Porter* magazine which allows the reader to 'shop the issue' and move seamlessly from fashion fantasy to purchase reality via its app. Launched in February 2014, and now in digital format only, the magazine comprises high-spec photography and long-form features, positioning itself as a luxury brand promoting luxury brands. Branded content is now a distinctive feature in the media packs or kits used to garner advertising interest. Returning to the *Vogue* example explored earlier they now offer a discrete *Vogue* Branded Content division "which allows advertisers to create world class bespoke campaigns and projects which sit seamlessly within *Vogue's* editorial environment across multiple platforms" (British Vogue Media Kit, 2020). This may include photography shoots art directed by *Vogue*, native advertising copy written by *Vogue*, video content and podcasts.

A close relation to branded content is native advertising but what distinguishes the two is the origin of the placement. If the content is created for the brand's own channel, as in the Red Bull example above, then it is deemed branded content. However, if it is created by an external party and adapted for their audience, then it is native advertising. Whilst branded content centres on storytelling and seeks to build brands, native seeks out more short-term goals and is aimed at driving sales. Therefore, native advertising is a "merger between an advert, advertorial and editorial content that uses a creative, but tailored, approach" (Hogarth, 2018, p. 137) and arises out of a collaboration of on one side the brand that wishes to promote and on the other a magazine's editorial and sales teams. The goal is to produce promotion that sits seamlessly within its surroundings, integrally placed within content that speaks to the magazine's target audience and distributed across the most appropriate channels. As with branded content, it is all about creating content audiences want to engage with but unlike branded content it is a form of 'paid' advertising rather than 'owned' media. Tagged as advertising, native is particularly effective online as it is perceived as non-disruptive, appearing alongside content that has already been actively searched for.

Verizon Media's recent study 'Redefining Native' surveyed 6,000 consumers from the UK, France and Germany, looked at 60 hours' worth of online content and interrogated 1.5 million data points. They found that native ads within a content page increase engagement by 63 per cent. And nearly 80 per cent of people would like to see ads to blend into the page as they seek more seamless experiences.

Simpson and Llewellyn, 2019

Two examples of native in magazine advertising that evidence the alignment of content and promotion is from the USA where in 2016 *The Atlantic* published a 2125 word sponsored post entitled 'The Ascent: Political Destiny and the makings of a first couple' ahead of the third season of the political drama 'House of Cards' whilst in the UK Mars worked with MediaCom UK to drive relevance of its products via an Easter native recipe campaign in *BBC Good Food, Olive* and *Delicious* magazines. This then returned as a competition to speak to the British nation in lockdown during Easter 2020.

As one of the fastest growing areas of digital advertising the IAB (Interactive Advertising Bureau) has developed 'The IAB Advertising Playbook 2.0' to map the various derivations of native advertising now emerging. Underpinned by three key principles or objectives namely "cohesive with the page content", "assimilated into the design" and "consistent with the platform behaviour" (www.iab.com), it is appealing to advertisers on the basis of both its targeting efficiency due to programmatic models discussed previously and an ability to track ROI through the measurement of click-through rates. As a result three distinct formats arise to meet the objectives set out above: in-feed native advertising, which is placed in an article and mimics the surrounding site design and aesthetics; in-content native advertising, which works with the articles on a page and mimics the design and ethics of the surrounding editorial content; and content recommendation native advertising, which appears alongside content but when clicked on takes you through to an external page.

The lifestyle market is one sector where in recent years, the elision between editorial and promotional content has increased and in so doing throws up ethical challenges. The Committee on Advertising Practice (UK) clearly stipulates that "marketing communications must be obviously identifiable as such" (CAP, 2010: Rule 2.1). However, as Hardy (2018, p. 115) indicates "research shows a wide spectrum of responses to branded content and native advertising, from positive endorsement, when communications are relevant for users, to confusion and failure to identify advertising, and criticism of stealth marketing practices".

A consistent theme circulating this chapter centres on the magazine as brand: magazines that are surviving in the toughest of conditions do so on the basis of crafting an identity synonymous with any other successful brand in any other market sector. That is to say, it has a strong brand personality and consistent brand values which allow for the cultivation of loyal consumers on the basis of them developing a sense of trust. In the magazine industry that sense of trust is generated through the editorial line: that readers trust what they see in the magazine both in terms of editorial content and the promotional content that

PHOTO 5.2 Competing promotional environments: advertisements shining bright in Piccadilly Circus at night. Photo: OfrPeterz.

sits alongside it. This has been noted by Alexandra Shulman (2017, p. 3) former editor of *Vogue UK,* who defined her role as follows: "It's *Vogue*'s voice, not mine. Although I do, of course, have a choice in what the voice says." However, what sense of criticality does an editor still hold as arbiters of content control when there is the pressure of revenue generation constantly present? Indeed, it has been noted (Magnetic, 2017b) that advertisements gain greater attention when situated in magazines in all formats due to the surrounding context and are trusted more on the basis of this context. This is due to the "brand rub effect" (ibid.) whereby trust in the magazine translates into perceptions of trust in the brands that advertise there. Key themes articulated by Magnetic that are commensurate in crafting levels of trust is that the content of the magazine exercises expertise, objectivity and reliability. Nowhere is this more acute than in the fiercely competitive lifestyle sector. For example, Tesco wished to raise the fashion credentials of its fashion brand F&F, reaching out to budget-conscious, fashion-forward young women. Exposure to the brand in magazine environments saw "an average brand trust uplift of 94 per cent" (ibid.).

Conclusion: where now for magazine advertising?

Prior to the global pandemic of 2020, the magazine market saw a continual decline in circulation, with digital growth failing to offset declining print sales despite the introduction of subscription platforms such as Readly, Magzter and Apple's News+.

The major challenge magazines now face is the wealth of free content available and to counter this brand identity is more important than ever, offering its reader specialist curated content that informs, educates and entertains in a robust manner. To fund such publications, magazines can no longer rely purely on advertising in its traditional sense, although the attraction of specialisation allowing for tailored print campaigns, can still produce strong ROI for advertisers. The evolution of the communications industry accounts for the fragmentation of what constitutes advertising. Nevertheless, advertising is still held together by two key principles: to tell stories with an emotional pull that audiences identify with and are affected by and secondly, to draw on culture as a key tool of communication to embed meaning and currency. Indeed, readers engage with a magazine in a particular mindset and this in itself informs how the advertising is consumed. And yet to achieve these aims advertising too is adopting new approaches as the exploration of branded content and native advertising highlighted. Magazines must also expand their revenue generating potential offering up innovative additional touchpoints for relationship building and developing a community of readers, including events, with their qualitative experiential dimension. These can no longer be positioned as add-ons but rather an integral part of the magazine brand offer as both a cultivator of loyalty and survival. And yet "despite the downturn trend in magazine circulation nearly seven in ten people have read magazines" in the last six months of 2019 and eight in ten of those paid for a print copy (King, 2019, p. 3). King, category director for technology and media at Mintel, further elaborates on the opportunities this presents for the magazine industry arguing that "with so much content available online, the act of paying for an issue or subscribing can act as a greater motivation to read each issue" (ibid., p. 5).

When 'life on screen' becomes the norm that then directly offers up opportunities for points of difference that takes us away into a tactile environment commensurate with the slower pace of relaxation and exploration. The impact of COVID-19 in the UK has shown us that print is not dead. Rather it becomes an alter-world, a third space when the life–work balance and its boundaries are all too easily merging into one. As a result, those magazines whose USP centre on their high-end print quality, beautiful photography and a specific brand aesthetic will continue to attract advertising. As Holmes (2013, p. 173) has articulated "magazines have always been associated with promotion. The promotion of the self, the promotion of personal interests, the promotion of specialised knowledge, the promotion of commerce". It is the inter-related nature of the magazine as a mediated site for brand promotion and self-promotion, often enshrouded in a sense of fantasy and escapism on behalf of the reader, that continues to drive their appeal. Even in the most difficult of times. As Alexandra Shulman (2017, p. 199) claimed when seeking to contexualise and indeed validate the role of *Vogue* in an age of social media, and in particular Instagram:

> It seems that, more than ever, the strength of what *Vogue* can offer has to be in the uniqueness of the image. Our ability to be the informers of which

trends are the newest and strongest has obviously been diluted by the speed and reach of digital websites…but none of them has, as yet, managed to create the memorable imagery that we can.

It is this memorable imagery that prolongs life in print and is consequently of value to advertisers with brand messaging repeatedly accessed and endured. To be memorable relies on emotional triggers to generate feelings: media choice is key in enabling this to happen successfully. Carefully curated content is essential here to a magazine's future success. In line with this observation, and reinforced by the Magnetic 'I pay attention' campaign, is the importance of advertisers making considered media decisions based on evidence and proof rather than current trends in determining what works for them and their brand.

COVID-19 has also indicated that traditional models of consumption have been severely challenged, with many familiar high street faces dropping off the radar. Unless a brand can now offer a unique retail experience, then the ability to shop online supplants the need to leave the home and magazines can steal a march here. The model of Net-a Porter and *Porter* magazine can be extended across the sector through technology offering up the opportunity to see, interact and then buy. Magazine advertising will remain important in its role of informing choice and functioning as a filter in the decision-making process that now seems to impact all aspects of our lives. Magazine advertising does this effectively as it provides a meaningful and trusted environment or context that allows us to frame and shape our perceptions of a brand or service. However, the function here is more than simply guiding choice, it is also about affirmation beyond the point of purchase, whereby seeing the product again, framed appropriately, affirms that we have made the right choice.

In terms of evolving promotional strategies, the need is to move away from the binaries of "long and short, new and established, or digital and everything else. The way forward is to understand how all the elements work together to deliver improved business effects for clients" (Field, 2017, p. 2). In this context, magazine media should function to complement brand building across other channels but in and of itself "a magazine's features should be multi-faceted across print, digital and online…Each version should contain different strands to create content-rich experiences" (Hogarth, 2018, p. 102). One example where mobile technology is adding value to print magazines is *Cosmopolitan* (2018) which is using AR to connect its readers to brands in a more interactive manner. The magazine partnered with YouCam, an AR app, and Juicy Couture, allowing readers to use their mobiles to virtually apply make-up. An accompanying lookbook in the magazine included a QR code to seamlessly transform the reader into consumers, purchasing the items directly for the look they had just created.

Finally, sustainability now dominates the political agenda of global youth. Whilst magazine advertising has since modernity been inextricably aligned to a culture of consumption and economic growth, this has since been countered by a realisation of the consequences of such actions on the planet. As brands in the future will have to reappraise their sustainability credentials, so will magazines have to reconsider their print medium and its constitution, ensuring they are both fully recyclable and disregard their use of plastic wrapping. Nevertheless, this is countered by there being significant evidence of people's passion for tangible magazine collections: whether that be a tower at the side of the bed, displayed across a coffee table or even at Hymag, the world's largest collection of magazines situated in Woolwich Arsenal, London. Tory Turk, curator, archivist and Hymag's creative lead, expresses his passion for print magazines: "It's the luxurious nature of it, the way it lives forever" (Strunck, 2019, p. 41). This emphasis on longevity is interesting and encapsulates the essence of advertising's relationship with this particular medium. Contradictory in nature as whilst positioned as distraction artefacts, readers also see them as a necessary resource for the times in which we live and it is this distinct qualitative nature over other media that allows for their enduring appeal as a promotional vehicle.

A new state of existence emerged in the spring of 2020 – namely lockdown. It changed behaviours, work patterns, childcare arrangements and states of mind. 'Indoor media' as a term came into circulation with access to sport, theatres, cinemas, live music and shopping, in its physical sense, denied. As discussed, the notion of the brain's 'pleasure centre' began to take hold to counter the severity of the situation as people used their time to do the hobbies they loved and develop new skills. *Vogue* placed keyworkers on the cover of its July 2020 issue to underpin their value as superheroes and magazines adapted to the times through curating content that spoke to these new ways of living. That many magazines already focused on hobbies and leisure should surely have seen magazine sales rise in line with these changes in behavioural patterns. However, a decline in consumer spending coupled with access to traditional points to purchase stifled, now places print in a precarious position. Such a position is further exacerbated in the longer term. For even as we ease out of the first phase of lockdown, the impact that this global pandemic has had on major brands, who are now holding back on all forms of ad spend as recession looms and takes businesses back to memories of the 2008/9 financial crash, is worrying. With major players such as WPP, Omnicom and Publicis Groupe, right down to medium-sized and niche advertising players, all making staff cuts, the script on how all this impacts the long-term future of advertising as a business is currently being written, albeit with pessimistic undertones. As this chapter indicated at the outset, magazines were already facing challenges prior to the onset of a global pandemic. These challenges are now exacerbated by a struggling economy with brands significantly holding back on ad spend, historically the first area to feel the consequence of any economic crisis. However, despite the proliferation of free online content available, the appeal of magazines as dedicated 'pleasure centres' remains. Survival centres on strong brand identity and curated content that speaks to readers' interests in an informed, engaging and trusted manner. It is specifically these qualities that should lead media planners to continue to consider magazine advertising in any integrated brand campaign.

References

CAP [Committee on Advertising Practice] (2010), *The UK Code of Non-Broadcast Advertising and Direct & Promotional Marketing*. Available at: www.asa.org.uk/codes-and-rulings/advertising-codes/non-broadcast-code.html (accessed 15.07.2020)

Das, S. (2016), 'Magazine publishing innovation: two case studies on magazine creativity', *MDPI*, Vol.4 (2). Available at: www.mdpi.com/2304-6775/4/2/15/htm (accessed 17.11.2019)

Denegri-Knott, J., Jenkins, R., Yesiloglu, S., Oshima, S. and Arman, S. (2018), *Attention Please: The Whitepaper*. Bournemouth University in conjunction with Magnetic, November. Available at: https://darkroom.magnetic.media/original/b6ad7d94595b94d54d632492d9ee7fbd:b2459c6448949c44b85476462b320d63/attention-please-the-whitepaper.pdf (accessed 11.02.2020)

Dentsu Aegis Network (2019), *The Attention Economy: Exploring the Opportunity for a New Advertising Currency*. Available at: www.dentsuaegisnetwork.com/attention-economy. (accessed 04.03.2020)

Feldwick, P. (2019), 'How does advertising work?', *Advertising Association*, January. Available at: www.adassoc.org.uk (accessed 09.11.2019)

Field, P. (2017), 'Bridging the long/short-term divide: The role of magazine brands in the digital era', *Magnetic*, 21 November, pp. 1–9. Available at: https://magnetic.media/research/studies/bridging-the-long-short-term-divide (accessed 16.07.2020)

Goldhaber, M.H. (1997) 'Attention shoppers!', *Wired*, 12 January. Available at: www.wired.com/1997/12/es-attention (accessed 07.04.2020)

Hardy, J. (2018), 'Branded content: media and marketing integration', in J. Hardy, H. Powell and I. MacRury (eds.) *The Advertising Handbook* (4th edition), Abingdon: Routledge, pp. 102–122

Hays, K. (2019), 'Ads in the September Issues: A Multiyear Breakdown', www.wwd.com, 12 September. Available at: https://wwd.com/business-news/media/ads-in-the-september-issues-a-multiyear-breakdown-1203276718/ (accessed 07.07.2020)

Hogarth, M. (2018), *Business Strategies for Magazine Publishing: How to Survive in the Digital Age*, Abingdon: Routledge

Holmes, T. (2013), 'Magazines and promotion' in H. Powell (ed.), *Promotional Culture and Convergence*, Abingdon: Routledge

Holmes, T. (2019), 'Magazines in the digital world' in J. McKay (ed.), *The Magazine Handbook* (4th edition), Abingdon: Routledge, pp. 190–208

IAB (2019) 'IAB Native Advertising Playbook 2.0', 09 May. Available at: www.iab.com/insights/iab-native-advertising-playbook-2-0/ (accessed 16.07.2020)

Jenkins, H. (2008), *Convergence Culture: Where Old and New Media Collide*, New York, NY: New York University Press

King, M. (2019), 'Magazines: executive summary', *Mintel*, December. Available at: www.reports.mintel.com (accessed 06.02.2020)

Leiss, W. et al. (2018), *Social Communication in Advertising: Consumption in the Mediated Marketplace* (4th edition), New York: Routledge

MacRury, I. (2009), *Advertising*, Abingdon: Routledge

Magnetic (2017a), *The Power of Context and the Benefits of Published Media Environments for Advertisers*. Available at: https://magnetic.media/research/studies/the-power-of-context (accessed 04.03.2020)

Magnetic (2017b), *A Matter of Trust*. Available at: https://magnetic.media/research/studies/a-matter-of-trust-insight (accessed 19.04.2020)

Marchand, R. (1985), *Advertising and the American Dream: Making Way for Modernity, 1920–1940*. California: University of California Press

McKay, J. (ed.) (2018), *The Magazine Handbook* (4th edition), Abingdon: Routledge

McStay, A. (2018), 'Digital advertising and adtech: programmatic platforms, identity and moments' in J. Hardy, H. Powell and I. MacRury (eds.), *The Advertising Handbook* (4th edition), Abingdon: Routledge, pp. 88–101

Nobel, C. (2012), 'What neuroscience tells us about consumer desire', *Harvard Business School: Working Knowledge,* 26 March. Available at: https://hbswk.hbs.edu/item/what-neuroscience-tells-us-about-consumer-desire (accessed 16.07.2020)

Pena-Taylor, S. (2019), '*The Face* story: reviving a classic print title for the digital age' *WARC,* July. Available at: ww.warc.com (accessed 02.05.2020)

Powell, H. (2013), 'Introduction: promotion in an era of convergence', in *Promotional Culture and Convergence: Markets, Methods, Media,* Abingdon: Routledge, pp. 1–20

Rosengren, S. (2016), 'From advertising avoidance to advertising approach: rethinking attention in new advertising formats', in P. De Pelsmacker (ed.) *Advertising in New Formats and Media: Current Research and Implications for Marketers,* Bingley: Emerald Group, pp. 3–18

Sampson, A. (2019), 'The perception gap around magazine media: why advertisers are missing out', *WARC,* December. Available at: www.warc.com (accessed 16.04.2020)

Schulman, A. (2017), *Inside Vogue: My diary of Vogue's 100th Year,* UK: Penguin

Scott, A. (2014), 'The science of advertisement sales' in D. Stam and A. Scott (eds.), *Inside Magazine Publishing,* Abingdon: Routledge, pp. 195–225.

Simpson, G. and Llewellyn (2019), 'What's next for native?', *Campaign.* Available at: www.campaignlive.co.uk/article/whats-next-native/1668641 (accessed 26.07.2020)

Storr, F. (2017), 'Words from the editors', *Advertising Week Europe,* pp. 248–252.

Strunck, C. (2019), 'Mag for it!', *ES Magazine,* 13 September, pp. 41–42

Turow, J. (2011), *The Daily You: How the New Advertising Industry Is Defining Your Identity and Your Worth,* New Haven, CT: Yale University Press

Turow, J. (2015), 'Media buying: the power of advertising', in M.P. McAllister and E. West (eds.), *The Routledge Companion to Advertising and Promotional Culture.* New York: Routledge, 99–112

Young, M. (2017), *Ogilvy on Advertising in the Digital Age,* London: Goodman

Magazines featured

Esquire (2019), July/August

Good Housekeeping (1935), April

Good Housekeeping (2020), May

The Face (2019), Autumn, Vol.4 (1)

6
MAGAZINE PUBLISHING IN A GLOBAL WORLD

Andrew Blake

Introduction

At the end of the nineteenth century, magazine publishing was based on national markets; 120 years later, it is global in reach, and multinational, multilingual and multicultural in content and emphasis. Magazine publishers have responded to the emergence of new markets with new print, online and social media products, and with new ways of marketing and distributing their existing offerings, in what is often seen as a 'globalised' world.

By their nature, publishing businesses are now international both in outlook and operation, and among other things, this means that publishing businesses themselves are part of an international market. Even when magazines are apparently local in content and unavailable in translation, their publishers may be international businesses based elsewhere. For example, German companies such as Axel Springer, Bauer Media, Bertelsmann and Burda all bought significant stakes in Central and East European and Russian magazine publishers in the early 1990s, just as their economies were reorienting towards consumerism, and items such as fashion magazines were becoming more important (Sternadori, 2020, p. 448). As a result, Bauer Media dominates the magazine sector in Poland (Bauer 2020).

These companies were also competing in more complex markets. In early 2020, the UK market leaders in magazine publishing included, for the first time in a decade, a UK company, Future Publishing. Future had recently added IPC's magazine titles to its existing list. It bought these from the London-based private equity company Epiris – which had bought them from the American-owned Time Inc. only in 2017. But overall leader in the UK market was Bauer Media (which had a presence in the UK from 1987, and bought then second-largest UK publisher, EMAP in 2008) and third was Burda (which had bought Immediate, publisher of the *Radio Times* listings magazine, in 2017). The fourth and fifth biggest places belonged to the US-owned companies Hearst Media (which bought most of the French magazine group Hachette Filippachi's titles in 2010) and Condé Nast.

The American presence in UK markets had started when Condé Nast launched a UK edition of *Vogue* in 1916. Other Anglicised American titles followed; arguably the most influential of these, Hearst's *Harper's Bazaar,* was launched in 1929 as a direct rival to *Vogue UK.* This Anglo-American publishing world then became somewhat Europeanised, after a number of technological and political changes in the early 1980s made it easier for EC-based businesses to launch new publications in various national territories. Following the French company Hachette's successful introduction of *Elle UK* in 1985, Bauer Media launched its English-language version of *Bella* in the following year, while in 1987 the UK edition of *Hello!* was launched. The fact that all three publishers entered into UK territory with magazines for women is unsurprising, as that was then the core of the magazine market; whether this remains true of international publishing today is an important question.

'Globalisation' and 'international' are contested terms (and can even be taken back to prehistory: see Howe, 2002, p. 43), so for the purposes of this chapter, let us simply agree that trade, and the movement of people and information, across national boundaries and continents have become easier over the last 40 years, making the world feel 'smaller' and more connected. Those boundaries have weakened while global regulations and international relationships have strengthened, thanks to political, economic, social and technological developments which include (not in chronological order):

- The end of the Cold War in c.1990, which gave increasing freedom of movement to hundreds of millions of people who had in effect been imprisoned within the boundaries of the Soviet empire.
- The subsequent enlargement of the European Union as a free trade and free movement area.
- The deregulation of airlines and the encouragement of competition in air travel, which made flying cheaper and more easily available.
- The rise of first Japan and South Korea, and then Taiwan and mainland China, as global economic powerhouses, with the subsequent emergence of generations of wealthy and well-educated young people wishing to travel in order to study or work – or simply to enjoy spending their new wealth.
- The ubiquitous deployment of the internet as a source of relatively cost-free information.

'747 internationalism' and the travel magazine

Only the most avid conspiracy theorist would argue that any of these changes were planned. In other words, what we mean by 'international' or 'global' are always subject to change without notice. For example, while the massive growth in personal air travel owes much to deregulation, the attitude which produced it owes a great deal to the unexpected success of the Boeing 747 'jumbo jet' airliner, whose first commercial flights took place in 1970, and whose final retirement was under way as this book went to print in 2021 (Morris 2020). Before the 'jumbo', international air travel had been an exotic and expensive facility aimed at the wealthy, and the high-technology, small capacity supersonic airliner Concorde (whose commercial service started in 1976) was aimed at keeping it that way. Concorde's relative failure, and the growing success of the 747, helped make the case for airline deregulation, which took place in the USA in 1978, leading to an increase in relatively cheap flights within the USA and elsewhere.

There were many beneficiaries of this 'normalisation' of air travel. Europeans and North Americans now used air travel routinely, for holidays and short breaks, whether skiing, walking, urban-breaking or following their teams in the Champions League or the NFL. American and European students increasingly went on 'gap years', travelling around places like Australasia, Peru, Thailand and Vietnam. Middle-class professional North Europeans bought second homes in sunnier climes such as Spain, Portugal and Italy, flying there and back several times per year. And, South Asians living in the UK, the USA or Canada could now revisit their families and places of birth in India and Pakistan regularly. A typical beneficiary of this dem-ocratisation of flight was retired schoolteacher Thomas Brown, who recalled his 'inebriation on a Boeing 747' while travelling from London to his new home on the Caribbean island of Montserrat in 1988 (Brown, 2015, p. 21).

Our geographical and cultural understandings of the world have been signifi-cantly reshaped by this relative freedom of movement, and as soon as international flying became normal, magazines were there to highlight the possibilities of this '747 internationalism'. Since the early impact of deregulation, a genre of travel magazines has come into being; indeed it now includes micro-genres which address different segments of the travel market, from the backpacker on a limited budget who wants to see the world, to the five-star-hotel-hopping global elite who think they own it. Titles include *National Geographic Traveller* (which was founded in 1984); *Wanderlust* (1993); *Condé Nast Traveller* (1997); *Elite Traveller: The Private Jet Lifestyle Magazine* (2001); *Luxury Travel Magazine* (2003); and *Lonely Planet Travel Magazine* (2009).

Condé Nast Traveller is a typical example, in which the benefits of holiday travel to experience one or more of local people and customs, different weather, cuisine, architecture and the natural world, are taken for granted by all the contributors. These benefits are presented to a claimed five million monthly readers of editions of *Condé Nast Traveller* produced in India, China, Italy, Spain, the Middle East and the USA (Condé Nast, 2020).

The April 2020 UK print edition of this magazine is a publication on top form. The front cover photograph represents a fantasy holiday scenario of the 'paradise' to be found on a desert island: a single canoeist navigates the crystal sea in front of an otherwise empty Polynesian beach, with bleached sand fringing a stand of palm trees. An article inside tells you how to turn this fantasy into reality by getting and staying there (Misner, 2020, pp. 96–105). The UK magazine has a cover price of just under £5, so it is not just for the very wealthy (or those who aspire to be). Yes, the journalistic contents are interspersed with advertisements for expensive hotels, and very expensive watches, perfume and jewellery; and the effect of an account of a visit to the Antarctic, supported by spectacular photography, is somewhat tempered by the revelation that a similar visit would cost the reader about £70,000 – which is nearly three times the median household income in the UK, officially calculated at £26,600 (ONS, 2020). However, another feature in this issue reviews new hotels in European destinations from £60 to £130 per night. The magazine is for international travellers, and by implication, that's most of us.

Magazines as international brands

Of course, 'international' means more than adventurous holidays, and international publishers already produced magazines which cater for local markets as well as for global travellers. Many such magazines have become multiedition global brands in themselves, available in different regions and in different languages: as we have seen, *Condé Nast Traveller* has several such editions. *Men's Health*, published by American multimedia company Hearst, currently has 35 nationally based editions, and is available across all continents except Antarctica. Celebrity magazine ¡*Hola!* (*Hello!*), owned by Spanish family publisher Sanchez Junco, has 16 worldwide editions, across Europe, Latin America, the USA and Asia. On a smaller scale, women's monthly *Psychologies*, founded in France but currently owned by UK publishing house Kelsey Media, publishes in six languages, including Russian and Chinese editions.

While they might share the same brand name, the content of these magazines is not always the same for the purchaser in London or Lima. We can identify three distinct approaches:

1. *Standardisation*, in which the same product is distributed across several different markets (though the contents might be translated).
2. *Localisation*, in which a product with the same brand identifier and owned by the same company is entirely different in content in different locations.
3. *Glocalisation*, in which a product with the same brand identifier and owned by the same company has some content deliberately tailored for local markets but shares some editorial content, and/or a sense of shared values, with the 'home' edition.

It's relatively easy to identify a 'standardised' product. Weekly news magazine *Paris Match*, published by the now French-only group Hachette since 1949, has made no effort to move beyond its loyal Francophone readership; similarly, the London-based fortnightly satirical magazine *Private Eye*, founded in 1961, concerns itself only with the UK and has made no attempt to internationalise in content. You can buy *Paris Match* in London, and *Private Eye* in Paris, but in each case you will be buying one edition. Neither is available in translation.

Localisation and glocalisation can be more difficult to tell apart. One of the best-known and most culturally influential multinational magazine enterprises is the Condé Nast women's fashion magazine *Vogue*. Currently, the magazine has 27 editions: the long-established US, UK and Paris versions are complemented by those published in China, Hong Kong, Taiwan, Japan, Korea, India, Brazil, Mexico and Latin America, Thailand, Turkey, Russia, Ukraine, Italy, Spain, Portugal, the Netherlands, Germany, Greece, Poland, the Czech Republic and Slovakia, New Zealand, Australia, Arabia and most recently Singapore.

These editions are not translated carbon copies of the UK, US or Paris versions; indeed, they are different enough that the approach here might seem to be *localisation*. Each version of *Vogue* has its own, locally based, editorial and production staff, and each features locally based models, and local fashion news and other stories. In mid-2020, while all editions of both the print magazine and the website featured stories about the global coronavirus pandemic and its impact on the high-fashion world, they had very different national and regional emphases. *Vogue Arabia's* top fashion stories included 'Men's Fashion Week and Couture Week are Cancelled in Paris' alongside '16 Muslim Influencers with Modern Modest Fashion', and 'The Must-Have Pieces from this Ramadan's Exclusive Capsule Collections (vogue.me., 2020a). *Vogue Paris* also mixed the routine 'Quels sont les sacs stars du printemps-été 2020?' (Which handbags will be the star performers for spring and summer 2020?) alongside the more topical 'Les marques indépendantes se mobilise aussi pour lutter contre le coronavirus' (Independent brands are also gearing up for the fight against coronavirus) (Vogue.fr., 2020). Though there were coronavirus items elsewhere on its website, *Vogue India's* fashion stories were, as usual for this edition, purely celebrity-oriented, with '14 Pictures that Take You Inside Kiara Advani's Gym Wardrobe' and 'Sonakshi Sinha's Complete Style Evolution' (Vogue. in., 2020).

However, though they are different in many details and sometimes in areas of emphasis, the various national *Vogue* editions are not fully independent publications either in ownership or in editorial content. In effect, the current aim of the parent company is not to produce localised but *glocalised* magazines. Condé Nast has established a central 'editorial hub' tasked with steering the overall direction for these publications, all of which have to subscribe to a 'global mission statement':

> *Vogue* stands for thought-provoking imagery and intelligent storytelling. We devote ourselves to supporting creators in all shapes and forms. *Vogue* looks to the future with optimism, remains global in its vision, and stands committed to practices that celebrate cultures and preserve our planet for future generations. We speak with a unified voice across 26 editions standing for the values of diversity, responsibility and respect for individuals, communities and for our natural environment.
>
> *All the Editors-in-Chief, Vogue.me., 2020b*

The chief executive of the company, Roger Lynch, amplified this commitment:

> As the world's leading fashion title, *Vogue* has the ability to move, influence and inspire — and with that, a responsibility to lead on the issues that matter most … For over a century, Condé Nast's titles have driven the cultural conversation and propelled meaningful change around the world. This new commitment underscores what we can accomplish when we work together to leverage our global reach.
>
> *Vogue.me, 2020b*

An example of this hub group in action was the September 2020 issues of *Vogue*, which while, again, significantly different from edition to edition, shared the common theme of 'hope'. This would seem to be a generous and positive response in a time of crisis, expressing common aspirations at a time of global crisis. Nonetheless, the claims made by Mr Lynch, and the shared aims of the 'hub' editorial group, raise a number of issues which any student of international magazine publishing must address. Condé Nast is based in the USA, which necessarily inflects what Mr Lynch means by 'global reach', and what we might understand by a 'glocal' product. Are aspirations towards 'diversity' and 'universal' values an attempt to respect, and build on, local cultures and local differences? Or are they in fact a new form of American, or Western, cultural imperialism? Are new, hybrid forms of identity proposed here, or will the intended cultural outcome be that all *Vogue* readers, everywhere in the world, aspire to look and live like the magazine's typical cover model: a young, slim, white(ish), relatively wealthy, and conventionally beautiful woman?

Is international magazine publishing a new form of imperialism?

There can be no question that magazines played their part in a now discredited form of internationalism: Western colonialism and imperialism, which reached its peak in the generation before the First World War of 1914–18. The April 2018 edition of *National Geographic* opened with an apology. *National Geographic* was founded in 1888 by a scholarly society, which aimed to use the publication to bring American citizens knowledge of the world beyond the borders of the USA, well before the era of mass leisure travel. In doing so, editor Susan Goldberg said in that 2018 issue, the magazine had often reflected racist and colonialist attitudes to the rest of the world. It had identified peoples and cultures outside North America and Europe as racially inferior and technologically primitive compared with the imagined white American reader; until the 1970s, it had largely ignored African Americans; it had published articles on apartheid South Africa without identifying apartheid itself as a problem. The magazine had commissioned a report on its historic treatment of race by Professor John Mason, who said that

Americans got ideas about the world from Tarzan movies and crude racist caricatures … *National Geographic* wasn't teaching as much as reinforcing messages they already received and doing so in a magazine that had tremendous authority. *National Geographic* comes into existence at the height of colonialism, and the world was divided into the colonizers and the colonized. That was a color line, and *National Geographic* was reflecting that view of the world.

cited in Goldberg, 2018

National Geographic is now painfully aware of its own history. But at the height of this discrimination, it was a national product with a mainly white readership. Magazine publishers have, since the end of the Cold War and the collapse of apartheid South Africa, become truly global businesses, selling products like *Vogue* which are, as we have seen, at the same time generic, and crafted for differentiated markets, everywhere in the inhabited world. Clearly, the crude racism of the early twentieth century would be very unlikely to attract readers in Asia and Africa. However, one common response to the globalisation strategies of these Western-owned media organisations is to claim that while they no longer embody the obvious prejudices of the colonial era, their contents are a more insidious form of neocolonialism, which represents Western bodies and consumer capitalism as the global norm, and treats local physical and cultural differences and local and national traditions, as picturesque departures from that Western norm (if it treats them at all).

Some of the academic research which follows this line of thought is summarised by Leara D. Rhodes (2018). The author discusses magazine scholarship published after 1990 on a range of international issues, and also points to areas in which more research would be welcome. Taking as her definition of 'international' anything which is not directly concerned with magazines published in the USA (though it could have been written, researched and published there), Rhodes summarises and discusses some 60 scholarly works.

Most of the content examined by Rhodes concerns magazines published for young women in China, Japan and South Korea; and much of the scholarly interest is in advertising rather than editorial content. Scholars have examined ways in which such magazines have produced variations on local-global femininity (and also, in a few instances, masculinity), which while apparently respecting local laws and variations in ethical and religious beliefs – especially in relation to cover images – produces the readers of those magazines as Western-style consumers. Through their advertising and editorial content and through aggressive marketing techniques, some of the Western-based publishing houses have managed to produce and service these hybrid identities at the expense of magazines produced by nationally based publishers. Irene Yang, for example gives an overview of the establishment of localised versions of Western, and mainland Chinese, magazines in Taiwan, and their effects on local publishers (whose magazines have emulated Western ones in order to attract advertisers, and so become very like their Western counterparts). Yang concludes that 'International women's magazines, supported by international advertising agencies to sell international brand-name commodities, use their "international" language of human rights and sexual pleasure to articulate a popular version of feminism conducive to the workings of global capitalism' (Yang, 2004, p. 526). International women's magazines help to produce women who become Westernised consumers, at the expense of local and national traditions.

Such a stark manifestation of economic and cultural imperialism through magazine publishing is not always the experience in mainland China itself, according to Yang Feng and Katherine Frith (2008; see also Frith and Feng, 2009; Frith and Kavan, 2014). Feng and Frith examined advertising in Chinese women's magazines, each printed in Mandarin, though published by companies based in the USA and Japan as well as in China (in effect all 'international' titles available in China are co-published with local firms, in order to be licensed by the Chinese government: Ren, 2020, p. 419). They found that Western or 'Caucasian' models were largely used in Western-owned magazines, while Japanese and Chinese magazines used predominantly Asian models. They argue that "By including foreign fashion and lifestyle with skilfully designed editorial material and beautiful photos, international women's magazines in China attract foreign advertisers as well as Chinese readers away from existing [China-based] women's magazines" (Feng and Frith, 2008, p. 1). However, they conclude that the use of Asian models and beauty products has allowed Japanese magazines to take a greater market share than Western magazines, with their predominantly Caucasian models. They conclude that this "brings into question whether concepts like Western cultural imperialism and global media's hegemony hold sway" (Feng and Frith, 2008, p. 12).

These debates on representation and gender identity are typical of academic research on magazines published elsewhere in the world. Ngozi Akinro & Lindani Mbunyuza-Memani (2019), for example argue that Western-owned women's magazines published in Africa represent beauty ideals foreign to sub-Saharan Africans, while Loubna H. Skalli (2006) relays a similar argument in relation to magazines for women in Morocco, and Erin Massi da Casanova (2002) does so in relation to women in Ecuador, South America. Many of these arguments are summarised in Yan & Kim Bissell (2014).

While these important questions of representation and identity are often the focus of academic research on international magazines, a far broader range of issues is covered. In the final paragraph of Rhodes's survey, she identifies some of the relative absences in this recent material (Rhodes, 2018, p. 146). She concludes that the study of globalisation in relation to magazines is not yet global in coverage; there is far less academic research on magazines published in Central and South America; India; and Africa, or even on Australasia and Canada, than on magazines for Asian consumers. Rhodes also found few studies of magazines concerning topics such as health or new technology (despite the obvious international success of titles such as *Psychologies* and *Men's Health*).

But these areas, and issues, have not been ignored altogether. For example, Pratt, Ha and Pratt (2002) discuss the representation of HIV/AIDS within popular magazines *New African* and *Z-Magazine* (where it was commonly represented as a gay or 'white man's' disease, consequently stigmatised, and not seen as a genuine community issue). This negativity is contrasted to the *East African Medical Journal,* and the *Central Africa Journal of Medicine*, which were eager to impress on their readers the medical status of this potentially fatal, and inheritable, disease. However, the use of hard statistics and Latinate terminology in these journals was unhelpful in helping the general public to reach a compassionate and fully informed response to the disease. The authors conclude optimistically that popular magazines have a crucial role to play in the formation of positive community attitudes to health, and that they are capable of doing so: 'Armed with a community power approach to using health-advice columns or biographies, the media could assist audiences to participate and understand the issues in their own terms' (Pratt, Ha and Pratt, 2002, p. 903). In this view, international issues have to be addressed through terminology acceptable to local cultures; only if this happens can truly global solutions (to global issues such as HIV/Aids) emerge. It's a positive argument for the benefits of a glocal mode of publication, where international co-operation is vital in addressing global issues which have a local impact.

Magazines for internationalist advocacy

Magazines themselves are seldom a neutral medium in such debates, often ostentatiously setting the agenda in discussions about global and local policy. It is instructive to compare what could be called 'house magazines' for two very positive, but very different visions of a globalised world, *The Economist* and *New Internationalist*.

Those who argue in favour of frictionless 'free' trade in the interests of capital accumulation and, by association at least, continued significant income inequality, while claiming that this free trade will gradually improve the lives and opportunities for most humans, are served by weekly news magazine *The Economist*, whose principal shareholder is Exor, the investment group owned by the Agnelli family (who also own significant shares in Fiat Chrysler automobiles, and the most successful Italian football club, Juventus).

The Economist was founded in London in 1843 to promote ideals of free trade liberalism (including borders open to immigration as well as to capital, goods and services) when such ideas were politically radical. It continues to promote these liberal ideals by reporting and commenting on economic and political news from around the world. The principal edition is still edited from London, with substantial contribution from its New York office; there are separate American and European and Middle Eastern editions. The weekly print versions of *The Economist* are backed by website Economist.com, which includes an online version of the weekly issues; a daily newsletter delivered by email; and *Economist Espresso*, a daily microedition delivered to the subscriber's smartphone app. These are complemented by a bimonthly luxury lifestyle magazine, *1843*; an annual forecast of the state of the world in the following year; podcasts and films; discussion and networking events; and an online shop. Its commercial success is largely subscriber-driven, with audited circulation for the print issue of 909,476 as of December 2019; 737,246 of

TABLE 6.1 Advertising in *The Economist*, 20–26 June 2020, and *The New Internationalist*, March–April 2020.

The Economist, 20–26 June 2020	New Internationalist, March–April 2020
Jobs: Higher Education, teaching business studies	
Jobs: a recruitment agency CV-fishing	
Jobs: Administration x2	
Online seminars x 3	The *Guardian Weekly* news magazine
National branding (Mauritius)	Ethical online shopping x 2
Tender for development	Higher education courses in sustainable development
Ecologically sensitive coffee	Greenpeace (environmental lobbyists)
Luxury real estate x2	The Quakers (a religious group)
Financial computing services x2	Ethical investment trusts x 2

these readers were subscribers (ABC, 2020a). All print subscribers also have access to the digital versions, whose audited circulation at December 2019 was 748,459, including 277,652 digital-only subscribers (ABC, 2020b).

However, advertising is still significant to *The Economist*, both as a source of revenue and as a confirmatory statement of the magazine's influential readership. The print issue dated 20–26 June 2020 carried 20 adverts. Two were for finance-related computing; six for jobs (three in higher education, one from a recruitment agency fishing for CVs, two in high-level administration); one higher education corporate branding statement, and two for higher education courses; three for online seminar-based 'events'; one corporate branding statement; one national branding statement (by the island of Mauritius); one request to tender for development; two for luxury real estate; and one for an ecologically sensitive coffee brand.

Despite its advocacy of open-doors immigration in an integrated global economy, *The Economist* is often regarded as 'conservative'. Critics of this viewpoint include those who claim that this version of free trade is another form of imperialism, in which the free movement of goods and capital means businesses moving factories to where wages, and workers' rights, are lowest, while any profits made in these territories are transferred back to shareholders based in the West. Instead, they advocate more powers for national governments to control capital investment in the interests of their citizens, though in a world without any restrictions on the movement of people, in order to achieve equal opportunities for all humans. This would, apparently, tend to reduce income inequalities and eventually put an end to global poverty.

Such a viewpoint can be found in the pages of *New Internationalist*. This magazine was founded, and originally funded, in 1973 by a group of UK charities which were interested in the promotion of 'international development'. Its proponents see this as a benign process through which state and charitable aid from rich countries

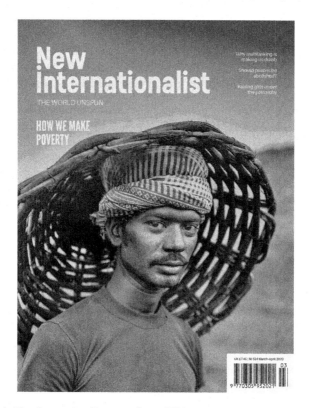

PHOTO 6.1 A *New Internationalist* cover from 2020.

is passed to poorer countries with a view to increasing their capacities for change towards equality of treatment in areas such as health, and equality of opportunity in areas such as education and careers. The prime aim of this process is economic growth to the general benefit, rather than the enrichment of nationally based kleptocrats.

Since the magazine's foundation, however, the latter has occurred. Despite apparently significant amounts of global wealth being allocated to the development process, in *New Internationalist*'s own words 'the global economic order has been reconfigured … to serve the interests of a class of untouchable and unaccountable offshore-based billionaires' (*NI*, March–April 2020, p. 28). The politics, possibilities and effects of all these processes are vigorously debated in what is now a bimonthly magazine produced by an editorial co-operative based in Oxford, England (with offices in Australia, Canada and New Zealand). It is funded largely by its subscriber base of c.75,000; the March–April 2020 issue carried advertisements from the magazine's own online shop; religious group The Quakers; the onevillage.com online global craft shop; the *Guardian Weekly* news magazine; two ethical investment trusts, Investing Ethically ltd., and Abundance Investment; environmental lobbyists and activists Greenpeace; and a suite of Masters programmes taught at the Graduate School of the Environment at the Centre for Alternative Technology, Snowdonia, Wales.

Magazines for international and transnational communities

The globalisation of magazine publishing was partly a reflection of the continuing global movement of readers. The increasing flow of people round the world for holiday and leisure purposes involving a brief stay rather than any change in residence, has been paralleled by the large-scale movement of people between countries, for life-change, business or other reasons. Many of these people have formed significant language-based communities in bigger cities, and magazines have catered for them. *Metropolis Japan*, for example was founded in 1994 as a brief listings sheet in English; it has since become the leading English-language magazine in Japan, catering mainly for Anglophone residents of Tokyo, introducing them to local news and events, with background on Japanese cultural norms and expectations. *10 Magazine* does a similar job for the growing number of English-speaking residents of South Korea's capital, Seoul.

Metropolis Japan and *10 Magazine* assume that most members of the Anglophone communities they address are not, and do not intend to become, permanent residents of the countries and cities they inhabit. These readers are *international*, usually changing residency but not national status or identity. Of course many people move, either by choice or by force of circumstance, in order to settle permanently away from their places of birth and education. But the ways in which these massive shifts affect peoples' identities have changed significantly. Over the last 50 years, patterns of immigration from poorer countries into North America and Europe, and the drift of young people from relatively poor Central and Eastern European countries to Western European countries with better-paid jobs, have been part of '747 internationalism'. They depend in part on the rise of easily available, affordable if not actually cheap, air travel, as well as the provision of information from and about everywhere, on the internet, on television and in magazines.

As a result of these changes, many people who are notionally permanently resident in one country are not just aware of, or practisers of, a 'cultural heritage' from their or their parents' or grandparents' former homes, but they are actively connected to two (or more) countries through regular travel and electronic communication. Whatever their passports might say about their citizenship status, such people are socially and culturally not national or international but *transnational*.

The normalisation of this type of life experience has produced an increasing emphasis on multiple, hybridised or 'hyphenated' identities (e.g. Irish-American, or British-Asian), and many magazines now cater for people inhabiting these relatively new worlds. Examples include the print and online magazine *Burnt Roti*, founded in London in 2018, which navigates the problems and possibilities of sexual and gender identity across British and South Asian political and economic systems. Similarly, *Brown Girl*, founded in New York as an online magazine in 2008, addresses

PHOTO 6.2 Bookstall display of Chinese magazines. Photo Todd Gipstein.

the experience of South Asian women in and across the USA, India, Pakistan and Sri Lanka (more recently, the magazine has also addressed men, through their own 'Brown Man' section of the magazine). *Hyphen* was founded in San Francisco in 2003 in order to represent the rapidly growing Asian-American community in the area with recent as well as generational ties to Japan, Korea and China. More generally, the Canadian magazine *Shameless* (founded in 2004) and the London-based online and print magazine *gal-dem* (founded in 2015), offer spaces for women and non-binary people of colour to express and explore their identities, offering them an increasingly influential voice in a world which still seems patriarchal and racist partly because of the heritage of colonialism, which is present in most of the world (Egbeyemi, 2020).

Magazines for the transnational elite

While there are now significant groups of people with transnational, hybrid identities, there is also, as *New Internationalist* pointed out, a new transnational plutocracy, and they too have been served by an emerging magazine genre. A range of luxury magazines cater for the very wealthy, including a number specifically for the emergent areas of wealth in the Far East. Whatever populations they address, magazines for the wealthy are essentially platforms for high-end advertising, so in order to approach them we have to consider ways of thinking about global branding and the luxury market.

Michel Chevalier and Gerald Mazzolo make four important points about the luxury market:

1. Luxury is a keyword whose use is becoming more frequent in our daily lives. We encounter it in all media; we use it more often in our discourses (Google Trends shows that its use has doubled between 2004 and 2010).
2. A luxury product must meet three main criteria. It must have a strong artistic content, it must be the result of craftsmanship and it must be international.
3. The luxury market today is based on a paradox. Luxury operates ... as a social distinction. It is ... reserved for the happy few and thus circumvents the masses. At the same time, contemporary luxury is promoted by many brands that remain linked to the logic of volume of production and product distribution. How, therefore, can distinction and selectivity be acquired?
4. The 'intermediate luxury' category is for the aspirant middle class to demonstrate their aspiration (Chevalier and Mazzolo, 2012, pp. 2–5).

The luxury market is the paradigm example of innovation in international magazine publishing. As this example indicates, brands and magazine writing often form a symbiotic bond:

> Louis Vuitton was able to find, in its historical identity, the elements of a 'fashion discourse'. The values of tradition associated with the luggage connote not so much conservatism as excellence and distinction – the nostalgic evocation of a time when travel was still an adventure and the privilege of a small circle of privileged individuals. "Nostalgic exoticism" is in vogue today in the fashion magazines, but style counts less than fantasy. The brand has made extensive use of this imaginative capital.
>
> *Chevalier and Mazzolo, 2012, p. 18*

Leading luxury magazines, which are basically a platform for the goods identified by Chevalier and Mazzolo, include well-established titles such as *The Economist's 1843*; the *Financial Times* newspaper's monthly magazine, unsubtly titled *How to Spend It;* and the London-based, Condé Nast owned monthly *Tatler*. In all of these, the same high-end brands predominate as advertisers (Klein, 2000, p. 117), though the markets addressed are somewhat different.

In particular, these magazines represent the impact of the growing economies of the Far East on international luxury marketing and consumption. The *Financial Times*, founded in London in 1888, is currently owned by Japanese media organisation the Nikkei Group. *Tatler* was originally targeted at the British upper and upper middle classes, and its print edition still largely reflects that demographic, but it now also has bespoke websites tailored for readers in Singapore, Hong Kong, China and Taiwan. The target readership may vary, but the brand and experiences

PHOTO 6.3 A 2020 cover from the monthly *Financial Times* magazine, *How to Spend It*.

offered are very similar. Though there are differences (e.g. the UK edition/website of *Tatler*, which still aims to reproduce its readers' social class through marriage, has more about weddings – and more gossip about the European royal families – than the others in this category), in each case these magazines provide advertising and editorial information about fashion; other luxury goods such as jewellery, watches, cars, private planes and yachts; and holidays. This is presented alongside editorial featuring entrepreneurial and business success stories, and those fantasy representations of luxury life and/as privileged adventure identified by Chevalier and Mazzolo.

All this is for the global wealthy, and particularly for those whose wealth is recent, and so are new to the game and therefore not quite sure yet 'how to spend it'. But spend it they must, in order to signal their arrival in the global elite: as Chevalier and Mazzolo state, the purchaser requires to indicate 'distinction'. This is a psychosocial imperative. Writing way back in 1899 in his book *The Theory of the Leisure Class*, the American sociologist Thorstein Veblen claimed that elite spending is deliberately, and functionally, 'conspicuous consumption', designed to show the spender's status both to their peers in the economic elite, and to the rest of us. His insight still stands (Veblen, 1899/2009).

PHOTO 6.4 Front cover of *Monocle*, December–January 2020. An intermediate luxury magazine for the creative class.

Intermediate luxury: magazines for the 'creative class'

Many others wish to be in this happy position, and in the meantime display to the world their *relative* distinction. The early 2000s saw the transformation of the cultural geography of urban life to accommodate these aspirants. In three key books, American academic Richard Florida identified and described a new 'creative class' of workers in the creative and technology industries (Florida, 2000, 2004, 2006). He claimed that up to 40 per cent of current US workers are 'creative' by lifestyle as well as work skills. Well-educated and ambitious, they are no longer prepared to don suits and work from 9 am until 5 pm for the same employer all their careers, or to live in 1950s-style heteronormative family units. This creative class is global in provenance and mobile in aspiration: they do not have any strong sense of national identity but just go with the flow, wherever that might take them, in order to earn more, or to live in a more pleasant, or fashionable, urban or semi-rural environment. British journalist David Goodhart has labelled such people 'anywheres'; they regard themselves as citizens of the world, tied to shared liberal values rather than national identity or any other strong sense of place (Goodhart, 2017).

A number of magazines provide entertainment and information for this relatively new, aspirant global cohort. For example, *Monocle* was founded in 2007 by Canadian journalist Tyler Brûlé (who had already founded, edited and sold on, the rather similar *Wallpaper**, a London-based Future publication). The fundamental belief system behind the magazine's editorial content can be summed up by the editor's confirmation of his own internationalist assumptions: 'Yes, we call ourselves CEOs, curators, designers, attorneys and architects but really we're just traders and tinkers, wanderers and hoarders, hustlers and chroniclers and we love nothing more than the freedom to roam this earth' (Brûlé, 2020). This is Florida's creative class, or Goodhart's anywheres, in a single sentence.

Monocle is based in London and Zurich, with offices in Toronto, Los Angeles, Hong Kong and Tokyo. In structure, *Monocle* goes well beyond the publication basics of a monthly print magazine and a detailed website. There is a comprehensive, free, daily newsletter emailed to anyone who subscribes. This publication serves as a taster like *Economist Espresso*, but is much more comprehensive, featuring not just mini-articles but medium-length essays, plus links to rich media (video, audio). The *Monocle* website offers links to several live and podcast-based radio channels. The company's London and Zurich shops offer ranges of carefully priced luxury goods, and coffee shops for readers to meet. There are regular discussion residencies and social events. *Monocle* has a number of 'site sponsors', who have significant advertorial space within the daily newsletter, as they do in the print magazine; even beyond these relationships, most of the advertising carried in print or online is bespoke for the publication.

Monocle typically represents, and reviews, what Chevalier and Mazzolo call 'intermediate luxury' – a semi-bespoke experience. Much of the magazine and newsletter content is about welcoming cities; indeed much of it precisely helps to make those cities the destinations for the aspirant elite. A typical piece from the newsletter discusses the kind of bespoke, personal, intermediate luxury experience every *Monocle* reader is assumed to want:

> Ever since I visited Budapest … I've lamented the lack of a spa culture in Canada … Tucked inside an unassuming shopping mall in Mississauga, a city of almost a million people that doubles as a suburb of western Toronto, is the Russian-inspired South-Western Bathhouse and Tea Room. Run by Victor and Valentina Tourianski and their two daughters, the spa houses a *banya* (a Russian sauna) erected by Victor himself, a dry Finnish sauna, a hammam, a cool plunge-pool and my favourite: a barrel-shaped water tank that releases teeth-chatteringly cold water upon your head at the pull of a chain … The lure of something more authentic – and more fun – than your average ultra-white, ultra-mundane spa has made the Tourianskis' *banya* a success. As we visit, the bathhouse

overflows with young Torontonians who have made the trek west for one of its unisex days. It's charming, it's social and, though I haven't spent my afternoon being thoroughly demoralised by a game of floating chess, I am eating a bowl of buttery *pierogies* while wearing a bathrobe. That suits me just fine.

Kitchens, 2020

Monocle is an international(ist) brand in its own right. Its advertisers offer goods and services in the 'intermediate luxury' bracket (many of which are available in

TABLE 6.2 Advertising in *Monocle*, December 2019–January 2020 double issue.

Monocle December 2019/January 2020, special edition on Japan. 238 pp.		
Feature Articles, all on aspects of Japanese life		
	Editorial welcoming the opening of Japan to tourism, long-term residence, and permanent immigration, and anticipating the presumed success of the 2020 Tokyo Olympics as part of that process	Culture 5 Business 4 Politics 5 Travel destinations 3
Advertisements		
	Jewellery	Men's watches 11 Women's jewellery 1
	Clothing etc.	Men 3 Women 2 Unisex 2 Spectacles 1
	Shoes	Men 2 Unisex 1
	Interiors	Furniture 6 Bathroom design 2 Kitchen design 1 Washing machine 1
	Food and drink	Champagne 2 Cognac 2
	Cars	Cars 1
	Finance	Business advice 1 Personal banking 2
Advertorials, all done in the *Monocle* house style		
	Travel	Thailand; Madrid; Paradores hotels; Japan House, London
	Other	Leuchtturm writing materials USM modular office

the *Monocle* shops), and this is backed up by reporting which emphases bespoke experiences such as the above, in cities all over the world. As such, it is read not only by existing members of the creative class, what could be called the 'intermediate elite', but also by what we might identify as the 'subaltern class' of that intermediate elite. In conversation with the *Observer* newspaper, Tyler Brûlé quoted an item of fan mail from a reader. "I am a 21-year-old studying economics and government in Australia. I have not achieved the means to live by the majority of the magazine's ideas, I'm simply writing to thank you for the … awesomeness of the magazine." Brûlé added, tellingly, "Now I would go to an advertising meeting and talk about that being the core reader … who is going to be with us for a long time … part of a different media generation" (Nicol, 2012). As Table 6.2 shows, advertisers seem only too willing to go with this particular flow.

Changing the direction of travel

Until this point, the chapter has discussed internationalisation with one implicit direction of travel: from the West to the Rest. As Asian economies become more important, the future may well see a reversal of direction.

Despite Japan's significant global economic power in the period from 1960 up to about 1990, Japanese culture only made it to the West in cult form such as Manga comics, films and fast sports coupés. (As Japan opens up to global tourism, *Monocle* is doing its best to make Japanese culture more accessible; but this remains a work in progress). South Korean culture is more globally culturally successful, with the Oscar for best picture for *Parasite* (2019) mirroring the intense worldwide interest in K-Pop (and the ubiquity of Samsung phones and LG televisions). Though there are some very interesting Korean magazines (such as the online atkmagazine.com and ksoulmag.com), no Asian publications have yet become international phenomena in the Condé Nast sense. But there is already significant investment. For example, in 2019 the long-running, but failing, British music title *New Musical Express* (*NME*) was bought by Singaporean company Bandlab Technologies. The new owners wasted no time, firstly reviving the magazine's print edition in Australia and then opening a new *NME* website dedicated to music in Singapore, Malaysia and the Philippines (BBC 2020).

Meanwhile the intensity of Chinese economic growth, which has included massive growth in both literacy and internet usage, has helped the development of some powerful and very innovative magazines, from indie products to the mainstream. For example, *Life Week's* continuous experiments with reader engagement using social media sites Weibo and WeChat have led to the launch of its own *San Liang Zhong Dhu* reading app, with the aim of attaining independence from other social media providers, and with the advantage of direct control over its many readers' data (Ren, 2020, pp. 422–3). If this, currently localised, model works there will be great potential for its globalisation.

Similarly India, with a big English-speaking middle class, and an increasing diaspora of well-educated transnational workers, might well ride the next wave of internationalisation. *The Caravan*, a niche political/cultural magazine founded in

Delhi in 2009, was quite deliberately set up to be a transnational publication, able to appeal to a reader in New York as much as someone reading it in Jaipur (Jain and Raman, 2020, p. 434). Its long-form journalism puts it (again, very deliberately) close to the style world of publications such as the *New Yorker*; but its concerns with the experience of Indian-heritage communities worldwide, as well as intra-Indian affairs, also mark it out as the inverse of publications such as *Burnt Roti*, by its very nature capable of addressing a transnational community. The internationalisation of magazine publishing may well have a very different direction of travel in the twenty-first century's second quarter.

References

ABC (2020a) www.abc.org.uk/Certificates/49687426.pdf (accessed 25.06.2020.

ABC (2020b) www.abc.org.uk/product/18768 (accessed 25.06.2020)

Akinro, N. and Lindani Mbunyuza-Memani, L. (2019), 'Black is not beautiful: Persistent messages and the globalization of "white" beauty in African women's magazines', *Journal of International and Intercultural Communication*, vol. 12 no. 4, pp. 308–324.

Bauer (2020), www.bauermedia.com/en/media/magazines/ (accessed 29.05.2020).

BBC (2020), 'NME Asia: British Music Brand Launches in Asia', www.bbc.co.uk/news/business-53816771 (accessed 17.08.2020)

Brown, T. (2015), *Memories of Paradise*, London: Amazon.

Brûlé, T. (2020), 'New Connections', *The Monocle Weekend Edition* (email), 1 March 2020.

Casanova, E.M. de (2002), Women's magazines in Ecuador: re-reading "la chica cosmo", *Studies in Latin American Popular Culture*, no. 22, pp. 89–102.

Condé Nast (2020), www.condenast.com/brands/cond%C3%A9-nast-traveller (accessed 27.03.2020).

Chavalier, M. and Mazzolo, G. (2012), *Luxury Brand Management: A World of Privilege*, 2nd Edition, Hoboken, NJ: John Wiley.

Egbeyemi, E. (2020), 'How *gal-dem* magazine succeeded where mainstream media failed', in Miglena Sternadori and Tim Holmes, eds., *The Handbook of Magazine Studies*, Hoboken, NJ: John Wiley, pp. 393–399.

Florida, R. (2000), *The Rise of the Creative Class and How It's Transforming Work, Life, Community and Everyday Life*, New York: Basic Books.

Florida, R. (2004), *Cities and the Creative Class*, London: Routledge.

Florida, R. (2006), *The Flight of the Creative Class: The New Global Competition for Talent*, New York: Harper Business.

Feng, Y. and Frith, K. (2008), 'The growth of international women's magazines in China and the role of transnational advertising', *Journal of Magazine and New Media Research*, vol. 10 No. 1, pp. 1–14.

Frith, K and Feng, Y. (2009), 'Transnational cultural flows: An analysis of women's magazines in China', *Chinese Journal of Communication*, vol. 2, Issue 2, pp. 158–173.

Frith, K, and Karan, K. (2014), 'Magazines and International Advertising', in Hong Cheng, ed., *The Handbook of International Advertising Research*, Hoboken, NJ: John Wiley, pp. 149–160.

Goldberg, S. (2018), 'For decades, our coverage was racist. To rise above our past, we must acknowledge it', *National Geographic*, 12 March 2018: www.nationalgeographic.com/magazine/2018/04/from-the-editor-race-racism-history/ (accessed 05.03.2020).

Goodhart, D. (2017), *The Road to Somewhere: The New Tribes Shaping British Politics*, London: Penguin.

Howe, S. (2002), *Empire: A Very Short Introduction,* Oxford: Oxford University Press.

Jain, S, and Raman, U (2020), 'Indian Magazines Revitalised in Response to Demand for Long-form Storytelling', in Sternadori, Miglena and Holmes, Tim, *The Handbook of Magazine Studies*, Hoboken, NJ: John Wiley, pp. 427–439.

Klein, N. (2000), *No Logo,* New York and London: Fourth Estate.

Kitchens, W. (2020), 'From Russia with Loofah", *The Monocle Weekend Edition* (email), 23 February 2020.

Misner, R. (2020), 'Scale up', *Condé Nast Traveller,* April 2020, pp. 96–105.

Morris, H. (2020), 'Farewell to the Boeing 747', www.telegraph.co.uk/visual-stories/farewell-to-the-boeing-747/ (accessed 25.08.2020).

Nicol, R. (2012), 'Tyler Brûlé: the Man who Sold the World', www.theguardian.com/media/2012/mar/17/tyler-brule-wallpaper-monocle-magazine (accessed 27.2.2017).

Pratt, C. B., Ha, L. and Pratt, C. A. (2002), 'Setting the public health agenda on major diseases in sub-Saharan Africa: African popular magazines and medical journals, 1981–1997', *Journal of Communication,* December 2001, pp. 889–904.

Ren, X. (2020), 'Chinese consumer magazines: digital transitions in an evolving cultural economy', in Miglena Sternadori and Tim Holmes, eds., *The Handbook of Magazine Studies*, Hoboken, NJ: John Wiley, pp. 417–426.

Rhodes, L. D.(2018), 'International magazine publishing: the transformative power of globalisation', in David Abrahamson and Marcia R. Prior-Miller, eds., *The Routledge Handbook of Magazine Research,* 2nd edition, London: Routledge, pp. 135–152.

Savyasaachi, J. and Rama, U. (2020), 'Indian magazines revitalised in response to demand for long-form storytelling', in Miglena Sternadori and Tim Holmes, eds., *The Handbook of Magazine Studies*, Hoboken, NJ: John Wiley, pp. 427–439.

Sternadori, M. (2020), 'From grit to glitz: magazine markets and ideologies in post-Communist Europe and Asia', in Miglena Sternadori and Tim Holmes, eds., *The Handbook of Magazine Studies*, Hoboken, NJ: John Wiley, pp. 440–452.

ONS (Office for National Statistics) (2020), www.ons.gov.uk/peoplepopulationand community/personalandhouseholdfinances/incomeandwealth/bulletins/householddisp osableincomeandinequality/financialyearending2019 (accessed 26.06.2020).

Skalli, L. H. (2006), *Through a Local Prism: Gender, Globalisation and Identity in Moroccan Women's Magazines*, Lanham, MD and Plymouth: Lexington Books.

Yan, Y. & Bissell, K. (2014), 'The globalization of beauty: How is ideal beauty influenced by globally published fashion and beauty magazines?', *Journal of Intercultural Communication Research,* Volume 43, Issue 3, pp. 194–214.

Yang, I. (2004), 'International Women's magazines and the production of sexuality in Taiwan', *The Journal of Popular Culture*, vol. 37, no. 3, pp. 505–530.

Veblen, T. (1899/2009), *The Theory of the Leisure Class. An Economic Study of Institutions,* Oxford: Oxford University Press.

Vogue.fr (2020), www.vogue.fr/mode (accessed 30.03.2020).

Vogue.in. (2020), www.vogue.in/fashion (accessed 30.03.2020).

Vogue.me. (2020a), en.vogue.me/category/fashion/ accessed 30.03.2020.

Vogue.me (2020b), '*Vogue* Values: All 26 Editions of *Vogue* Come Together to Announce a Global Mission Statement', https://en.vogue.me/culture/vogue-values/ (accessed 16.02.2020).

7

DIVERSITY IN MAGAZINES

Time to turn over a new leaf?

Andrew Blake and Simon Das

Introduction

Most studies of magazines and diversity have focused on representation and identity. What magazines say, and how they say it – the portrayal of people on their pages by words and semiotics – has dominated magazine-related debates on gender, race and identity in the last two decades. This chapter, however, is focused not on a cultural examination through magazines, but on looking inside them as organisations.

By looking specifically at racial diversity not through the pages of a magazine, but what's actually and humanly behind them, the chapter seeks to further address a large gap within the field of publishing studies. In the last decade, little has been published on race and creative workers in the UK other than large sector reports about mainstream news journalism such as those by Mark Spilsbury (2017, 2018). Magazine publishing as a less mainstream (and promotionally driven) adjunct to the journalism industry has therefore largely flown under the radar when it comes to the scrutiny of holding a mirror up to their organisations in terms of diversity both on and off the page.

While it is accepted by some that many key posts such as content creators, editors, designers, art directors and even publishers of magazines are more balanced in terms of gender diversity – race remains one of the most pernicious issues in media today. Acknowledging research around diversity and media (including Gooch, 2018 and Saha, 2018), this chapter explores an explicit link between the diversity of people *inside* magazines as a driver of better representation in media facing *outside* of magazines. By looking at data, reports and gathering first-hand insights, a snapshot will be provided about race in UK magazine publishing at a time when some of the major publishers have responded to the lack of BAME (black, Asian and minority ethnicity) cover stars and representation of their wider content.

The economics of magazine media and race

In recent years, magazine publishers have made some high-profile interventions in attempting to improve the diversity on their pages – and none more high profile than that of *Vogue UK's* editor. Condé Nast's appointment of black Briton Edward Enninful as editor of *Vogue* in 2017 was hailed by the media as praiseworthy, especially when he set about recruiting a more diverse staff and, as will be discussed, created more diverse content for the fashion bible. However, whether this reflects a wider change in the organisational culture at his publisher has come starkly into question, after Enninful himself reported being racially profiled by a company security guard when entering work in July 2020. The guard was subsequently dismissed (BBC, 2020).

In the US, the Asian-American editor, Lee Miller, of *Allure* magazine has commented that at the time of taking the editorship of the magazine, of 327 covers published over three decades, only two featured people of colour. In an interview about diversity, she admits the proactive nature of improving diversity, citing her July 2017 cover with model Halima Aden wearing a hijab. According to her, "it never happens by accident. Choosing people, ideas, covers, making it a priority – it's not something that happens automatically" (Lee, 2018).

This question of why diversity does not 'happen automatically', has been at the heart of decades of academic and critical analysis about race and representation. Much of this research reveals one overriding paradox – the split between what is often stated as desired by companies, policy makers and cultural industry spokes-people (mainly to improve diversity, inclusion and limit racism) and what is often said to be happening by media scholars – marginalisation, racialisation and the building-up of stereotypes. An overview by Gooch (2018) of representation and race in and around magazine media scholarship, for example cited scholarly studies that showed "limited ideas and images of marginalised social groups" (citing Rebecca Lind, 2013), the reinforcement of the assimilation ideal for immigrant groups in the US (Nguyen, 2013) and one damning study (Sengupta, 2006) that correlated race and types of representation in teenage girls' magazine advertisements – connoting what Gooch explains as "the white beauty ideal" compared with depictions of "hypersexual black women" (Gooch, 2018, p. 214).

This paradox is drilled down into by an analysis of cultural production by Anamik Saha (2018), who explores how society acknowledges racism and its causes, but how its very existence can maintain the present market and economic system. In his words:

> The paradox of living with racism in advanced capitalism is in how, on the one hand, racialized communities continue to be oppressed and their experiences and histories disavowed and, on the other, racial and ethnic differences become qualities used to distinguish products within a hypercompetitive market.
>
> *Saha, 2018, p. 7*

By this analysis, when it comes to magazine publishing, racism may be challenged by the industry, yet also tacitly encouraged within its pages and publications (or lack of them) for reasons of the unguided hand of sales, circulations and the differentiation of audiences through segmentation.

Perhaps a history of the existence of a largely independent organisation of black and 'ethnic media' in Britain (magazines, newspapers, radio stations), is proof that 'mainstream' magazine publishers have treated race in a way that has suited economic reasons in the past – and not any moral commitments to diversity. In the

PHOTO 7.1 *Touch* launched the careers of many UK black music artists between 1990 and 2006.

case of magazines that have struggled to reach out to larger multicultural audiences, Noughties black music monthly *Touch* magazine (see the case study below) provides a telling story of the advertising industry's endorsement for black music artists, at the expense of its exclusion to other advertisers without the weight of a 'white' champion brand such as *Time Out* (its publisher the late Tony Elliott being a supporter of *Touch* and its contribution to London's black music heritage and culture).

A TOUCH OF PREJUDICE

Before becoming a magazine academic, Simon Das was a music journalist and the penultimate managing editor of Touch from 2002 to 2006, before its closure in 2008.

I took over at the helm of *Touch* during the summer of 2002, just at the cusp of the digital era. Having already worked in digital media during the first wave Dot Com boom at a multimedia lifestyle portal, I was well aware of the power and potential of the cultural industries at that moment in time. *Touch* was an exciting prospect to work for – by 2002, it was already one of the most established black music 'brands' in the UK, alongside magazines such as *Echoes* (formerly *Black Echoes*), *Hip Hop Connection*, *Blues & Soul*, and to an extent, jazz periodical *Straight no Chaser*.

In the years preceding this, I had freelanced for a number of magazines (including *Touch*), and I was aware that its covers had launched the careers of black music artists who would go-on to enjoy mainstream appeal in the UK and elsewhere. A few examples of cover stars before the mainstream press adopted them included everyone from Alesha Dixon (as Mis-Teeq), Talvin Singh, Dizzee Rascal (his first ever magazine cover), Prince Naseem and even stage and screen actress Thandie Newton. However, regardless of its following and brand 'awareness', in the early Noughties, *Touch* was no *Mixmag* (EMAP's giant dance music monthly*)*, no *Muzik* magazine (launched by nightclub superbrand Ministry of Sound) and certainly no match to the fashion and lifestyle icons of *i-D* magazine or *Dazed & Confused* when it came to one crucial publishing area: advertising and sponsorship revenues. When it came to the media sales market, *Touch* was not so much in the slow lane, as marginalised in a side road in a horse and cart marked 'ethnic minority media'.

I knew what I was taking on within a short time of getting the job. Being given the reins as a managing editor to a nationally and even internationally known magazine (a magazine that was brought to the fore by the best-known Kiss FM DJs such as Trevor Nelson) it was not the start most would expect. On my first day, I had no team, no computer, no archive of images and no salesperson (he'd just walked out). I was shown a shabby office shared with *Non League Football* and a reprographics firm on the tenth floor of a tower block in north London, before being walked through a tiny editorial budget by a white middle-aged, middle-class man who used to print the magazine. There were no journalists, no people from the black music 'scene', no PR people on the phone and no-one from its near 15-year past. You see, *Touch* had already, albeit quietly, 'gone under' – and had been bought by its repro-graphics supplier-turned-publisher, the founding publishers having failed in their attempts at expanding the brand in the UK and then ultimately going broke through costly international expansion (mainly in Holland).

Despite the interest in the magazine in the UK and abroad, and having consistently sold more copies that many other independents, nothing could save *Touch* version 1 from the lack of advertising revenue – as they relied almost entirely on the revenues made from a once a year edition in conjunc-tion with *Time Out* (who partly owned *i-D* at the time) for the Notting Hill Carnival. In the mid-1990s, *Time Out* was purchased regularly by around a quarter of a million Londoners, and it was only during this once a year issue that major brands would advertise products such as Red Stripe beer, Cockspur rum, clothing and sportswear brands related to a 'black' audience. For the other 11 months of the year. *Touch* only received advertising interest from the recorded music industry – keen to launch its black and 'urban music' artists from a street or ground-up way, whether a rapper or by the Millennium, even artists like Amy Winehouse.

It was my job to capitalise on this, and also to help court a new advertising base – now *Touch* had been purchased by a small print and reprographics firm with no experience in this area. It was a job that required bringing back the community around it, the buzz, and at the same time, to turn out a quality 88-page colour glossy magazine every month that at least 30,000 readers demanded. It had been off the shelves for a little while, and the clock was ticking. I would help make this work with the aid of the previous commercial director, Joe Pidgeon, who was kept-on as a consultant – a man who knew the black music scene, the clubs, the brands. Having worked with *Touch* since its second year in existence (when it was little more than a Brixton-based fanzine called *Free*), he was a man who wasn't afraid to ask the media planners (the people who spend advertisers' money for them) why *Touch* wasn't better than the *Face* or *i-D* for an advertiser's return on investment.

When asked about this, Joe Pidgeon recently explained:

> To stand a chance of competing with The Face and Sky *magazine, it was a real struggle, as when it came to the agencies – I encountered a lot of racism. The only reason that I was successful at the time was probably because I wasn't of colour. When I walked into the agencies I wasn't a threat to this public school world. They'd never come across people of colour. I was successful because I wasn't afraid to go in and say: "Are you racist? Are you not advertising with Touch because you think it's black?" I educated them*

that you didn't have to be black to like black music – you just had to be
open-minded. For ten years I did that.

Personal interview, 2019

In the end, the relaunched *Touch* went on to receive a number of awards
and accolades, and started to court some of the brand spending from a
changing media planning world – a tight-knit Soho-based sector of media
planners and marketing managers. As *Touch's* covers began looking more and
more like the diverse UK Top 40 music charts (unlike the separation in the US
with a separate Billboard R&B chart), so did the faces of the brand managers
such as *Touch's* best clients – Nike and Adidas. However, while sports brands
might have understood the power of what Paul Mackenzie (the next editor
of *Touch* after myself) described in *The Guardian* (4 November 2006) as the
power of "the black Pound", it never translated into the mainstream advertising revenues. These much needed revenues from lifestyle brands or high-
end consumer products such as cars or package holidays might have provided
a buttress against what was ultimately more toxic to *Touch* than marginalisation with the industrial sales market: the rise of the internet and the demise of
traditional music journalism with it.

The story of *Touch* ends, therefore, like many other music magazines –
failing in its attempt to become a digital-first brand, only more depressingly
during a period where black and urban music became the mainstay of the UK
music charts. This may itself not seem like a problem of diversity, race or even
racism – however, when you consider the longevity in the publishing sector
of other more marginal music magazine genre magazines such as *Mixmag,*
Kerrang!, or the almost exclusively 'indie' rock music *New Musical Express*
(NME), it amazes me that during *Touch's* 20 years of strong black music leadership, it was never invested-in, bought and sold or even copied by a major
publishing company. Operating in a market much wider than any one community, the financial or even political independence that might be argued as
a reason for independence in a black publication such as newspaper *The Voice,*
cannot be levelled at *Touch* – a magazine that often pre-empted the 'what's
next' youth music and fashion movements from soul, techno, hip-hop, drum
n bass and contemporary pop R&B.

By 2010's *NME* relaunch via considerable investment by IPC (now TI Media),
Touch was a brand with no digital footprint and little investment, unlike its
sister brand *Kiss FM* (which became part of Bauer Media's EMAP era radio
drive) – featuring the DJs who themselves started *Touch*. As people who in the
1990s set about reinventing pop music culture itself as racially diverse and
inclusive, it seemed that only radio broadcasters, and not publishers, seemed
to understand the cultural and commercial value of black music media. By this
estimation, one can only conclude that diverse faces on pop magazine covers

were, amazingly, too much of a hard sell for mainstream publishers only a decade ago.

Today, with the *NME* long gone from the newsstands, and still reeling from its freesheet give-away failure, and digital-only soft relaunch, it seems poignant that founding *Touch* magazine columnist and club DJ, Trevor Nelson, is today the host of a daily classic black music show on BBC Radio 2. 30 years on from his *Kiss FM* and *Touch* days, what could be more mainstream in entertainment than being the soul generation's evening equivalent of Housewives' Choice?

PHOTO 7.2 BBC Radio 2's Trevor Nelson was one of the Kiss FM DJs who helped to promote *Touch* in the mid-1990s.

Ethnic media: an emergent phenomenon

While *Touch* may have failed in the end, other attempts to represent black culture through magazines had succeeded. In the USA, the African-American magazine *Ebony* was a particularly important trailblazing publication because of its deliberate attempt to represent black successes which were otherwise ignored by the media. *Ebony* addressed the emergent black middle class, following the post-war Great Migration from the southern to the northern States of the USA. Publisher John H. Johnson was himself part of this migration, moving from Arkansas to Chicago. Realising that there was "no consistent coverage of black Americans in northern newspapers and magazines" (Bloyd–Peskin and Whitaker, 2020, p. 148), in 1942 Johnson had set up *Negro Digest*, which was based on *Readers Digest*; then in 1945 he launched *Ebony*, which was modelled on the lifestyle feature magazine *Life*. *Ebony* provided this 'consistent coverage' about black success in the bourgeois professions (law, medicine, accountancy, church leadership) as well as in sports and entertainment. Early success for *Ebony* led to the launch of another Johnson publication, the weekly news magazine *Jet*, in 1951. In the early 1950s, Johnson made huge efforts to get mainstream advertisers for his suite of titles; eventually the mainly white-owned corporates produced advertising tailored specifically for the magazines' readers (Bloyd-Peskin and Whitaker, 2020, p. 149). Indeed, the success of the Johnson magazines meant that advertisers – however powerful – had to respond to specific demands made by the publisher. For example, adverts for hair straighteners or skin bleachers disappeared from the magazines after the civil rights campaigns of the 1960s – which all the Johnson magazines supported (Bloyd-Peskin and Whitaker, 2020, p. 149).

Ebony, which was bought by the Clear View group in 2016, remains a historic example of 'ethnic media' produced by and for people of colour, and its story has been successfully copied elsewhere. The UK equivalent is arguably *Pride*, a black British women's fashion magazine, which was set up in 1991 and is published by the largest black-owned media company in the UK. The magazine says of itself that

> Pride has fed the spirit of the woman of colour for the best part of three decades, offering information that is important to her, such as career, health, hair and beauty, and advice on issues ranging from dealing with cultural racism to updates on the latest braid sprays – issues that are not found in any other lifestyle title.
>
> *Pride, 2020*

Pride was by no means alone. In 2002–6, an EU-funded research study examined the growing presence across Europe of media produced by and for members of ethnic minorities within nation states. As the project's researchers reported, despite the enormous growth of academic research in media studies in the preceding 20 years, "Minority ethnic and diasporic media, which have … developed to an unprecedented extent within this context, are still at the periphery of such research." Yet, they insisted, "minority media in their production, consumption and in the consequences of their existence are of growing importance for communication, identity and participation in local, national and transnational communities" (LSE, 2006). As part of their research across both broadcast media and publications, they identified significant numbers of newspapers and magazines serving ethnic minorities within nation states: for example they found 106 of these in the UK; 72 in Germany; 54 in Austria; and 21 in the Irish Republic (LSE, 2006).

Among the recent success stories of this rapidly growing genre is the UK magazine *gal-dem,* which was founded in 2015 as a print annual and website specifically made by and aimed at its key demographic of women and non-binary people of colour aged 18–34. Though the representation of black faces was increasing throughout the UK media – for example in September 2018, black women featured on the covers of seven British mainstream women's magazines (Egbeyemi, 2020, p. 397) – like John H. Johnson in the USA of the 1940s, *gal-dem's* founder–publisher

Liv Little was aware that this did not reflect ownership or production. In the words of Tobi Oredein, who runs the online UK magazine *Black Ballad*, "[magazines] think that if they do a beauty story with one or two token black and brown people, or have a freelancer every other month that's writing around race, that's serving people. But people want genuine inclusion" (Egbeyemi, 2020, p. 398). Answering this plea, *gal-dem* was successful enough for the team to edit an issue of the *Guardian Weekend* magazine in August 2018.

DOING IT FOR OURSELVES

By Sharan Dhaliwal – The Founder and Editor-in-Chief of Burnt Roti

PHOTO 7.3 A 2018 cover from independent title *Burnt Roti*.

In 2016, when I conceived the idea behind *Burnt Roti*, it came out of frustration and selfishness. There was little in terms of representation for the South

Asian reader, especially those who weren't interested in conservative politics, wedding dresses or Bollywood.

Not long before creating *Burnt Roti*, I had been asked to talk about my nose job for *Cosmopolitan* magazine; a journalist was covering the subject of ethnic plastic surgery (Wilder, 2016). I remember picking up the printed issue from the shelves of WH Smith and noticed how it was adorned with mostly white models. I wondered what it would be like to have a whole magazine dedicated to stories like mine.

It's a harsh reality that for many womxn of colour, products aren't created for our consumption, whether it be in publishing, beauty or art. Many womxn and specifically black womxn are placed on the forefront of marketing campaigns to give the illusion of inclusion, yet behind the scenes, most strings are pulled by elite cis white men.

When our stories are told, they are hiding inside magazines and restricted to just a handful of manageable pages. On national holidays, a whole section is dedicated to celebrating us. And when that's over, we're hidden again. This is also true with LGBTQ+ issues, as we see an outpouring of content during Pride month and then silence the rest of the year.

When our accomplishments are discussed in publishing, through interviews, journalism or reporting, they are typed by white hands, with little understanding of our focus and energy. I'm not alluding to the suggestion that only black people should talk about black people, but when an industry (when I say 'an industry', I mean 'every industry') benefits from the hard work of people of colour, then publishing should pay those very people to talk about us.

There should be an attempt to address the imbalance, and to recognise the contradiction in representation. The Publishers Association is largely made up of membership from book and journal publishers and they publish a useful diversity report on an annual basis. The numbers published for 2019 show 55 per cent of senior leadership is held by women, 13 per cent identify as BAME, 10.3 per cent identify as LGB+, 0.6 per cent transgender and 7 per cent identify as having a disability or impairment (Publishers Association, 2019). Whilst noting that this survey reflects book publishing, is there any reason to believe that the metrics for magazine houses will be significantly different?

So this isn't just about telling our stories, it's about letting us tell our stories; letting us become writers, photographers, editors, art directors. The financial reparations we deserve is a big conversation here, because money is difficult to talk about and interestingly, a lot of immigrant communities have the illusion that as long as our work output is excellent, we don't say how much we get in return from it. But when we do, we show it off. Many South Asian communities can attest to this aesthetic wealth positioning. Unless you have it, hide from the conversation.

Many of us have transferred this on to our professional life and are convinced that merely being part of the conversation is enough remuneration.

So, the question is: "how do we get beneficial representation that we can profit from, both financially and emotionally?"

The answer so far has been: "create it yourself."

The rise of independent magazines created by womxn of colour, has been a recent phenomenon, recognised by many institutes and news outlets. Somerset House put on a summer-long exhibition in 2018 called Print! Tearing It Up, which drew its focus to radical publishing. Although historically many publications were created by men (especially in music), a remarkable trans- formation was recognised.

The Guardian ran a story in 2017 called "Zine queens: how women's magazines found new life via indie publishing" and although there is a striking erasure of people of colour in many of these instances, the change in publishing still cannot go unnoticed (Jamieson, 2017).

While we have a rise in womxn-led publishing, the largest percentage of those who are making a stamp in the industry, tend to be cis white women. The emphasis is on the comfortable; whiteness is believed to be the strongest marketing force, when held by either cishet men or women.

This all sounds very defeatist, but when you look at the black, Asian and queer womxn focused publications that have made a difference, you begin to feel hope again. *gal-dem* magazine has been one of *Burnt Roti*'s biggest inspirations. We've watched them sell-out their issues, work with amazing names, guest edit on *The Guardian's* weekend issue and publish books.

They are the pinnacle of hard-working black queer womxn and non-binary people, giving a space to themselves and others for representation. But as many will admit, creating spaces ourselves comes with a barrage of cons. Two of the biggest ones are funding and fatigue.

There's a heavy burden in becoming one of the few faces of representation for whichever community you stand with causes a kind of fatigue that you've never had to face before. It's not just the pressure of creating content, it's the pressure to represent a whole community as a singular divisive person. A North Indian cannot understand the injustice faced by South Indians because of the privilege North Indians hold. So, you need to learn, study, speak to others and become uncomfortable.

And saying "one of the few faces of representation" isn't a gloat – there truly is such little representation of South Asian queer people in publishing, that you become held at high esteem for your work.

The fatigue comes hand in hand with funding, because most independent publishers I know have had to work full time to fund their projects. I worked 9am until 6pm Monday to Friday and then every evening and weekend would be filled with work on my magazine. There was little time for rest and when rest was allowed, the guilt of not working set in.

The possibilities of funding are small, the UK government's traditional support for the arts is disappointing so there is no real surprise there. When I visited Toronto to do a talk on my magazine at Magazines Canada Conference 2019, I was struck by the support that the arts sector received. A lot of the work I discovered were of indigenous people, creating spaces for their stories – very much like what I was doing with *Burnt Roti*. (It is reassuring, however, to see the fiscal purse open for the arts in the UK to help them survive lockdown.)

When you look for funding, you're faced with antiquated forms, which seem to be written in Olde Ye English and it's the forms with the penchant for drama I promise, it's not me. A lot of the requirements to tick their boxes don't fall as neatly in communities that haven't been spotlighted by the media. Asian communities that aren't going to talk about music, dance or food are not sellable to white audiences, so our efforts are quickly dismissed.

Unless it makes someone look good to fund you, they will probably not do it. And South Asians just aren't sexy enough for them.

Working full time, freelance, balancing many projects, unable to hire a team due to no finances – leads to the entirety of cons involved with running your own magazine and until the publishing industry is inclusive of creators of colour in their business and financial models, we won't see significant change in this.

So, starting your own magazine in terms of radical publishing has its imbalance pros and cons with nuance on individual identity and marketing criteria. Nonetheless, the community that is represented become driven. Since the start of *Burnt Roti*, there has been a significant rise in South Asian magazines and people carving their own spaces, no matter their identity.

When there is a significant rise in those who are most disenfranchised, those in power have no choice but to pay attention.

Race and transnational identity

Adding more nuance to the meaning of 'race', culture and backgrounds, the phenomena of transnational ethnicities are clearly also part of magazine publishing's diversity challenge. *Burnt Roti*, with its concerns for politics both in India and Britain, is a pointer to a significant shift in the experience of identity, and the ways in which it is represented by magazines. As Chapter 6 argues, the last 50 years have seen several intertwined shifts in the ways in which immigration and emigration are experienced. The relative ease of travel, and the growth of new communications technologies, have made it easy for people to maintain physical as well as emotional contact with their country and culture of origin. The resulting 'transnational' identities imply that we need to think very carefully about the concept 'diaspora' and what is often called 'diasporic identity'.

The word 'diaspora' was first used in relation to the historic experience of displacement which has happened to Jewish people, and it has often been used since in such examples as the African or Irish diasporas, which are associated with slavery, famine, violent or forced displacement and colonialism. It has sometimes been used more broadly to describe any significant movement of peoples. The experience of emigration (whether forceful or voluntary) used to mean that people or their immediate ancestors had left the homeland for good. Partly because they were not fully accepted by the host society, they maintained an imaginative link with their ancestral homeland, thus preserving a communal sense which emphasised their difference from the hosts. This used to mean a collectively imagined but mythical homeland, often accompanied with an acknowledged wish to 'return', which in most cases was for political or economic reasons, a fantasy; feeling like this about an impossible 'home' was part of a diasporic identity. However, transnationals today are in touch *not* with a mythologised homeland of shared stories, fading photographs and blurred memories, but the real thing. They visit friends and relatives in the homeland regularly, and they are often politically engaged with both host and homeland states, as is the case with *Burnt Roti*. Diaspora, in its traditional meaning, is perhaps no longer quite the term to describe this new status: people no longer fully 'leave' anywhere, and their links with the homeland are not imaginary but real.

Diversity 'drivers' in the creative industries

Explained as a direct result of society living with and to a certain extent 'understanding' immigration, internationalisation and the global movement of people (see Chapter 6), there now exists huge racial diversity in the UK's population, with BAME as a group comprising of 16 per cent of England and Wales by the 2011 census (ONS 2018). Within most large cities, this figure is at least twice as large – presenting the statistical truth of ethnic 'majorities' and not minorities across entire postcodes of major cities. 'Ethnic media' such as *gal-dem* and *Burnt Roti* are one of the products of this shift. But the presence of ethnic media should not blind us to the need for more mainstream media to represent their populations more completely.

This is not to say there has been no improvement in diversity in society or progress against racism – it's important to note that within the UK in the last two decades, there has been positive change in this area. When two decades ago, the media and political scientists might have talked about the more distanced problem of 'race relations' – today this term seems utterly outdated, the debate having moved-on to a widely held belief in racial 'equality'. With it, the agenda of diversity exists on the mainstream agendas of all spheres of daily life. But while this change seems relatively seismic and even radical (at the time of the writing the BLM movement sparked by the death of George Floyd in the USA has led to civic statues of figures associated with the historical slave trade removed by protesters), things have moved very slowly in specific areas within the British workplace in recent years. When professions such as journalism (across all mediums) have been surveyed, the representation in employment of black and ethnic minority workers is woeful.

While a few sectors, such as the UK's NHS (National Health Service) might represent a high percentage of BAME staff throughout the echelons (i.e. from porter to professor), the picture is not replicated when it comes to private sector industries – and especially within the wider media and cultural industries, which have been areas of huge new economic growth during the last two decades. According to the model of inner city digital and tech growth first 'predicted' by Richard Florida (2004), British BAME communities might be represented in many fields and areas of everyday life, but in fact they seem to be stubbornly excluded from Florida's 'creative class'. In a recent report by Spilsbury on 'Journalists at Work', diversity in overall employment in journalism, for example was found to be so poor that the figure cited of 90 per cent of all journalists being white is confessed as being "less positive than even this would suggest" (Spilsbury, 2018, p. 7), given media concentration in cities such as London. To be '90 per cent white' as a profession, when 55 per cent of the entire London population in the census data reported being non-'White British' (ONS 2018) indicates industry bias on a significant scale.

Although the seemingly sincere diversity 'drives' have attempted to address this issue, critical theorist of the media and creative industries Anamik Saha attributes the underlying problem with diversity drives as a form of unspoken tokenism, one driven according to him, by the neoliberal agenda that has

> stress[ed] the benefits of diversity for competition and economic growth, rather than for political, let alone ethical or moral, reasons. While this rationale, with its clear appeal to corporate (and public) interests, has seen the issue of diversity placed high on the policy agendas across the media, diversity initiatives have arguably failed, in that film studios, broadcasters, major record labels and publishing houses remain overwhelmingly white.
>
> *Saha, 2018, p. 87*

Diversity in magazine publishing today

In 2017, two accounts of this lack of diversity in the UK workplace called for immediate action. Baroness Ruby McGregor-Smith (2017) reported on BAME people in the workplace in general, while Mark Spilsbury (2017) wrote about the lack of diversity both in journalism, and journalism training. Spilsbury concluded that

> those working as journalists six months after graduation are, when compared with the rest of the student body, more likely to be white, more likely to have attended a private school, more likely to be from higher socio-economic backgrounds and more likely not to be from low HE participation neighbourhoods. When compared with the general population, the lack of diversity is more stark, since the HE student population already under-represents people from poorer backgrounds, state schools and low participation neighbourhoods.
>
> *Spilsbury, 2017, p. 22; compare Holmes, 2020, p. 66*

This lack of diversity was equally expressed in the senior staffing of magazine publishers. In early 2021, the global boards of directors of the five leading magazine

publishers in the UK (Bauer, Future, Burda, Hearst and Condé Nast) listed 49 individuals. Company website profiles and their publicly available social media accounts
indicates that of these 49, 30 were white men, and 13 white women; there were 4
BAME men and 2 BAME women. At the level below this, the UK-based executive
leadership teams included 14 white men, 14 white women, 1 BAME man and 2
BAME women. So at the senior management level, ethnic diversity would appear
to be tokenist at best.

Meanwhile, in mid-2020, *Vogue USA* editor Anna Wintour publicly apologised
for the lack of diversity in her production staff (Cohen 2020), and her most
prominent black colleague, Leon Talley, confirmed that an apology was called
for (Flanagan 2020). This is not to deny that some significant changes have been
made. In one of the most important of these, as we have seen Condé Nast UK
deliberately changed a successful product in order to address these issues, through
the appointment of Edward Enninful as editor of British *Vogue* in 2017. Before
Enninful's appointment *Vogue UK*, which had been edited for a quarter of a century
by Alexandra Shulman, featured content which reflected both its staffing and readership. While Shulman was a generalist (who had previously edited men's magazine
GQ), and her *Vogue* was not *just* a fashion magazine, it was principally focused on
the high fashion industry, which serves the consumer desires of relatively wealthy
white middle-class women – such as *Vogue's* employees (Shulman, 2017 is an
interesting and honest account of this set of relationships). This virtuous circle,
which was financially successful, was repeated endlessly to an extent which perhaps
inhibited commitment to innovation both in diversity of representation, and in the
creative use of new technology to address potential new cohorts of readers in the
age of Instagram influencers.

THE RE-LAUNCHED *FACE* AND ITS DIVERSITY DRIVE

By Dan Flower – Managing Director, The Face

From Day 1, we built the team at *The Face* to represent the best of contemporary culture and that means diversity is a fundamental principle of how we
operate. We put together a very tight multidisciplinary team of permanent staff
working incredibly closely with a retained creative council comprising some of
the most influential creatives across the worlds of fashion, music and art.

Currently, BAME employees account for just over 30 per cent of that core
team and 50 per cent of our senior management team. We have the first gay
editor of *The Face*, and 50 per cent of our leadership team are women. In addition, we are constantly vigilant about ensuring the writers, photographers and
directors we commission represent the diverse community we aim to serve.
Moments like the Issue 2 cover with Naira Marley shot by Bolade Banjo are
really important to us because it's vital that black excellence is represented in
front of, and behind, the camera.

In changing the staffing, and immediately relaunching Vogue's own Instagram account, Edward Enninful and his colleagues have necessarily also changed the content of *Vogue*, which as well as representing a more diverse range of faces in fashion shoots, is now more inclusive across a wider range of subject matter, reaching out to new age and ethnic groups, and highlighting current political and social topics. For example, the September 2020 issue (which is normally the best-selling issue of the year, thanks to the fashion calendar), was made by an all-black production team, was headlined *Activism Now: the Faces of Hope*, and featured political activists and writers on the cover and inside, with a lead article on the consequences of the BLM movement by the journalist Afua Hirsch. Enninful's editorial commentary in this issue concludes that "When all is said and done, it's clear that 2020 will be remembered as a tough year, but also as a moment of necessary change" (Enninful, 2020).

However, elsewhere in the Condé Nast publishing empire the pace of 'necessary change' seemed somewhat slower. In December 2018, the UK edition of Condé Nast's *GQ* magazine ran a very anti-stereotypical front cover image and inside feature interview with a well-known, popular and successful black man, the British boxer Anthony Joshua, and his son Joseph. The inside feature, echoing the cover image, focused not on Joshua's profession, or his celebrity, but on his thoughts as a parent in contemporary Britain (Parsons, 2018). This was an important issue of *GQ*, which celebrated 30 years of the magazine in the UK, and which was dedicated to the discussion of the state of contemporary masculinity; indeed, this was the very first issue of this long-running magazine which had featured father and son together.

But this positive representation was not reflected behind the scenes. The print magazine's masthead for the issue identified, as usual, an editorial team in various roles from editor, online editor and so on down to junior design editor (these are all roles which would normally be full-time, salaried and pensionable employment rather than the casual 'freelance' status of most of the contributing writers and photographers). An examination of public profiles and social media accounts indicated that this list of permanent employees included just 2 BAME men, alongside 25 white men and 8 white women.

Eighteen months after this anniversary issue *GQ* ran a powerfully angry story by Ciaran Thapar, about the necessity for the BLM movement and its accompanying mini Cultural Revolution (Thapar, 2020). At this time, the magazine's website listed 21 white men, 9 white women, 1 BAME man and 1 BAME woman among its permanent officials. However, much *GQ* might claim enthusiastic commitment to the principles of decolonisation and diversity, its employment structures would seem to tell a different story.

It would be naively simplistic to conclude from this that the editorial team at *GQ* were hypocrites, or to call for the wholesale replacement of magazine staff or boards of directors. But these snapshots of data do appear to indicate a structural problem, one which echoes Wintour's apology about the staffing of *Vogue USA*, as well as the conclusions and recommendations made in the Spilsbury report on *Diversity in*

Journalism (Spilsbury, 2017). *GQ* is not alone in producing positive images of, and articles about, an increasingly diverse population, while those in charge of producing the representations were largely products of the interlocked class, family and education systems through which power has been held and reproduced in the UK since the nineteenth century. Most power is held by people who have attended one of a few private schools and either Oxford or Cambridge universities. A witty and interesting account of the ways in which this power structure works, and reproduces itself, is *The Glossy Years*, in which Nicholas Coleridge reflects on his distinguished career as director of CondéNast Britain and CondéNast International (Coleridge, 2019). Coleridge was educated at the exclusive British private school Eton College, and attended Cambridge University (two of the last three UK Prime Ministers had been at Eton; as with four of the last five Prime Ministers, they also went to Oxford University). Two of Coleridge's godchildren are supermodels Cara Delevingne and Edie Campbell.

Given the powerful reach of these educational and family structures, it is perhaps unsurprising that the changes at *Vogue* have been the exception, but not the rule. On the whole, while magazine publishing has made big strides towards gender equality, this has not been replicated by significant movement in the direction of ethnic or cultural diversity. It is no wonder, then, that the editors of innovative magazines such as *gal-dem* and *Burnt Roti* feel they have to go it alone in representing the rapidly changing populations of the early twenty-first century, while the staff at *The Face* report a sense of missionary zeal in HR matters as well as in contributions.

For the wider industry's moral and financial future standing, it's high time for twenty-first century magazine publishers to turn the page, and to write a new chapter for its digitally mediated diverse future audiences: they might depend on them. Today, new moral and economic arguments for structural (and less tokenistic) interventions are becoming clearer to publishers. As pointed out by the CEO of FIPP (the International Federation of Periodical Publishers):

> Diversity is no longer an option. No longer in some CSR [corporate social responsibility] plan. It has to be embedded into every aspect of companies because that is what workers expect. With all the changes happening in the world, if you're not a diverse company, you're not in a position to find new ways of working and uncover a new revenue stream you hadn't thought of.
>
> *Hewes, 2020*

References

BBC (2020), 'Edward Enninful: British Vogue editor 'racially profiled' at work', *BBC News*, 16 July. Available at www.bbc.co.uk/news/uk-53425148 (accessed 20.07.2020)

Bloyd-Peskin, S. and Whitaker, C. (2020), 'On Johnson's shoulders: the lessons and legacy of *Ebony* magazine', in Miglena Sternadori and Tim Holmes, eds., *The Handbook of Magazine Studies*, Hoboken, NJ: John Wiley, pp. 146–153

Cohen, S. (2020), 'Vogue's Anna Wintour Admits "Hurtful" Mistakes, But Is Her Apology On Race More Than Just Fashionable?', available at www.forbes.com/sites/sethcohen/2020/06/10/vouges-anna-wintour-admits-hurtful-mistakes/ (accessed 10.08.2020)

Coleridge, N. (2019), *The Glossy Years. Magazines, Museums and Selective Memories,* London: Fig Tree

Egbemyi, E. (2020), 'Case study: how *gal-dem* magazine succeeded where mainstream magazines failed', in Miglena Sternadori and Tim Holmes, eds., *The Handbook of Magazine Studies,* Hoboken, NJ: John Wiley, pp. 393–399'

Enninful, E. (2020), 'Editor's Letter September 2020', available at www.vogue.co.uk/news/article/september-2020-issue-editors-letter (accessed 05.08.2020)

Flanagan, H. (2020), "Andre Leon Talley critiques Anna Wintour Apology to Vogue Staffers: Name what Your Mistakes Were', available at https://people.com/style/andre-leon-talley-critiques-anna-wintour-apology-to-vogue-staffers/ (accessed 10.08.2020)

Florida, R. (2004), *The Rise of the Creative Class... And How It's Transforming Work, Leisure, Community and Everyday Life,* New York: Basic Books.

Gooch, Cheryl Renee (2018), 'Gender, Race and Ethnicity: Magazines and the Question of Self-Identity', in Abrahamson, David and Prior-Miller, Marcia, *The Routledge Handbook of Magazine Research: the Future of the Magazine Form.* 2nd edition, New York: Routledge, pp. 211–223.

Holmes, T. (2020), 'Case study: where industry and academia meet', in Sternadori, M. and Holmes, T. (eds.), *The Handbook of Magazine Studies,* Hoboken, NJ: John Wiley, pp. 65–74

Hewes, J. (2020), FIPP *Insider Podcast Season 1.* [podcast] March 2020. Available at www.fipp.com/news/features/fipp-launches-insider-podcast (accessed 21.03.2020)

Jamieson, R. (2017), 'Zine queens: how women's magazines found new life via independent publishing', available at: www.theguardian.com (accessed 27.08. 2020).

Lee, M. (2018), Media Voices podcast. Available at https://whatsnewinpublishing.com/podcast-allure-editor-in-chief-on-diversity-and-how-it-became-magazine-of-the-year/ (accessed 20.07.2020)

Lind, R. (2013), *Race/Gender/Class/Media 3.0: Considering Diversity Across Content, Audiences and Production.* New York: Pearson

LSE (2006), 'Introduction' to 'Diasporic Minorities and Their Media in the EU: A Mapping', www.lse.ac.uk/media@lse/research/EMTEL/minorities/reports.html (accessed 15.07.2020)

McGregor-Smith, Baroness Ruby (2017), *Race in the workplace. The McGregor-Smith Review,* available at https://assets.publishing.service.gov.uk/government/uploads/system/uploads/attachment_data/file/594336/race-in-workplace-mcgregor-smith-review.pdf (accessed 05.08.2020).

Nguyen, T. H. (2013), 'AudreyMagazine.com portrayals of Asian American women online by Asian American women', in Lind, R. *Race/Gender/Class/Media 3.0 Considering Diversity Across Content, Audiences and Production.* New York: Pearson, pp. 269–273

Office for National Statistics (2018), *Population of England and Wales.* Available at www.ethnicity-facts-figures.service.gov.uk/uk-population-by-ethnicity/national-and-regional-populations/population-of-england-and-wales/latest#full-page-history (accessed 15.07. 2020)

Parsons, Tony (2018), 'When GQ met AJ and JJ', *GQ* December 2018, pp. 206–221.

Pride (2020), www.pridemagazine.com/about-us/ (accessed 05.08.2020)

Publishers Association (2019), Diversity and Inclusion Report 2019, London: Publishers' Association

Saha, A. (2018), *Race and the Cultural Industries*, London: Polity

Shulman, A. (2017), *Inside Vogue: My Diary of Vogue's 100th Year,* London: Penguin

Sengupta, R. (2006), 'Reading representations of Black, East Asian and White women in magazines for adolescent girls', *Sex Roles,* vol. 54 no. 11, pp. 799–808

Spilsbury, M. (2017), *Diversity in Journalism,* London: National Council for the Training of Journalists. Available at www.nctj.com/downloadlibrary/DIVERSITY%20 JOURNALISM%204WEB.pdf (accessed 10.08.2020)

Spilsbury, M. (2018), *Journalists at Work*. London: National Council for the Training of Journalists. Available at www.nctj.com/downloadlibrary/JaW%20Report%202018.pdf. (accessed 10.05.2020)

Thapar, C. (2020), 'Fear, fury and a failed state: "Black people are hurt and killed by police without repercussions in the UK Too"', www.gq-magazine.co.uk/politics/article/ george-floyd-uk-racism (accessed 17.07.2020)

Wilder, R. (2016), 'Why we need to talk about ethnic plastic surgery', Available at: www. cosmopolitan.com (accessed 27.07.2020)

8

INDEPENDENT THINKING

David Stam

Is T-Post an online T-shirt fashion merchant or a magazine? The company website claims it is "the world's first wearable magazine, or a story driven clothing brand, whichever you prefer". Each month up to 2000 subscribers worldwide receive a limited edition shirt for Euro 35. Neatly packaged in a creative outer sleeve, the T-shirt has a stunning front design and a related story or interview printed inside the garment itself. Shirts are issue numbered. 151 has content about the power of social media and 152 about fake news. Founded in 2004, T-Post is now a well-established and respected brand and has played its part in redefining what a magazine is in the early years of the twenty-first century. Indeed, its founder, Peter Lundgren, says that the business was created after a heated discussion about "whether or not the classic magazine could be given a new life if combined with something completely different" (T-Post, 2020). Whilst pushing the boundaries of the print medium the company is firmly seen as a magazine by the prestigious *Wall Street Journal* who call T-Post "the magazine we wear" (Losowsky, 2009).

This chapter will look at independent magazines, known throughout as indies, and the role that they play through the creative use of storytelling and innovative design in ensuring that publishing remains relevant to changing technological and sociocultural trends. The author will explore what is meant by an independent magazine, where their origins lie and the factors which have allowed the sector to flourish. As contributors have noted in other chapters of this book, finding a sustainable business model is not easy for any publisher nowadays, but by looking at examples of successful commercial businesses, a route through the minefields of distribution and advertisement sales can be found.

What is an independent magazine?

The Editor or Publisher of an independent title will almost certainly be its founder, the guardian of the initial creative idea, vision and voice. He or she may have started their career in a mainstream publishing house before finding that these larger businesses could not keep them motivated and were a barrier to creativity and expression. Above all, there will be love and a passion for magazines in print and a strong desire to use the medium to explore their life's interest, commitment or view of the world. Start-up would doubtless have been tough as banks or financial institutions are unlikely to make loans to speculative media ventures, money may have been borrowed from family and friends and savings dipped into.

The publishing house is independent with no circulation or advertisement team already in place at launch to drive the commercials and no financial back office. In her excellent 2012 paper, Megan Le Masurier invites readers to envisage a publishing spectrum with the indies "occupying a zone of small-scale commercial publishing between DIY zines and mainstream niche consumer magazines" (Le Masurier, 2012, p. 384). Some may only last an issue or two whilst a very small handful may go on to reasonable commercial success, for example *Kinfolk* (as described below) or the UK title *The Gentlewoman*.

Independent publishers celebrate the printed form. Visit the magCulture store in London and you will enter a different world – a cornucopia of over 400 beautifully printed artefacts. Not confined to the rigidity of a traditional newsagent's shelves, publishers' experiment with different page sizes far beyond the normal A4. Paper stock will be superior and can vary from gloss to matt within the same issue, while designers will experiment with cover treatments that often require careful study with few concessions to impulse purchase. These high production standards coupled with short print runs obviously drive high prices; specialist independent magazine distributor Stack has few titles available on its website for less than £10, and many for considerably more. Writing in *The Guardian*, industry observer Mark Hooper contrasts the permanence of print to the immediacy of online, and likens the experience of reading indie magazines to books (Hooper, 2012).

What are independent magazines by way of content? Le Masurier tries to answer as follows – "The editorial focus of the indies tends to be a celebration of the under-represented manifestations of popular culture and creative work" (Le Masurier, 2012, p. 384). Retail websites suggest that the main topic clusters are art and design, photography, lifestyle including food and drink, fashion, female and male lifestyle, LGBT, slow journalism, travel and indies supporting ethnic groups. For a full spectrum, readers are advised to read Walter Loetscher's review, 'The 100 best magazines you have (probably) never heard of' (Loetscher, 2018). One factor that the independent market has in common with the mainstream is the purchasing importance of women. The magCulture website has 44 titles in that category, close to ten per cent of the total range (accessed 6 June 2020). Amongst the better known are *Frankie*, *Riposte* and *The Gentlewoman*. Editors and the contributors are key members of the communities which they serve and write and communicate with a knowledge and passion that only inside knowledge can bring. Indies are likely to market to their specialist or niche communities through social media, word of mouth and just being out there with effective PR. Readership is international, independent magazines travel well with the main centres of publication the creative metropolitan hubs of London, Amsterdam, Copenhagen, Berlin, Barcelona, Johannesburg and Sydney. A good example of this is Danish title *Kinfolk* – a quarterly lifestyle title distributed in 100 countries in 4 languages which celebrates home and work lifestyles with the emphasis on quality of life and time spent with family and friends. It also runs international events and has a gallery space in Copenhagen.

The size of the independent magazine market is difficult to quantify. Titles are not audited and do not rely on published readership research to sell advertisement space. Indeed, it is hard to estimate the number of independent titles there are in publication around the world but a figure of close to 3000 established titles is generally accepted as reliable. This century has seen a proliferation of titles and the chapter will shortly describe the factors which fostered this. But before that a look at the historical roots of the genre.

Underground to overground

Publishing alternative views to the mainstream press is as old as the eighteenth-century pamphleteers in the coffee houses described by Christine Stam in Chapter 2. The story is taken up here after the austerity and paper rationing of the Second World War and the 1950s with the alternative and counterculture of the 1960s. Radical magazines were called 'underground' with long dormant titles named *Ink*, *IT* and *Frendz*. One of the best known was *Private Eye*, launched in 1961 as a satirical, news-driven fortnightly and a title which remains highly successful to this day. Possibly, the most notorious was the underground magazine *Oz* with its editorial agenda of gay rights, anti-racism, profeminism and anti-Vietnam war. The editors made the headlines in an obscenity trial over an issue called '*Schoolkids Oz*' and were all handed jail terms. With a more than a hint of irony, the trial judge gave co-editor Felix Dennis what he considered to be a lenient sentence as he seemed 'very much less intelligent' than his colleagues. The convictions were quashed on appeal – and Felix went on to become one of the richest and most successful magazine entrepreneurs of modern times until his sad death in 2014.

In the 1970s, just as progressive rock gave way to punk, so the alternative underground press gave way to punk zines or fanzines. *Sniffin' Glue* edited by Mark Perry was one of the strongest sellers with a strong distribution network of sales at gigs and record shops. Stores were so keen to secure orders they would pay in advance. Production was basic, photocopied or duplicated pages stapled together. Danny Baker, a writer on the paper who went on to become a BBC broadcaster, reminisced to the *Guardian* newspaper in 2019:

> There would be thousands of copies of each page arranged in piles on a table. We'd come back from a night out… walk round the table all night, taking a

page from each pile. You'd get to the end, put a staple through them, then start again. In the morning, you'd have 10,000 *Sniffin' Glues*.

Wray, 2019

The punk zines of the 1970s were totally removed from the lavishly produced indie titles of today. However, they showed that magazines – and successful ones at that – could be produced by folk with little media knowledge or professional journalism training. A die had been cast.

As the 1980s dawned, punk music slid into commercialism and record sales gave way to the polished musical tones of the new romantics. The punk zine movement ended. Now, students of modern magazine history can start to draw direct lines from magazines of the 1980s to the indie movement of today. magCulture founder Jeremy Leslie highlights the importance of four titles (*The Face, Blitz, Tempo* and *i-D*). Leslie comments of the first three that "these independently published glossy magazines … were able to match or exceed the major publisher's magazines in terms of quality of content and production" (Leslie, 2013, p 7). But special mention

PHOTO 8.1 Robert Maxwell on the cover of *Private Eye*, November 1986.

is reserved for street fashion magazine *i-D*. At launch with just two colours and stapled, the magazine was deliberately low-tech, as such reflective of its editorial content but under its ex-Vogue founder Terry Jones, design boundaries soon became pushed. Leslie reveals that at a conference of indie publishers in 2009, *i-D* was the most cited as inspiration. He concludes:

> It marked the point at which it was no longer simply a case of the bigger, glossier and slicker the better. The entire history of magazine publishing was now a toolbox from which a single publisher/editor could pick and choose to create their publication.

Leslie, 2013, p. 7

Technology was just about to radically change not only the way magazines would be created but also who would be in charge of the process.

---

i-D: INDEPENDENCE WITH A KNOWING WINK

Mark Hooper was deputy editor at i-D from 2000 to 2005. Here, he reveals how founder Terry Jones ensured the magazine set a template for independent titles.

i-D was unique in that its founder, Terry Jones, reversed the tried-and-tested publishing career trajectory. Rather than starting with a stapled-together fanzine assembled in his kitchen and ending up being poached to work on a fashion glossy, Jones was working as art director at the glossiest of fashion magazines – *British Vogue* – when he decided to throw it all in to staple together his own fanzine instead.

In 1977, while working at *Vogue*, Jones commissioned the photographer Steve Johnston to document the nascent punk scene that was emerging in the streets of London. When Johnston's photos arrived – shot in what Jones christened as 'straight-up' style (head-to-toe portraits, captured in the street) – they were rejected by the editor, Beatrix Miller. It should be noted that Jones credited Miller as an 'amazing' editor who often encouraged him to break the rules – most notably when he picked a heavily cropped image by Willie Christie of a model's teeth sinking into a slab of green jelly as the February 1977 cover. Despite advice from the marketing department that 'green covers don't sell', Miller backed Jones' decision. It turned out to be one of the year's best-selling issues. However, when Miller decided that the punk story wasn't '*Vogue*' enough, Jones decided he was more excited by the current street fashion than the glossy version, and quit.

Eventually, in 1980, he launched his own magazine in order to capture the street spirit that so inspired him. Embracing the DIY punk ethos, he went back to basics. The first issues were assembled at his home with wife Tricia and a team of willing volunteers. The famous logo doubled as a trademark 'smiley' face if turned on its side – to this day Jones swears he invented the emoji.

That instinct – to take inspiration from the street rather than the catwalk, to apply an impish eye and a punk attitude to convention – was still evident two decades later, when I joined the *i-D* staff as deputy editor in 2000. Jones was a hands-on and ever-present owner, constantly driving us up the wall with his last-minute and seemingly arbitrary changes. And yet, we knew he was always right. He would always choose the image no-one else would; chop and crop words and text, suggest provocative themes and coverlines simply because he enjoyed rocking the boat. His motivation was always – why do it if you're not going to do it differently?

We learned to have an entire set of drawers filled with fashion stories, ready for when he would walk in the day before our print deadline and announce we had another 20 pages to fill. I distinctly remember the night when he and I concocted a ludicrous front section story about horses being the season's hottest fashion accessory – solely to justify running a beautiful image of a white horse across a double page spread. Of course, the next month, all the fashion magazines were rehashing our invented trend. On another occasion, for the March 2004 issue, he changed our coverline at the last moment to read, "Voted the world's favourite fashion magazine". When the editorial team questioned whether that was entirely legal, his response was pure Terry Jones: "Let's have a show of hands", he announced. "Who thinks we're the best?" After the unanimous response, he smirked and muttered, "We never said voted by *who*, did we?"

Today's independent editors often talk about how *i-D* has been an inspirational influence on them. I think this is down to a number of factors:

Timing: Having launched in 1980, *i-D*'s shelf-life spans much of modern youth culture, meaning most of today's editors grew up reading it, absorbing its content and visual language. In addition, it has employed a 'Who's Who' of creative talent – including Dylan Jones, Edward Enninful, Caryn Franklin, Judy Blame and countless others – all of whom have gone on to shape the media landscape in their own ways.

Attitude: *i-D* has always instilled that punk, DIY mindset – inclusive, positive, welcoming of creativity in all forms. Where many supposedly 'aspirational lifestyle' titles come across as cynical and excluding as well as exclusive, *i-D* has always sought to seek out new, inspiring talent – and always with a social conscience at its heart: lifestyles that people can genuinely aspire to.

Design: *i-D* has an unparalleled track record for commissioning the best new photographic talent around – from Mark LeBon, Wolfgang Tillmans and Nick Knight to Alasdair McLellan – and designing it brilliantly. Despite the magazine's early, highly influential graphic experimentation (often a case of necessity being the mother of invention, when available imagery was less than inspiring) – that often means understanding when less is more. Where appropriate, images have always been given breathing space, with plenty of pages and minimal design interference.

Budget: The fact that *i-D* was historically run on a shoestring meant that the staff always had to come up with innovative ways of making things happen – and making them look more professional than they really were: inspiration for any aspiring indie editor.

Expansion – favourable winds of change

In Chapter 1, Simon Das explains the importance of external factors in shaping innovation and industry make-up. Following this lead, what were and indeed remain the technological, structural and sociocultural factors which have given so many founders of indie titles the confidence to launch magazines about their passions and interests?

Technology

How does an indie title get produced? Barriers to entry to the magazine publishing world have never been large and were largely confined to obtaining launch funding, printer's credit and securing distribution. Development of desktop publishing technology and software, largely courtesy of Apple and Adobe, helped lower those hurdles even further and started to offer magazine makers an array of choice in the look and feel of their titles. In an important book published in 2006 *Wired Magazine* Editor-in-Chief Chris Anderson articulated what has become known as 'long tail' theory. Whilst writing principally about the music and movie business, there is relevance for magazine publishers. Anderson states that niche markets have become both easier and cheaper to reach. One of the enablers of this is that the tools of production have become 'democratised'. He argues: "The power of the PC means that the ranks of 'producers' – individuals who can now do what just a few years ago only professionals could do – have swelled a thousandfold" (Anderson, 2006, p. 54). For a number of would be magazine editors, the ability to write and publish from a laptop allowed them to use blogs as a stepping stone to a print title. Using the example of *It's Nice That*, Jeremy Leslie notes that it was "launched as a biannual print edition to balance the disposability of their daily posts with a more precise editorial voice" (Leslie, 2013, p. 214).

Applying the long tail work to the magazine world is not without its problems, particularly when it comes to distribution. But emerging technologies have made it easier for editors and designers to produce the independent magazine they are passionate about. They can do it anytime, anyplace, anywhere. So, if a creative from a mainstream publisher wants to write or design a magazine at home in the evenings or weekends they can – if they have a PC and software suites such as Photoshop or InDesign as there is no need for a dedicated art and design studio or production department. But it is important to emphasise that these newly 'democratised' producers are highly professional in the practice of their crafts. These sophisticated packages give journalists and designers tremendous flexibility, but they still have to know how to use them and use them well. As Leslie states, this understanding can push the boundaries of the concept of a traditional magazine to its limits and allow creatives to think out of the box.

> Technology has undoubtedly improved magazines. The smooth integration of layout, photographic manipulation and illustration software, allied with the increased processing power of the desktop computer, has meant the editor and designer now have a degree of control unthinkable even ten years ago.
>
> *Leslie, 2013, p. 214*

Publishing a magazine, be it a mass selling mainstream title or a niche indie, is a team effort. And here, we find yet another example of digital innovations bringing down another potential barrier to entry. Social media sites, especially those aimed at professionals, allow editors to find and reference contributors and designers. Instagram is a brilliant platform for photographers to showcase their work. Cloud services allow collaborators to share copy with each other remotely (that is how, in the midst of a pandemic, Das, Stam and Blake edited the book which you are now reading). You can sit in London and subedit an article written in Sydney with photographs transmitted from New York. Minutes later, you can create pdfs and whiz them over to a printer in Holland. Making a magazine has never been easier; alas the same cannot be said for distributing it – as this chapter will shortly discuss.

Industry structure

As was widely explored by Andrew Scott and David Stam in the pages of *Inside Magazine Publishing* (Routledge 2014), from the 2008 financial crisis onwards the industry has faced two major challenges. As already observed in previous chapters, there was a severe downturn in advertising revenues as consumer marketers cut back sharply on marketing spend. At the same time publishers found it imperative to make significant investments in their digital presence, whether that be websites, apps or on-screen editions. This point cannot be undervalued. Total focus was on launching on new platforms as quickly as possible to protect and develop existing brands. Pre-2008 a persistent editor may have persuaded financial management to back a relatively low-cost 'pet' print project, in the hard world of digital investment necessity he or she had no chance to launch. If a niche title wanted to see light of day, it had to be through the independent route.

In the classic dystopian novel *Fahrenheit 451*, Ray Bradbury describes a world devoid of books and magazines with firemen despatched to burn them. (The book's title refers to the temperature at which paper burns.) He depicts culture as being mass and monolithic and devoid of diverse opinion, saying that "the bigger the market the less you handle controversy" and "magazines became a nice blend of vanilla tapioca". This is of course a picture of a totally extreme parallel world. Major titles in this country are now making strides to manage diversity but back in the 1990s mainstream titles did come across at times as 'samey' with few concessions to niche interests or beliefs. Focus on mass by the main players was yet another catalyst for the launch of indie titles which offered space for new and diverse content both in words and pictures.

These new magazine makers started to become ultracreative and began to think out of the box, particularly from a design perspective. In the mainstream market, page sizes were traditionally clustered around A4 to both save paper costs and maximise display on standardised retailers' shelves. Reds and yellows were the dominant cover colours, especially for womens' titles, because they worked. The logo was almost always top left and cover lines ranged left. All were very sensible ploys to drive sales in retail newsagents and supermarkets; but these standard and uniform ways of doing things did somewhat strangle creativity in the overall market. Moreover, the decline in magazine advertisement revenue forced many mainstream magazine houses to increase their cover prices as the circulation revenue stream became increasingly important. This overall trend has aided independent publishers, as the reading consumer has slowly become accustomed to paying more for a quality print product.

The importance of the niche

As both Christine Stam and Simon Das have described in previous chapters, the magazine market has been moving from mass to niche ever since the 1980s. In that decade, increased leisure time and disposable income allowed innovative publishers such as EMAP (now part of Bauer UK) and Future plc to take advantage of new web offset printing presses which delivered good quality short print runs at a sensible price. Opportunities for specialist titles exploded, particularly in the areas of leisure such as motoring, sport, home computing and technology. Publishing is a spectrum of enterprises and there is a relatively fine line between a niche title at the specialist end of the mainstream market and an indie title. Both types of magazines influenced and reflected leisure trends and societal change but there is a cut-off point, in terms of market size and content, where the mainstream market seemed happy to watch the indies grow. Putting it simply, if the numbers were too small or the content too controversial then leave it to the little guys.

Generation X (children born between roughly 1965 and 1990) did not want uniformity, they wanted choice. There was a desire for their chosen media to reflect the sociocultural changes happening around them. In the mainstream market, this gave rise to the shooting stars of lads' mags; in the indie market, voice was given to the LGBT movement. Members of the various communities making up LGBT will argue that progress towards acceptance has not been fast enough or gone far enough but there have been significant changes in understanding, awareness and acceptance since the start point of the late 1980s. Set up in 1989 to fight prejudice and lobby for inclusion, Stonewall has been at the forefront of demands for change. There is a timeline chronicling progress on its excellent website ranging from early Pride events (1990) to the passing of legislation for Civil Partnerships (2004) and same sex marriage (2013) in the UK. The movement was largely overlooked by mainstream magazine publishers who seemed to underplay the importance of lesbians and gays in society, within politics and also to the economy with what became known as the 'pink pound'. Indies, however, soon took up the cause.

On Loetscher's 100 Best List (mentioned above), he highlights five LGBT titles, Stack Distribution also list five and the magCulture store fifteen (all sites accessed 6 June 2020). There will doubtless be more. *gal-dem* has grown a strong community after just four annual issues. Described on its own website as "committed to telling the stories of women and non-binary people of colour," the title was founded by ex-Bristol University students and has print, online and social media platforms with an impressive following of close to 130,000 on Instagram and 50,000 on Facebook. Their outside image is strong with strong political content. *The Guardian* featured them in 2018 and concluded:

> *gal-dem* attracts the audience it does, and the brands desperate to resonate with that audience, because of what's often described as 'authenticity'. But the gal-dem team see it in less grandiose terms, as being true to their own experience.
>
> *Hirsch, 2018*

Individual independent titles may be small and struggle to make ends meet– as this chapter will discuss next – but as a genre they give voice to a huge range of minority interests, lay bare some of the undoubted prejudices in Western society and create markets and communities overlooked by mainstream media. Whilst much content is passionate and serious, the sector will also give ideas on new and unspoilt travel destinations (*Suitcase*) and cover sports both leisurely (*Fallon's Angler*) or more energetic (*The Surfer's Journal*). But to whatever example one looks to, two key attributes stand out. First, a deep love and passion for design on the printed page and second a complete dedication to the served community. This is best summed up by Le Masurier:

> These editors and journalists see themselves as participants in a cultural com- munity…the magazine becomes a part of the culture, a way to develop the culture, not a neutral reporter.
>
> *Le Masurier, 2012, p. 388*

But is there a sustainable business model for the sector – and does it matter?

PHOTO 8.2 Lifestyle and cultural title *Huck.* Published by TCO London.

Independent magazines – the business model

Independent magazines are thriving largely without the support of structured commercial teams generating circulation and advertisement revenues. To do so, they have had to be innovative and to 'think outside of the box' as to how they both reach and market their audiences. How have they achieved this?

Retail distribution

Despite the undoubted growth of the indie sector in the last ten years, it remains hard to buy one's chosen title at retail, apart from the heart of metropolitan centres. There are two sets of reasons behind this problem relating to both the intrinsic nature of the genre and the general magazine supply chain.

Indie magazines serve niche communities. For many titles, these communities are just too niche for a high street or neighbourhood newsagent to support. It is an industry norm that retailers earn around 25 per cent of the cover price. Whilst at first glance, high cover prices may make the title profitable for the store to stock this is soon eroded by the fact that the sales per issue of an individual title may be tiny. Shelf space is finite for all retailers and large mainstream titles with marketing budgets will win over. Indie titles are often published to bimonthly, quarterly or biannual frequencies meaning that one issue can take up shelf space for a long time, reducing the retail stock turnover.

A key characteristic of this aspect of publishing is creative experimentation and innovation. This often means that magazine titles and cover treatments will not appeal to or be understood by the impulse reader – customers may well need to browse and reflect before making a what is a relatively expensive purchase. This is not always the customer experience within a traditional newsagent. The traditional structure of the UK magazine supply chain is not 'indie friendly'. Larger distribution companies and wholesalers also work on a percentage share of cover price, in the case of the former this will be a single figure percentage. Long publishing frequencies coupled with small sales per title have traditionally not excited these businesses where costs are largely fixed but supported by revenues that are highly variable.

Whilst acknowledging the above commercial blockers, there are ways to make sure that indie and small specialist titles find a route to retailers' shelves. London-based Central Books offers a magazine distribution service with particular focus on gallery and museum shops and specialist bookshops. Similarly, UK distributor Magazine Merchandising Services offer direct deliveries to 700 retail outlets and encourage stocking by offering extended credit terms. Titles at the more commercial end of the indie sector can achieve reasonable levels of retail availability. *Huck*, *Little White Lies*, *Delayed Gratification*, *Suitcase* and *The Gentlewoman* are available in certain WH Smith outlets but these listings will be supported by trade marketing spend.

The specialist magazine shop is a rare breed. The costs of high street retailing do not help the economics of these ventures and their success is normally limited to metropolitan areas with a cultural centre and student population. magCulture (see below) is the 'must go to' store in London but there are other well-stocked retailers in Brighton, Bath and Bristol to name three. International distribution is important for indies: a niche market opportunity in just one country may not be commercially viable but adding a cluster of opportunities from different parts of the world may create a profitable market. In the Netherlands, Athenaeum Nieuwscentrum Amsterdam offers a unique customer experience for the magazine devotee. Founded in 1969 and located in the literary area of the Dutch city, passers-by will often see magazines neatly stacked in displays outside the store, space inside being limited for the range of indie titles they wish to stock. Marc Robbemond of the Amsterdam retailer believes the ability to browse along with careful selection of range to be fundamental to success. For customers who are unable to visit in person mail order is also available.

PHOTO 8.3 Athenaeum Nieuwscentrum store in Amsterdam. Magazines are attractively displayed outside the shop.

INNOVATIVE ROUTES TO MARKET

When this chapter's author was a circulation trainee, he was told by a highly experienced wholesaler that "good product will always find a way to market." Such is the case with the indie sector. What innovations in distribution and sales have helped niche titles seek out their communities?

magCulture

magCulture is the focal point of the London indie magazine scene and is best described from its own website.

> magCulture is a design studio, an online resource, a magazine shop and events producer. 'We love magazines' is our rallying cry; this reflects

> our belief that editorial design is an ever-developing discipline that con-
> tinually adapts to new technologies and circumstances. Everything we
> do celebrates magazines while questioning what their future might be.
> *magCulture, 2020*

At the centre of the business is the store. The terrazzo floored space, to
the north of London's Clerkenwell district, was a traditional newsagent but
is now one of the principal UK retailers for the indie magazine sector. On
opening in 2015 magCulture's founder, Jeremy Leslie, was quoted in the
New York Times:

> When you travel, you see magazine stores that are really impressive and
> it always upset me that London didn't have something similar. This is
> meant to be somewhere to visit, take your time, browse. People will
> come in and buy four or five magazines and spend the best part of £100.
> They deserve the chance to flick through in peace.
> *Moshakis, 2015*

magCulture also operates a healthy international online sales business
(which was essential during the coronavirus crisis of 2020), bespoke office
deliveries to design studios and subscription boxes. As quoted above, the
reach of the business goes far beyond just selling copies. A design studio
offers consultancy and advice on branding and redesign, prior to the 2020
crisis, it ran a successful live events business (which is currently running virtually) and has its own magCulture journal along with regular podcasts and
newsletters.

Stack distribution

Stack is a unique business serving the indie sector with a simple and effective
model. Founded in 2008, it offers a different title every month with copies
posted direct to the customer's door. Curation is by Stack itself; readers are
unaware of the monthly title until the packet arrives. The surprise element
is seen as a key attribute in introducing new magazines and widening
magazine experiences. At a 2020 UK price of £7 per month, the service
offers excellent value for money taking into consideration cover prices of
indie titles. Around 3500 magazines are dispatched every month. Single
copy sales are also available online and Stack produces excellent podcasts
interviewing editors and publishers of selected titles. Anyone working in
magazines enjoys a great night out and the Stack Awards provide just this.
Hosted annually but unfortunately cancelled for 2020, expert judges present awards across ten categories including Magazine, Launch and Cover
of the Year.

The move to subscriptions

The 2020 lockdown of society and the prolonged closure of many retail stores further accelerated a trend that was already gathering pace – the move from retail sales to subscriptions. Print and digital bundles (see Chapter 3) and pure play digital magazines required a far greater level of direct marketing skills than publishers had demonstrated prior to the watershed of the 2008 financial crash. Mainstream publishers quickly began to make significant investment in people, customer management systems and digital marketing.

During the 2020 lockdown supermarkets, neighbourhood newsagents and certain WH Smith stores remained open. But as explained, such retail outlets offer few opportunities for indie magazines. Bookshops, specialist shops, museums and galleries were all closed. Indie publishers had to look to the internet for their main source of both single-copy sales and subscriptions.

The benefits to publishers of subscription sales are well rehearsed. Subs customers receive every issue, whereas even loyal retail customers may miss the occasional one. The annual subscription paid upfront is a huge benefit for cash flow to many publishers but especially smaller independent ones. But above all, the publisher knows who their subscription customer is, their geographical and social demographics and their digital footprint. Through incentive and digital marketing, publishers can discover more and more about their readers' lives, their likes and dislikes, their shopping habits and their lifestyles. By doing so, they can market additional products to these their most loyal of customers by putting them at the centre of every commercial activity the publishing house undertakes.

Around the turn of the millennium, this author attended a conference at which the charismatic Felix Dennis gave a memorable address in which he loudly trumpeted that for publishers, the main benefit of the internet will be to sell print subs. The now late Felix was of course too restrictive in his then digital vision but he had a point. E-mail marketing, social media posts and tweets linking to subs pages, clever targeting of interest groups through database management are now important weapons in the modern subscription manager's armoury.

These weapons come with costs, and subscription marketing for the main players is now a high budget activity. The size and diversity of this sector makes generalisation difficult but it would not be unfair to say that, prior to 2020, many indies were not giving subscription marketing the focus and attention it deserved. Too many websites did not feature a BUY A SUBSCRIPTION icon with prominence and the customer journey to purchase a sub could be poor. As the preface to this textbook portrays, much of its research, content creation and editing was carried out during the health crisis of 2020. Interestingly, in preparing this chapter, the author noted a distinct quickening of pace by indie publishers to reach out to subscription customers through their websites and social media. With a retail lockdown, it was do or die.

At the time of his thundering speech, Felix Dennis almost certainly could not have predicted the scope and power of social media today – with large titles having millions of followers and social media serving as a key lever for publishers to learn more about their served communities and, in time, to market to them. Click on a post or tweet and you are switched into the publisher's world and into their microsystem; they can then find out more about you and start to market. Indie publishers' social followings may not be huge but they are loyal and committed. Learning the subtleties of marketing through social media will be a useful next step towards building a robust subscription driven business model. (Ironically after spending time on the internet researching *Suitcase,* a sponsored post from them appeared on this author's Facebook stream. *Suitcase* are clearly on the case!)

Advertisements and content marketing

Back in 2014, Andrew Scott argued that whilst the advertisement sales role in a publishing company was becoming more scientific, there remained a place for traditional selling skills built around the uniqueness of the magazine product and the editorial environment offered to potential advertisers (Stam & Scott, 2014, p. 197). A successful selling operation within mainstream print and digital media relies on quality circulation and readership data with agency performance monitored by external auditors. Qualitative plus points sit alongside the quantitative as publishers stress the diverse benefits of reader relationships, the quality of their content and design and paper quality.

Those selling advertisements into the journals of the independent sector have few, if any, statistical pillars to lean on. It has already been noted that public domain readership numbers do not exist for these magazines. The limited number of pages which are sold will be based upon the judgement made by advertisers that this magazine is the right place for their brands to be seen, the editorial and paid space sit comfortably together, the magazine has the right look and feel and the niche community is one which they wish to reach. It is all about the quality of the magazine environment.

This chapter has already described the universe size and diverse nature of indie magazines and how difficult this makes generalisations. Advertisement sales are clearly not top of mind for many editors and publishers. The issue of *Suitcase* purchased immediately pre-pandemic hosted nine advertisement pages, a number considered healthy for the sector; *The Gourmand* just two. Frequently, a publisher's website will fail to offer an invitation to enquire about advertising at all – however, many seem keen to pursue branded content.

The studio model

Forward thinking niche publishers are increasingly looking to what is now known as the studio model. Here, editors use the resources of the magazine (the studio) to write and curate paid for branded content for advertiser clients. This content may well appear in the media owned by said publisher – and obviously, there are clear commercial advantages to this. But the client may wish to use the content be in print, digital, video or audio as stand-alone promotional material. With paid for advertising space hit badly by the pandemic, this is a clear and sensible route for indie publishers to tread.

Turning once again to *Suitcase* magazine, their issue 29 included a tidily designed and printed A5 supplement *Gentleman's Journal* in partnership with American Express. Featuring exclusive restaurants and bars from around the world the branding was subtle and relatively low key; a one-page advertisement and a few paragraphs of editorial copy about their Platinum Card. Branded content extends to the magazine's website with a guide to Copenhagen sponsored by the premium luggage and travel accessories firm Horizn Studios. In both examples, the branding is a good fit, the exclusivity of American Express and Horizn being enhanced by the quality of Suitcase and the discerning nature of its travelling readership.

A new type of media company

The area immediately to the north east of London's financial district is becoming increasingly popular with the creative industry, small business start-ups and tech companies. In one of its side streets, readers will find a new type of media company called TCO London. The initials TCO herald from the firm's first name The Church of London but now more snappily shortened. What is new about it? TCO successfully blends independent magazine publishing and the provision of full creative and marketing agency services for commercial clients. The business uses its experienced and professional network of journalists, designers, photographers and filmmakers to create and project authentic branded content to communities of influential trendsetters.

Founded in 2006, the published titles are *Huck* and *Little White Lies*. Inspired by the rebellious culture of surf and skate, *Huck* has broadened out to become a premium cultural lifestyle brand featuring news, current affairs and arts. Sister title *Little White Lies* is a movie magazine but with a difference – featuring film reviews, features and interviews. It is famed for its iconic covers. Both titles have high quality websites with podcasts and videos available. It is fair to say that the magazines would consider themselves to be at the commercial end of the indie magazine spectrum and are available in selected WH Smith stores.

In a lecture to London College of Communication students in 2019, TCO's founder Vince Medeiros highlighted the relevance of the launch date of the business, 2006. Online advertisement spend was starting to take a very significant share of the advertisement market, a market which was to be badly affected by the financial crisis of 2008. He became convinced that a new business model was needed for niche titles, a model which had content marketing at its heart. As such, its history has made it flexible and responsive to the need for change in uncertain times.

Vince Medeiros believes that there are a number of key advantages to content marketing as a business model for publishers. With the traditional advertisement market increasingly driven by price, the media owner can control pricing of branded content and at its centre is the value proposition of quality content and audience delivery. The paid-for space market is oversupplied with inventory, especially digital, and branded content escapes ad blocking and 'user blindness' towards digital advertising. The company's showreel is highly impressive and features blue chip clients such as Levis, Nike, Facebook, London store group Selfridges, Vans and Destination Canada (accessed 30 May 2020). Written and design storytelling skills honed on magazines are transferred to the commercial world with creativity, technical knowledge and skill. Some of the branded content will appear in TCO's titles, some will feature independently in other media, print and online. The business is also able to offer research and insight for clients. In 2019, TCO produced a highly informative booklet *The Future of Brand Activism*, demonstrating how brands can safeguard and harness their images by playing a positive role in the causes that matter in people's lives.

The studio model as described here is not for every independent magazine publisher. To be successful, the host titles must enjoy trust and authority with their audiences in their chosen fields. Successful implementation of the model also requires investment in people and kit. At this author's first meeting with Vince Medeiros, he said he had just signed a sizeable cheque for filmmaking and video equipment! Editorial teams and content creators do not always have the commercial skills needed to gain and manage client demands and expectations and it may well be necessary to hire a commercially minded colleague to fulfil this role. On a deeper level, some of the purists of the indie magazine movement may consider that

PHOTO 8.4 *The Future of Brand Activism* report from TCO London.

engaging in branded content activities is not for them; there are issues of editorial independence versus commercial need. Some editors may argue that they 'escaped' mainstream publishing in order to avoid such conflicts. On this point, it should be noted that the author of this chapter was an executive in large publishing houses for over 30 years and may have had sympathy with this view. Research for this book has impressed upon him that much branded content produced by the indie sector is creative, thoughtful, technologically clever and can add real value for stakeholders.

GO SHOPPING WITH INDIE MAGAZINES

Many publishers use retail and live events to support their business models. The latter have been severely affected by the pandemic and virtual meetings have supplanted face to face where possible. Unable to hold its annual New York conference, magCulture moved the event online. *Delayed Gratification* successfully ran online seminars on how to launch an independent magazine as well as Zoom classes on its award-winning infographics designs. Despite such innovative workarounds, titles used to banking a revenue stream through face to face interaction will have been adversely affected by an as yet unquantifiable sum.

To make up the shortfall online shopping opportunities abound. *Delayed Gratification* offers coffee mugs and a set of its acclaimed infographics in a tin: tinfographics. *Hole & Corner* sells signed prints and on offer from *The Gentlewoman* are its cover stories printed in miniature alongside high quality T-shirts. Readers are encouraged to browse indie magazine's websites at leisure to view and partake of the scores of online shopping opportunities. As is the case with all product extension merchandising, the core values of the brand are reflected in range and quality.

Independent magazines – business or pleasure?

The short answer to this closing question is both. And anyway, it does not really matter. Why so?

It is self-evident that indie magazine makers enjoy and take pleasure from their craft. Driven by their commitment to the served communities, they devote huge amounts of time to its perfection, often balancing a second job and having invested savings in the outset. They do the overall publishing business a great service. At a time when the mainstream world was under financial and platform pressure, indies helped keep print journalism and innovative design alive and very much kicking. The clever combination of regular social media coupled with long frequency print offerings has engaged younger audiences as mass magazines have drifted older in demographic terms. Witness *gal-dem* for that. So, indie publishing is a pleasure.

The business model is complex and it is hard to see it getting significantly easier. Speaking with 40 years' experience, much of it running a major distributor, this author can testify to niche distribution being tough, very tough. There are excellent beacons of niche retailing as this chapter has demonstrated but they are few and far between. Publishers will have to embrace the subs model and database and digital marketing that is now aligned to that discipline. Paid-for space is not going to develop, but advertisers can be persuaded to value the economic power of niche communities and the indies have the storytelling skills to help them connect. With sensible dialogue, this can be created in a way that delivers value to the client brand whilst maintaining editorial trust and authority. Indie magazine making may not be easy, but it can be a business.

Business or pleasure, it does not seem to matter. They are indie closures but most months they are surpassed by launches. Somehow the financial ends are met and the next issue comes out. The team takes a deep breath and starts all over again. What is our theme for the next edition?

Useful web resources

www.magculture.com
www.stackmagazines.com
www.tcolondon.com
www.athenaeum.nl
www.stonewall.org.uk

References

Anderson, C., (2006). *The Long Tail*. London: Random House.
Hirsch, A., (2018). *Inside gal-dem Magazine*. [Online] Available at: www.theguardian.com [Accessed 6 June 2020].
Hooper, M., (2012). *Who Says Print Is Dead?* [Online] Available at: www.theguardian.co.uk [Accessed 17 June 2020].
Le Masurier, Megan, (2012). Independent magazines and the rejuvenation of print. *International Journal of Cultural Studies,* 13 January, Volume (15) 4, pp. 383–398.
Leslie, J., (2013). *The Modern Magazine – Visual Journalism in the Digital Era*. London: Lawrence King Publishing.
Loetscher, W., (2018). *The 100 Best Magazines You Have (Probably) Never Heard of*. [Online] Available at: www.insidehook.com [Accessed 4 June 2020].
Losowsky, A., (2009). *Reinventing the Magazine*. [Online] Available at: www.wsj.com [Accessed 5 March 2020].
magCulture, (2020). *magCulture*. [Online] Available at: www.magculture.co.uk [Accessed 25 May 2020].
Moshakis, A., (2015). *One-Thing Shops*. [Online] Available at: www.newyorktimes.com [Accessed 25 May 2020].
Stam, D. & Scott, A., (2014). *Inside Magazine Publishing*. Oxford: Routledge.
T-Post, (2020). *All About T-Post*. [Online] Available at: www.T-Post.com [Accessed 5 March 2020].
Wray, D. D., (2019). *How We Made Punk Fanzine Sniffin' Glue*. [Online] Available at: www.theguardian.com [Accessed 7 June 2020].

INDEX